Zami: A New Spelling of My Name

Audre Lorde

CROSSING PRESS
Berkeley

Parts of this book in earlier versions have appeared in *Heresies,*
Conditions, Sinister Wisdom, Azalea, The Iowa Review, and *Callaloo.*

ISBN-13: 978-0-89594-123-7
ISBN-13: 978-0-89594-122-0 (pbk.)

Printed in the U.S.A.

Cover design by Lizzie Allen
Cover illustration by Alexis Eke
Text design by Pat McGloin

43 42 41 40 39 38
First Crossing Press Edition

Acknowledgments

May I live conscious of my debt to all the people who make life possible.

From the bottom of my heart I thank each woman who shared any piece of the dreams/myths/histories that give this book shape.

In particular I wish to acknowledge my gratitude to: Barbara Smith for her courage in asking the right question and her faith that it could be answered; Cherríe Moraga for listening with her third ear and hearing; and to them both for their editorial fortitude; Jean Millar for being there, when I came up for the second time, with the right book; Michelle Cliff for her Island ears, green bananas, and fine, deft pencil; Donald Hill who visited Carriacou and passed the words on; Blanche Cook for moving history beyond nightmare into structures for the future; Clare Coss who connected me with my matrilineage; Adrienne Rich who insisted the language could match and believed that it would; the writers of songs whose melodies stitch up my years; Bernice Goodman who first made a difference of difference; Frances Clayton who holds it all together, for never giving up; Marion Masone who gave a name to forever; Beverly Smith for reminding me to stay simple; Linda Belmar Lorde for my first principles of combat and survival; Elizabeth Lorde-Rollins and Jonathan Lorde-Rollins who help keep me honest and current; Ma-Mariah, Ma-Liz, Aunt Anni, Sister Lou and the other Belmar women who proofread my dreams; and others who I can not yet afford to name.

To Helen, who made up the best adventures

To Blanche, with whom I lived many of them

To the hands of Afrekete

In the recognition of loving lies an answer to despair.

Zami: A New Spelling of My Name

*To whom do I owe the power behind my voice, what strength I
have become, yeasting up like sudden blood from under the
bruised skin's blister?*

My father leaves his psychic print upon me, silent, intense,
and unforgiving. But his is a distant lightning. Images of women
flaming like torches adorn and define the borders of my journey,
stand like dykes between me and the chaos. It is the images of
women, kind and cruel, that lead me home.

To whom do I owe the symbols of my survival?

Days from pumpkin until the year's midnight, when my sisters
and I hovered indoors, playing potsy on holes in the rosy linoleum that covered the living-room floor. On Saturdays we fought
each other for the stray errand out of doors, fought each other
for the emptied Quaker Oats boxes, fought each other for the
last turn in the bathroom at nightfall, and for who would be the
first one of us to get chickenpox.

The smell of the filled Harlem streets during summer, after a
brief shower or the spraying drizzle of the watering trucks released the rank smell of the pavements back to the sun. I ran to
the corner to fetch milk and bread from the Short-Neck Store-
Man, stopping to search for some blades of grass to bring home
for my mother. Stopping to search for hidden pennies winking
like kittens under the subway gratings. I was always bending
over to tie my shoes, delaying, trying to figure out something.
How to get at the money, how to peep out the secret that some
women carried like a swollen threat, under the gathers of their
flowered blouses.

3

To whom do I owe the woman I have become?

DeLois lived up the block on 142nd Street and never had her hair done, and all the neighborhood women sucked their teeth as she walked by. Her crispy hair twinkled in the summer sun as her big proud stomach moved her on down the block while I watched, not caring whether or not she was a poem. Even though I tied my shoes and tried to peep under her blouse as she passed by, I never spoke to DeLois, because my mother didn't. But I loved her, because she moved like she felt she was somebody special, like she was somebody I'd like to know someday. She moved like how I thought god's mother must have moved, and my mother, once upon a time, and someday maybe me.

Hot noon threw a ring of sunlight like a halo on the top of DeLois's stomach, like a spotlight, making me sorry that I was so flat and could only feel the sun on my head and shoulders. I'd have to lie down on my back before the sun could shine down like that on my belly.

I loved DeLois because she was big and Black and special and seemed to laugh all over. I was scared of DeLois for those very same reasons. One day I watched DeLois step off the curb of 142nd Street against the light, slow and deliberate. A high yaller dude in a white Cadillac passed by and leaned out and yelled at her, "Hurry up, you flat-footed, nappy-headed, funny-looking bitch!" The car almost knocking her down. DeLois kept right on about her leisurely business and never so much as looked around.

To Louise Briscoe who died in my mother's house as a tenant in a furnished room with cooking privileges—no linens supplied. I brought her a glass of warm milk that she wouldn't drink, and she laughed at me when I wanted to change her sheets and call a doctor. "No reason to call him unless he's real cute," said Miz Briscoe. "Ain't nobody sent for me to come, I got here all by myself. And I'm going back the same way. So I only need him if he's cute, real cute." And the room smelled like she was lying.

"Miz Briscoe," I said, "I'm really worried about you."

She looked up at me out of the corner of her eyes, like I was making her a proposition which she had to reject, but which she appreciated all the same. Her huge bloated body was quiet beneath the grey sheet, as she grinned knowingly.

"Why, that's all right, honey. I don't hold it against you. I know you can't help it, it's just in your nature, that's all."

To the white woman I dreamed standing behind me in an airport, silently watching while her child deliberately bumps into me over and over again. When I turn around to tell this woman that if she doesn't restrain her kid I'm going to punch her in the mouth, I see that she's been punched in the mouth already. Both she and her child are battered, with bruised faces and blackened eyes. I turn, and walk away from them in sadness and fury.

To the pale girl who ran up to my car in a Staten Island midnight with only a nightgown and bare feet, screaming and crying, "Lady, please help me oh please take me to the hospital, lady..." Her voice was a mixture of overripe peaches and doorchimes; she was the age of my daughter, running along the woody curves of Van Duzer Street.

I stopped the car quickly, and leaned over to open the door. It was high summer. "Yes, yes, I'll try to help you," I said. "Get in."

And when she saw my face in the streetlamp her own collapsed into terror.

"Oh no!" she wailed. "Not you!" then whirled around and started to run again.

What could she have seen in my Black face that was worth holding onto such horror? Wasting me in the gulf between who I was and her vision of me. Left with no help.

I drove on.

In the rear-view mirror I saw the substance of her nightmare catch up with her at the corner—leather jacket and boots, male and white.

I drove on, knowing she would probably die stupid.

To the first woman I ever courted and left. She taught me that women who want without needing are expensive and sometimes wasteful, but women who need without wanting are dangerous—they suck you in and pretend not to notice.

To the battalion of arms where I often retreated for shelter and sometimes found it. To the others who helped, pushing me into the merciless sun—I, coming out blackened and whole.

To the journeywoman pieces of myself.
Becoming.
Afrekete.

Prologue

I have always wanted to be both man and woman, to incorporate the strongest and richest parts of my mother and father within/into me—to share valleys and mountains upon my body the way the earth does in hills and peaks.

I would like to enter a woman the way any man can, and to be entered—to leave and to be left—to be hot and hard and soft all at the same time in the cause of our loving. I would like to drive forward and at other times to rest or be driven. When I sit and play in the waters of my bath I love to feel the deep inside parts of me, sliding and folded and tender and deep. Other times I like to fantasize the core of it, my pearl, a protruding part of me, hard and sensitive and vulnerable in a different way.

I have felt the age-old triangle of mother father and child, with the "I" at its eternal core, elongate and flatten out into the elegantly strong triad of grandmother mother daughter, with the "I" moving back and forth flowing in either or both directions as needed.

Woman forever. My body, a living representation of other life older longer wiser. The mountains and valleys, trees, rocks. Sand and flowers and water and stone. Made in earth.

1

Grenadians and Barbadians walk like African peoples. Trinidadians do not.

When I visited Grenada I saw the root of my mother's powers walking through the streets. I thought, this is the country of my foremothers, my forebearing mothers, those Black island women who defined themselves by what they did. "Island women make good wives; whatever happens, they've seen worse." There is a softer edge of African sharpness upon these women, and they swing through the rain-warm streets with an arrogant gentleness that I remember in strength and vulnerability.

My mother and father came to this country in 1924, when she was twenty-seven years old and he was twenty-six. They had been married a year. She lied about her age in immigration because her sisters who were here already had written her that americans wanted strong young women to work for them, and Linda was afraid she was too old to get work. Wasn't she already an old maid at home when she had finally gotten married?

My father got a job as a laborer in the old Waldorf Astoria, on the site where the Empire State Building now stands, and my mother worked there as a chambermaid. The hotel closed for demolition, and she went to work as a scullery maid in a teashop on Columbus Avenue and 99th Street. She went to work before dawn, and worked twelve hours a day, seven days a week, with no time off. The owner told my mother that she ought to be glad to have the job, since ordinarily the establishment didn't hire "spanish" girls. Had the owner known Linda was Black, she would never have been hired at all. In the winter of 1928, my mother developed pleurisy and almost died. While my mother was still sick, my father went to collect her uniforms from the teahouse to wash them. When the owner saw him, he realized my mother was Black and fired her on the spot.

9

In October 1929, the first baby came and the stockmarket fell, and my parents' dream of going home receded into the background. Little secret sparks of it were kept alive for years by my mother's search for tropical fruits "under the bridge," and her burning of kerosene lamps, by her treadle-machine and her fried bananas and her love of fish and the sea. Trapped. There was so little that she really knew about the stranger's country. How the electricity worked. The nearest church. Where the Free Milk Fund for Babies handouts occurred, and at what time—even though we were not allowed to drink charity.

She knew about bundling up against the wicked cold. She knew about Paradise Plums—hard, oval candies, cherry-red on one side, pineapple-yellow on the other. She knew which West Indian markets along Lenox Avenue carried them in tilt-back glass jars on the countertops. She knew how desirable Paradise Plums were to sweet-starved little children, and how important in maintaining discipline on long shopping journeys. She knew exactly how many of the imported goodies could be sucked and rolled around in the mouth before the wicked gum arabic with its acidic british teeth cut through the tongue's pink coat and raised little red pimples.

She knew about mixing oils for bruises and rashes, and about disposing of all toenail clippings and hair from the comb. About burning candles before All Souls Day to keep the soucoyants away, lest they suck the blood of her babies. She knew about blessing the food and yourself before eating, and about saying prayers before going to sleep.

She taught us one to the mother that I never learned in school.

Remember, oh most gracious Virgin Mary, that never was it known that anyone who fled to thy protection, implored thy help, or sought thy intercession, was ever left unaided. Inspired with this confidence I fly unto thee now, oh my sweet mother, to thee I come, before thee I stand, sinful and sorrowful. Oh mother of the word incarnate, despise not my petitions but in thy clemency and mercy oh hear and answer me now.

As a child, I remember often hearing my mother mouth these words softly, just below her breath, as she faced some new crisis or disaster—the icebox door breaking, the electricity being shut off, my sister gashing open her mouth on borrowed skates.

My child's ears heard the words and pondered the mysteries of this mother to whom my solid and austere mother could whisper such beautiful words.

And finally, my mother knew how to frighten children into behaving in public. She knew how to pretend that the only food left in the house was actually a meal of choice, carefully planned.

She knew how to make virtues out of necessities.

Linda missed the bashing of the waves against the sea-wall at the foot of Noel's Hill, the humped and mysterious slope of Marquis Island rising up from the water a half-mile off-shore. She missed the swift-flying bananaquits and the trees and the rank smell of the tree-ferns lining the road downhill into Grenville Town. She missed the music that did not have to be listened to because it was always around. Most of all, she missed the Sunday-long boat trips that took her to Aunt Anni's in Carriacou.

Everybody in Grenada had a song for everything. There was a song for the tobacco shop which was part of the general store, which Linda had managed from the time she was seventeen.

3/4 of a cross
and a circle complete
2 semi-circles and a perpendicular meet. . .

A jingle serving to identify the store for those who could not read T O B A C C O.

The songs were all about, there was even one about them, the Belmar girls, who always carried their noses in the air. And you never talked your business too loud in the street, otherwise you were liable to hear your name broadcast in a song on the corner the very next day. At home, she learned from Sister Lou to disapprove of the endless casual song-making as a disreputable and common habit, beneath the notice of a decent girl.

But now, in this cold and raucous country called america, Linda missed the music. She even missed the annoyance of the early Saturday morning customers with their loose talk and slurred rhythms, warbling home from the rumshop.

She knew about food. But of what use was that to these crazy people she lived among, who cooked leg of lamb without washing the meat, and roasted even the toughest beef without water and a cover? Pumpkin was only a child's decoration to

them, and they treated their husbands better than they cared
for their children.

She did not know her way in and out of the galleries of the
Museum of Natural History, but she did know that it was a
good place to take children if you wanted them to grow up
smart. It frightened her when she took her children there, and
she would pinch each one of us girls on the fleshy part of our
upper arms at one time or another all afternoon. Supposedly, it
was because we wouldn't behave, but actually, it was because beneath the neat visor of the museum guard's cap, she could see
pale blue eyes staring at her and her children as if we were a
bad smell, and this frightened her. *This* was a situation she
couldn't control.

What else did Linda know? She knew how to look into people's faces and tell what they were going to do before they did
it. She knew which grapefruit was shaddock and pink, before
it ripened, and what to do with the others, which was to throw
them to the pigs. Except she had no pigs in Harlem, and sometimes those were the only grapefruit around to eat. She knew
how to prevent infection in an open cut or wound by heating
the black-elm leaf over a wood-fire until it wilted in the hand,
rubbing the juice into the cut, and then laying the soft green
now flabby fibers over the wound for a bandage.

But there was no black-elm in Harlem, no black oak leaves
to be had in New York City. Ma-Mariah, her root-woman grandmother, had taught her well under the trees on Noel's Hill in
Grenville, Grenada, overlooking the sea. Aunt Anni and Ma-Liz,
Linda's mother, had carried it on. But there was no call for this
knowledge now; and her husband Byron did not like to talk
about home because it made him sad, and weakened his resolve
to make a kingdom for himself in this new world.

She did not know if the stories about white slavers that she
read in the *Daily News* were true or not, but she knew to forbid
her children ever to set foot into any candystore. We were not
even allowed to buy penny gumballs from the machines in the
subway. Besides being a waste of precious money, the machines
were slot machines and therefore evil, or at least suspect as connected with white slavery—*the most vicious kind*, she'd say ominously.

Linda knew green things were precious, and the peaceful,
healing qualities of water. On Saturday afternoons, sometimes,
after my mother finished cleaning the house, we would go looking for some park to sit in and watch the trees. Sometimes we

went down to the edge of the Harlem River at 142nd Street to
watch the water. Sometimes we took the D train and went to
the sea. Whenever we were close to water, my mother grew
quiet and soft and absent-minded. Then she would tell us wonderful stories about Noel's Hill in Grenville, Grenada, which
overlooked the Caribbean. She told us stories about Carriacou,
where she had been born, amid the heavy smell of limes. She
told us about plants that healed and about plants that drove
you crazy, and none of it made much sense to us children because we had never seen any of them. And she told us about
the trees and fruits and flowers that grew outside the door of
the house where she grew up and lived until she married.

Once *home* was a far way off, a place I had never been to but
knew well out of my mother's mouth. She breathed exuded
hummed the fruit smell of Noel's Hill morning fresh and noon
hot, and I spun visions of sapadilla and mango as a net over my
Harlem tenement cot in the snoring darkness rank with nightmare sweat. Made bearable because it was not all. This now,
here, was a space, some temporary abode, never to be considered forever nor totally binding nor defining, no matter how
much it commanded in energy and attention. For if we lived
correctly and with frugality, looked both ways before crossing
the street, then someday we would arrive back in the sweet
place, back *home.*

We would walk the hills of Grenville, Grenada, and when the
wind blew right smell the limetrees of Carriacou, spice island
off the coast. Listen to the sea drum up on Kick'em Jenny, the
reef whose loud voice split the night, when the sea-waves beat
upon her sides. Carriacou, from where the Belmar twins set
forth on inter-island schooners for the voyages that brought
them, first and last, to Grenville town, and they married the
Noel sisters there, mainlander girls.

The Noel girls. Ma-Liz's older sister, Anni, followed her Belmar back to Carriacou, arrived as sister-in-law and stayed to become her own woman. Remembered the root-truths taught her
by their mother, Ma-Mariah. Learned other powers from the
women of Carriacou. And in a house in the hills behind L'Esterre she birthed each of her sister Ma-Liz's seven daughters.
My mother Linda was born between the waiting palms of her
loving hands.

Here Aunt Anni lived among the other women who saw their
men off on the sailing vessels, then tended the goats and ground-
nuts, planted grain and poured rum upon the earth to streng-

then the corn's growing, built their women's houses and the
rainwater catchments, harvested the limes, wove their lives and
the lives of their children together. Women who survived the
absence of their sea-faring men easily, because they came to
love each other, past the men's returning.

*Madivine. Friending. Zami. How Carriacou women love each
other is legend in Grenada, and so is their strength and their
beauty.*

In the hills of Carriacou between L'Esterre and Harvey Vale
my mother was born, a Belmar woman. Summered in Aunt
Anni's house, picked limes with the women. And she grew up
dreaming of Carriacou as someday I was to dream of Grenada.

Carriacou, a magic name like cinnamon, nutmeg, mace, the
delectable little squares of guava jelly each lovingly wrapped in
tiny bits of crazy-quilt wax-paper cut precisely from bread
wrappers, the long sticks of dried vanilla and the sweet-smelling
tonka bean, chalky brown nuggets of pressed chocolate for
cocoa-tea, all set on a bed of wild bay laurel leaves, arriving every Christmas time in a well-wrapped tea-tin.

Carriacou which was not listed in the index of the *Goode's
School Atlas* nor in the *Junior Americana World Gazette* nor appeared on any map that I could find, and so when I hunted for
the magic place during geography lessons or in free library time,
I never found it, and came to believe my mother's geography
was a fantasy or crazy or at least too old-fashioned, and in reality maybe she was talking about the place other people called
Curaçao, a Dutch possession on the other side of the Antilles.

But underneath it all as I was growing up, *home* was still a
sweet place somewhere else which they had not managed to
capture yet on paper, nor to throttle and bind up between the
pages of a schoolbook. It was our own, my truly private paradise
of blugoe and breadfruit hanging from the trees, of nutmeg and
lime and sapadilla, of tonka beans and red and yellow Paradise
Plums.*

---

*Years later, as partial requirement for a degree in library science, I did
a detailed comparison of atlases, their merits and particular strengths. I
used, as one of the foci of my project, the isle of Carriacou. It appeared
only once, in the *Atlas of the Encyclopedia Brittannica*, which has always
prided itself upon the accurate cartology of its colonies. I was twenty-six
years old before I found Carriacou upon a map.

2   I have often wondered why the farthest-out position always feels so right to me; why extremes, although difficult and sometimes painful to maintain, are always more comfortable than one plan running straight down a line in the unruffled middle.

What I really understand is a particular kind of determination. It is stubborn, it is painful, it is infuriating, but it often works.

My mother was a very powerful woman. This was so in a time when that word-combination of *woman* and *powerful* was almost unexpressable in the white american common tongue, except or unless it was accompanied by some aberrant explaining adjective like blind, or hunchback, or crazy, or Black. Therefore when I was growing up, *powerful woman* equaled something else quite different from ordinary woman, from simply "woman." It certainly did not, on the other hand, equal "man." What then? What was the third designation?

As a child, I always knew my mother was different from the other women I knew, Black or white. I used to think it was because she was my mother. But different how? I was never quite sure. There were other West Indian women around, a lot in our neighborhood and church. There were also other Black women as light as she, particularly among the low-island women. *Redbone*, they were called. *Different how?* I never knew. But that is why to this day I believe that there have always been Black dykes around—in the sense of powerful and women-oriented women—who would rather have died than use that name for themselves. And that includes my momma.

I've always thought that I learned some early ways I treated women from my father. But he certainly responded to my mother in a very different fashion. They shared decisions and the making of all policy, both in their business and in the family. Whenever anything had to be decided about any one of the three of us children, even about new coats, they would go into the bedroom and put their heads together for a little while. *Buzz buzz* would come through the closed door, sometimes in english, sometimes in patois, that Grenadian poly-language which was their lingua franca. Then the two of them would emerge and announce whatever decision had been arrived upon. They spoke all through my childhood with one unfragmentable and unappealable voice.

After the children came, my father went to real-estate school, and began to manage small rooming-houses in Harlem. When he came home from the office in the evening, he had one quick glass of brandy, standing in the kitchen, after we greeted him and before he took off his coat and hat. Then my mother and he would immediately retire into the bedroom where we would hear them discussing the day's events from behind closed doors, even if my mother had only left their office a few hours before.

If any of us children had transgressed against the rule, this was the time when we truly quaked in our orthopedic shoes, for we knew our fate was being discussed and the terms of punishment sealed behind those doors. When they opened, a mutual and irrefutable judgment would be delivered. If they spoke of anything important when we were around, Mother and Daddy immediately lapsed into patois.

Since my parents shared all making of policy and decision, in my child's eye, my mother must have been *other* than woman. Again, she was certainly not man. (The three of us children would not have tolerated that deprivation of womanliness for long at all; we'd have probably packed up our *kra* and gone back before the eighth day—an option open to all African child-souls who bumble into the wrong milieu.)

My mother was different from other women, and sometimes it gave me a sense of pleasure and specialness that was a positive aspect of feeling set apart. But sometimes it gave me pain and I fancied it the reason for so many of my childhood sorrows. *If my mother were like everybody else's maybe they would like me better.* But most often, her difference was like the season or a cold day or a steamy night in June. It just *was*, with no explanation or evocation necessary.

My mother and her two sisters were large and graceful women whose ample bodies seemed to underline the air of determination with which they moved through their lives in the strange world of Harlem and america. To me, my mother's physical substance and the presence and self-possession with which she carried herself were a large part of what made her *different*. Her public air of in-charge competence was quiet and effective. On the street people deferred to my mother over questions of taste, economy, opinion, quality, not to mention who had the right to the first available seat on the bus. I saw my mother fix her blue-grey-brown eyes upon a man scrambling for a seat on the Lenox Avenue bus, only to have him falter midway, grin abashedly, and, as if in the same movement, offer it to the old woman standing on the other side of him. I became aware, early on, that sometimes people would change their actions because of some opinion my mother never uttered, or even particularly cared about.

My mother was a very private woman, and actually quite shy, but with a very imposing, no-nonsense exterior. Full-bosomed, proud, and of no mean size, she would launch herself down the street like a ship under full sail, usually pulling me stumbling behind her. Not too many hardy souls dared cross her prow too closely.

Total strangers would turn to her in the meat market and ask what she thought about a cut of meat as to its freshness and appeal and suitability for such and such, and the butcher, impatient, would nonetheless wait for her to deliver her opinion, obviously quite a little put out but still deferential. Strangers counted upon my mother and I never knew why, but as a child it made me think she had a great deal more power than in fact she really had. My mother was invested in this image of herself also, and took pains, I realize now, to hide from us as children the many instances of her powerlessness. Being Black and foreign and female in New York City in the twenties and thirties was not simple, particularly when she was quite light enough to pass for white, but her children weren't.

In 1936-1938, 125th Street between Lenox and Eighth Avenues, later to become the shopping mecca of Black Harlem, was still a racially mixed area, with control and patronage largely in the hands of white shopkeepers. There were stores into which Black people were not welcomed, and no Black salespersons worked in the shops at all. Where our money was taken, it was taken with reluctance; and often too much was asked. (It was these conditions which young Adam Clayton Powell, Jr., addressed in his boycott and picketing of Blumstein's and Weissbecker's market in 1939 in an attempt, successful, to bring Black employment to 125th Street.) Tensions on the street were high, as they always are in racially mixed zones of transition. As a very little girl, I remember shrinking from a particular sound, a hoarsely sharp, guttural rasp, because it often meant a nasty glob of grey spittle upon my coat or shoe an instant later. My mother wiped it off with the little pieces of newspaper she always carried in her purse. Sometimes she fussed about low-class people who had no better sense nor manners than to spit into the wind no matter where they went, impressing upon me that this humiliation was totally random. It never occurred to me to doubt her.

It was not until years later once in conversation I said to her: "Have you noticed people don't spit into the wind so much the way they used to?" And the look on my mother's face told me that I had blundered into one of those secret places of pain that must never be spoken of again. But it was so typical of my mother when I was young that if she couldn't stop white people from spitting on her children because they were Black, she would insist it was something else. It was so often her approach to the world; to change reality. If you can't change reality, change your perceptions of it.

Both of my parents gave us to believe that they had the whole world in the palms of their hands for the most part, and if we three girls acted correctly—meaning working hard and doing as we were told—we could have the whole world in the palms of our hands also. It was a very confusing way to grow up, enhanced by the insularity of our family. Whatever went wrong in our lives was because our parents had decided that was best. Whatever went right was because our parents had decided that was the way it was going to be. Any doubts as to the reality of that situation were rapidly and summarily put down as small but intolerable rebellions against divine authority.

All our storybooks were about people who were very different from us. They were blond and white and lived in houses with trees around and had dogs named Spot. I didn't know people like that any more than I knew people like Cinderella who lived in castles. Nobody wrote stories about us, but still people always asked my mother for directions in a crowd.

It was this that made me decide as a child we must be rich, even when my mother did not have enough money to buy gloves for her chilblained hands, nor a proper winter coat. She would finish washing clothes and dress me hurriedly for the winter walk to pick up my sisters at school for lunch. By the time we got to St. Mark's School, seven blocks away, her beautiful long hands would be covered with ugly red splotches and welts. Later, I remember my mother rubbing her hands gingerly under cold water, and wringing them in pain. But when I asked, she brushed me off by telling me this was what they did for it at "home," and I still believed her when she said she hated to wear gloves.

[handwritten margin notes: "watching her mother deal w/ racism w/ her leaving it — I don't agree"]

[handwritten margin notes: "if they behaved they would have it all"]

At night, my father came home late from the office, or from a political meeting. After dinner, the three of us girls did our homework sitting around the kitchen table. Then my two sisters went off down the hall to their beds. My mother put down the cot for me in the front bedroom, and supervised my getting ready for bed.

She turned off all the electric lights, and I could see her from my bed, two rooms away, sitting at the same kitchen table, reading the *Daily News* by a kerosene lamp, and waiting for my father. She always said it was because the kerosene lamp remind-ed her of "home." When I was grown I realized she was trying to save a few pennies of electricity before my father came in and turned on the lights with "Lin, why you sitting in the dark so?" Sometimes I'd go to sleep with the soft chunk-a-ta-chink of her foot-pedal-powered Singer Sewing Machine, stitching up sheets and pillow-cases from unbleached muslin gotten on sale "under the bridge."

I only saw my mother crying twice when I was little. Once was when I was three, and sat on the step of her dental chair at the City Dental Clinic on 23rd Street, while a student dentist pulled out all the teeth on one side of her upper jaw. It was in a huge room full of dental chairs with other groaning people in them, and white-jacketed young men bending over open mouths. The sound of the many dental drills and instruments made the place sound like a street-corner excavation site.

Afterwards, my mother sat outside on a long wooden bench. I saw her lean her head against the back, her eyes closed. She did not respond to my pats and tugs at her coat. Climbing up upon the seat, I peered into my mother's face to see why she should be sleeping in the middle of the day. From under her closed eyelids, drops of tears were squeezing out and running down her cheek toward her ear. I touched the little drops of water on her high cheekbone in horror and amazement. The world was turning over. My mother was crying.

The other time I saw my mother cry was a few years later, one night, when I was supposed to be asleep in their bedroom. The door to the parlor was ajar, and I could see through the crack into the next room. I woke to hear my parents' voices in english. My father had just come home, and with liquor on his breath.

"I hoped I'd never live to see the day when you, Bee, stand up in some saloon and it's drink you drinking with some club-house woman."

"But Lin, what are you talking? It's not that way a-tall, you know. In politics you must be friendly-friendly so. It doesn't mean a thing."

"And if you were to go before I did, I would never so much as look upon another man, and I would expect you to do the same."

My mother's voice was strangely muffled by her tears.

These were the years leading up to the Second World War, when Depression took such a terrible toll, and of Black people in particular.

Even though we children could be beaten for losing a penny coming home from the store, my mother fancied a piece of her role as lady bountiful, a role she would accuse me bitterly of playing years later in my life whenever I gave something to a friend. But one of my earlier memories of World War II was just before the beginning, with my mother splitting a one-pound tin of coffee between two old family friends who had come on an infrequent visit.

Although she always insisted that she had nothing to do with politics or government affairs, from somewhere my mother had heard the winds of war, and despite our poverty had set about consistently hoarding sugar and coffee in her secret closet under the sink. Long before Pearl Harbor, I recall opening each cloth five-pound sack of sugar which we purchased at the market and pouring a third of it into a scrubbed tin to store away under the sink, secure from mice. The same thing happened with coffee. We would buy Bokar Coffee at the A&P and have it ground and poured into bags, and then divide the bag between the coffee tin on the back of the stove, and the hidden ones under the sink. Not many people came to our house, ever, but no one left without at least a cupful of sugar or coffee during the war, when coffee and sugar were heavily rationed.

Meat and butter could not be hoarded, and throughout the early war, my mother's absolute refusal to accept butter substitutes (only "other people" used margarine, those same "other people" who fed their children peanut butter sandwiches for lunch, used sandwich spread instead of mayonnaise and ate pork chops and watermelon) had us on line in front of supermarkets all over the city on bitterly cold Saturday mornings, waiting for the store to open so we each could get first crack at buying our allotted quarter-pound of unrationed butter. Throughout the war, Mother kept a mental list of all the supermarkets reachable by one bus, frequently taking only me because I could ride free. She also noted which were friendly and which were not, and long after the war ended there were meat markets and stores we never shopped in because someone in them had crossed my mother during the war over some precious scarce commodity, and my mother never forgot and rarely forgave.

3 When I was five years old and still legally blind, I started school in a sight-conservation class in the local public school on 135th Street and Lenox Avenue. On the corner was a blue wooden booth where white women gave away free milk to Black mothers with children. I used to long for some Hearst Free Milk Fund milk, in those cute little bottles with their red and white tops, but my mother never allowed me to have any, because she said it was charity, which was bad and demeaning, and besides the milk was warm and might make me sick.

The school was right across the avenue from the catholic school where my two older sisters went, and this public school had been used as a threat against them for as long as I could remember. If they didn't behave and get good marks in schoolwork and deportment, they could be "transferred." A "transfer" carried the same dire implications as "deportation" came to imply decades later.

Of course everybody knew that public school kids did nothing but "fight," and you could get "beaten up" every day after school, instead of being marched out of the schoolhouse door in two neat rows like little robots, silent but safe and unattacked, to the corner where the mothers waited.

But the catholic school had no kindergarten, and certainly not one for blind children.

Despite my nearsightedness, or maybe because of it, I learned to read at the same time I learned to talk, which was only about a year or so before I started school. Perhaps *learn* isn't the right word to use for my beginning to talk, because to this day I don't know if I didn't talk earlier because I didn't know how, or if I didn't talk because I had nothing to say that I would be

allowed to say without punishment. Self-preservation starts
very early in West Indian families.

I learned how to read from Mrs. Augusta Baker, the children's
librarian at the old 135th Street branch library, which has just
recently been torn down to make way for a new library building
to house the Schomburg Collection on African-American History and Culture. If that was the only good deed that lady ever
did in her life, may she rest in peace. Because that deed saved
my life, if not sooner, then later, when sometimes the only
thing I had to hold on to was knowing I could read, and that
that could get me through.

My mother was pinching my ear off one bright afternoon,
while I lay spreadeagled on the floor of the Children's Room
like a furious little brown toad, screaming bloody murder and
embarrassing my mother to death. I know it must have been
spring or early fall, because without the protection of a heavy
coat, I can still feel the stinging soreness in the flesh of my upper arm. There, where my mother's sharp fingers had already
tried to pinch me into silence. To escape those inexorable fingers I had hurled myself to the floor, roaring with pain as I
could see them advancing toward my ears again. We were waiting to pick up my two older sisters from story hour, held upstairs on another floor of the dry-smelling quiet library. My
shrieks pierced the reverential stillness.

Suddenly, I looked up, and there was a library lady standing over me. My mother's hands had dropped to her sides.
From the floor where I was lying, Mrs. Baker seemed like yet
another mile-high woman about to do me in. She had immense,
light, hooded eyes and a very quiet voice that said, not damna-
tion for my noise, but "Would you like to hear a story, little
girl?"

Part of my fury was because I had not been allowed to go to
that secret feast called story hour since I was too young, and
now here was this strange lady offering me my own story.

I didn't dare to look at my mother, half-afraid she might say
no, I was too bad for stories. Still bewildered by this sudden
change of events, I climbed up upon the stool which Mrs. Baker
pulled over for me, and gave her my full attention. This was a
new experience for me and I was insatiably curious.

Mrs. Baker read me *Madeline*, and *Horton Hatches the Egg*,
both of which rhymed and had huge lovely pictures which I
could see from behind my newly acquired eyeglasses, fastened
around the back of my rambunctious head by a black elastic
band running from earpiece to earpiece. She also read me an-

other storybook about a bear named Herbert who ate up an entire family, one by one, starting with the parents. By the time she had finished that one, I was sold on reading for the rest of my life.

I took the books from Mrs. Baker's hands after she was finished reading, and traced the large black letters with my fingers, while I peered again at the beautiful bright colors of the pictures. Right then I decided I was going to find out how to do that myself. I pointed to the black marks which I could now distinguish as separate letters, different from my sisters' more grown-up books, whose smaller print made the pages only one grey blur for me. I said, quite loudly, for whoever was listening to hear, "I want to read."

My mother's surprised relief outweighed whatever annoyance she was still feeling at what she called my whelpish carryings-on. From the background where she had been hovering while Mrs. Baker read, my mother moved forward quickly, mollified and impressed. I had spoken. She scooped me up from the low stool, and to my surprise, kissed me, right in front of everybody in the library, including Mrs. Baker.

This was an unprecedented and unusual display of affection in public, the cause of which I did not comprehend. But it was a warm and happy feeling. For once, obviously, I had done something right.

My mother set me back upon the stool and turned to Mrs. Baker, smiling.

"Will wonders never cease to perform!" Her excitement startled me back into cautious silence.

Not only had I been sitting still for longer than my mother would have thought possible, and sitting quietly. I had also spoken rather than screamed, something that my mother, after four years and a lot of worry, had despaired that I would ever do. Even one intelligible word was a very rare event for me. And although the doctors at the clinic had clipped the little membrane under my tongue so I was no longer tongue-tied, and had assured my mother that I was not retarded, she still had her terrors and her doubts. She was genuinely happy for any possible alternative to what she was afraid might be a dumb child. The ear-pinching was forgotten. My mother accepted the alphabet and picture books Mrs. Baker gave her for me, and I was on my way.

I sat at the kitchen table with my mother, tracing letters and calling their names. Soon she taught me how to say the alphabet forwards and backwards as it was done in Grenada. Although

she had never gone beyond the seventh grade, she had been put
in charge of teaching the first grade children their letters during
her last year at Mr. Taylor's School in Grenville. She told me
stories about his strictness as she taught me how to print my
name.

I did not like the tail of the Y hanging down below the line in
Audrey, and would always forget to put it on, which used to
disturb my mother greatly. I used to love the evenness of
AUDRELORDE at four years of age, but I remembered to put
on the Y because it pleased my mother, and because, as she always insisted to me, that was the way it had to be because that
was the way it was. No deviation was allowed from her inter-
pretations of correct.

So by the time I arrived at the sight-conservation kindergarten, braided, scrubbed, and bespectacled, I was able to read
large-print books and write my name with a regular pencil.
Then came my first rude awakening about school. Ability had
nothing to do with expectation.

There were only seven or eight of us little Black children in a
big classroom, all with various serious deficiencies of sight.
Some of us were cross-eyed, some of us were nearsighted, and
one little girl had a patch over one of her eyes.

We were given special short wide notebooks to write in, with
very widely spaced lines on yellow paper. They looked like my
sister's music notebooks. We were also given thick black crayons to write with. Now you don't grow up fat, Black, nearly
blind, and ambidextrous in a West Indian household, particularly my parents' household, and survive without being or becoming fairly rigid fairly fast. And having been roundly spanked on
several occasions for having made that mistake at home, I knew
quite well that crayons were not what you wrote with, and
music books were definitely not what you wrote in.

I raised my hand. When the teacher asked me what I wanted,
I asked for some regular paper to write on and a pencil. That
was my undoing. "We don't have any pencils here," I was told.

Our first task was to copy down the first letter of our names
in those notebooks with our black crayons. Our teacher went
around the room and wrote the required letter into each one
of our notebooks. When she came around to me, she printed a
large A in the upper left corner of the first page of my notebook, and handed me the crayon.

"I can't," I said, knowing full well that what you do with
black crayons is scribble on the wall and get your backass beat-

en, or color around the edges of pictures, but not write. To write, you needed a pencil. "I can't!" I said, terrified, and started to cry.

"Imagine that, a big girl like you. Such a shame, I'll have to tell your mother that you won't even try. And such a big girl like you!"

And it was true. Although young, I was the biggest child by far in the whole class, a fact that had not escaped the attention of the little boy who sat behind me, and who was already whispering "fatty, fatty!" whenever the teacher's back was turned.

"Now just try, dear. I'm sure you can try to print your A. Mother will be so pleased to see that at least you tried." She patted my stiff braids and turned to the next desk.

Well, of course, she had said the magic words, because I would have walked over rice on my knees to please Mother. I took her nasty old soft smudgy crayon and pretended that it was a nice neat pencil with a fine point, elegantly sharpened that morning outside the bathroom door by my father, with the little penknife that he always carried around in his bathrobe pocket.

I bent my head down close to the desk that smelled like old spittle and rubber erasers, and on that ridiculous yellow paper with those laughably wide spaces I printed my best AUDRE. I had never been too good at keeping between straight lines no matter what their width, so it slanted down across the page something like this: A

      U

    D

      R

        E

The notebooks were short and there was no more room for anything else on that page. So I turned the page over, and wrote again, earnestly and laboriously, biting my lip, L

        O

          R

            D

              E

half-showing off, half-eager to please.

By this time, Miss Teacher had returned to the front of the room.

"Now when you're finished drawing your letter, children," she said, "Just raise your hand high." And her voice smiled a big smile. It is surprising to me that I can still hear her voice but

I can't see her face, and I don't know whether she was Black or white. I can remember the way she smelled, but not the color of her hand upon my desk.

Well, when I heard that, my hand flew up in the air, wagging frantically. There was one thing my sisters had warned me about school in great detail: you must never talk in school unless you raised your hand. So I raised my hand, anxious to be recognized. I could imagine what teacher would say to my mother when she came to fetch me home at noon. My mother would know that her warning to me to "be good" had in truth been heeded.

Miss Teacher came down the aisle and stood beside my desk, looking down at my book. All of a sudden the air around her hand beside my notebook grew very still and frightening.

"Well I never!" Her voice was sharp. "I thought I told you to draw this letter? You don't even want to try and do as you are told. Now I want you to turn that page over and draw your letter like everyone. . ." and turning to the next page, she saw my second name sprawled down across the page.

There was a moment of icy silence, and I knew I had done something terribly wrong. But this time, I had no idea what it could be that would get her so angry, certainly not being proud of writing my name.

She broke the silence with a wicked edge to her voice. "I see." she said. "I see we have a young lady who does not want to do as she is told. We will have to tell her mother about that." And the rest of the class snickered, as the teacher tore the page out of my notebook.

"Now I am going to give you one more chance," she said, as she printed another fierce A at the head of the new page. "Now you copy that letter exactly the way it is, and the rest of the class will have to wait for you." She placed the crayon squarely back into my fingers.

By this time I had no idea at all what this lady wanted from me, and so I cried and cried for the rest of the morning until my mother came to fetch me home at noon. I cried on the street while we stopped to pick up my sisters, and for most of the way home, until my mother threatened to box my ears for me if I didn't stop embarrassing her on the street.

That afternoon, after Phyllis and Helen were back in school, and I was helping her dust, I told my mother how they had given me crayons to write with and how the teacher didn't want me to write my name. When my father came home that evening, the two of them went into counsel. It was decided that my mother would speak to the teacher the next morning when she brought me to school, in order to find out what I had done wrong. This decision was passed on to me, ominously, because of course I must have done something wrong to have made Miss Teacher so angry with me.

The next morning at school, the teacher told my mother that she did not think that I was ready yet for kindergarten, because I couldn't follow directions, and I wouldn't do as I was told.

My mother knew very well I could follow directions, because she herself had spent a good deal of effort and arm-power making it very painful for me whenever I did not follow directions. And she also believed that a large part of the function of school was to make me learn how to do what I was told to do. In her private opinion, if this school could not do that, then it was not much of a school and she was going to find a school that could. In other words, my mother had made up her mind that school was where I belonged.

That same morning, she took me off across the street to the catholic school, where she persuaded the nuns to put me into the first grade, since I could read already, and write my name on regular paper with a real pencil. If I sat in the first row I could see the blackboard. My mother also told the nuns that unlike my two sisters, who were models of deportment, I was very unruly, and that they should spank me whenever I needed it. Mother Josepha, the principal, agreed, and I started school.

My first grade teacher was named Sister Mary of Perpetual Help, and she was a disciplinarian of the first order, right after my mother's own heart. A week after I started school she sent a note home to my mother asking her not to dress me in so many layers of clothing because then I couldn't feel the strap on my behind when I was punished.

Sister Mary of Perpetual Help ran the first grade with an iron hand in the shape of a cross. She couldn't have been more than eighteen. She was big, and blond, I think, since we never got to see the nuns' hair in those days. But her eyebrows were blonde, and she was supposed to be totally dedicated, like all the other Sisters of the Blessed Sacrament, to caring for the Colored and Indian children of america. Caring for was not always caring about. And it always felt like Sister MPH hated either teaching or little children.

She had divided up the class into two groups, the Fairies and the Brownies. In this day of heightened sensitivity to racism and color usage, I don't have to tell you which were the good students and which were the baddies. I always wound up in the Brownies, because either I talked too much, or I broke my glasses, or I perpetrated some other awful infraction of the endless rules of good behavior.

But for two glorious times that year, I made it into the Fairies for brief periods of time. One was put into the Brownies if one misbehaved, or couldn't learn to read. I had learned to read already, but I couldn't tell my numbers. Whenever Sister MPH would call a few of us up to the front of the room for our reading lesson, she would say, "All right, children, now turn to page six in your readers." or, "Turn to page nineteen, please, and begin at the top of the page."

Well, I didn't know what page to turn to, and I was ashamed of not being able to read my numbers, so when my turn came to read I couldn't, because I didn't have the right place. After the prompting of a few words, she would go on to the next reader, and soon I wound up in the Brownies.

This was around the second month of school, in October. My new seatmate was Alvin, and he was the worst boy in the whole class. His clothes were dirty and he smelled unwashed, and rumor had it he had once called Sister MPH a bad name, but that couldn't have been possible because he would have been suspended permanently from school.

Alvin used to browbeat me into lending him my pencil to draw endless pictures of airplanes dropping huge penile bombs. He would always promise to give me the pictures when he was finished. But of course, whenever he was finished, he would decide that the picture was too good for a girl, so he would have to keep it, and make me another. Yet I never stopped hoping for one of them, because he drew airplanes very well.

He also would scratch his head and shake out the dandruff onto our joint spelling book or reader, and then tell me the flakes of dandruff were dead lice. I believed him in this, also, and was constantly terrified of catching cooties. But Alvin and I worked out our own system together for reading. He couldn't read, but he knew all his numbers, and I could read words, but I couldn't find the right page.

The Brownies were never called up to the front of the room; we had to read in anonymity from our double seats, where we scrunched over at the edges, ordinarily, to leave room in the middle for our two guardian angels to sit. But whenever we had to share a book our guardian angels had to jump around us and sit on the outside edge of our seats. Therefore, Alvin would show me the right pages to turn to when Sister called them out, and I would whisper the right words to him whenever it came his turn to read. Inside of a week after we devised this scheme of things, we had gotten out of the Brownies together. Since we shared a reader, we always went up together to read with the Fairies, so we had a really good thing going there for a while.

But Alvin began to get sick around Thanksgiving, and was absent a lot, and he didn't come back to school at all after Christmas. I used to miss his dive-bomber pictures, but most of all I missed his page numbers. After a few times of being called up by myself and not being able to read, I landed back in the Brownies again.

Years later I found out that Alvin had died of tuberculosis over Christmas, and that was why we all had been X-rayed in the auditorium after Mass on the first day back to school from Christmas vacation.

I spent a few more weeks in the Brownies with my mouth almost shut during reading lesson, unless the day's story fell on page eight, or ten, or twenty, which were the three numbers I knew.

Then, over one weekend, we had our first writing assignment. We were to look in our parents' newspaper and cut out words we knew the meaning of, and make them into simple sentences. We could only use one "the." It felt like an easy task, since I was already reading the comics by this time.

On Sunday morning after church, when I usually did my homework, I noticed an ad for White Rose Salada Tea on the back of the *New York Times Magazine* which my father was reading at the time. It had the most gorgeous white rose on a red background, and I decided I must have that rose for my picture—our sentences were to be illustrated. I searched through the paper until I found an "I," and then a "like," which I dutifully clipped out along with my rose, and the words "White," "Rose," "Salada," and "Tea." I knew the brand-name well because it was my mother's favorite tea.

On Monday morning, we all stood our sentence papers up on the chalk-channels, leaning them against the blackboards. And there among the twenty odd "The boy ran," "it was cold," was "I like White Rose Salada Tea" and my beautiful white rose on a red background.

That was too much coming from a Brownie. Sister Mary of PH frowned.

"This was to be our own work, children," she said. "Who helped you with your sentence, Audre?" I told her I had done it alone.

"Our guardian angels weep when we don't tell the truth, Audre. I want a note from your mother tomorrow telling me that you are sorry for lying to the baby Jesus."

I told the story at home, and the next day I brought a note from my father saying that the sentence had indeed been my own work. Triumphantly, I gathered up my books and moved back over to the Fairies.

The thing that I remember best about being in the first grade was how uncomfortable it was, always having to leave room for my guardian angel on those tiny seats, and moving back and forth across the room from Brownies to Fairies and back again.

This time I stayed in the Fairies for a long time, because I finally started to recognize my numbers. I stayed there until the day I broke my glasses. I had taken them off to clean them in the bathroom and they slipped out of my hand. I was never to do that, and so I was in disgrace. My eyeglasses came from the eye clinic of the medical center, and it took three days to get a new pair made. We could not afford to buy more than one pair at a time, nor did it occur to my parents that such an extravagance might be necessary. I was almost sightless without them, but my punishment for having broken them was that I had to go to school anyway, even though I could see nothing. My sisters delivered me to my classroom with a note from my mother saying I had broken my glasses despite the fact they were tied to me by the strip of elastic.

I was never supposed to take my glasses off except just before getting into bed, but I was endlessly curious about these magical circles of glass that were rapidly becoming a part of me, transforming my universe, and remaining movable. I was always trying to examine them with my naked, nearsighted eyes, usually dropping them in the process.

Since I could not see at all to do any work from the blackboard, Sister Mary of PH made me sit in the back of the room on the window seat with a dunce cap on. She had the rest of the class offer up a prayer for my poor mother who had such a naughty girl who broke her glasses and caused her parents such needless extra expense to replace them. She also had them offer up a special prayer for me to stop being such a wicked-hearted child.

I amused myself by counting the rainbows of color that danced like a halo around the lamp on Sister Mary of PH's desk, watching the starburst patterns of light that the incandescent light bulb became without my glasses. But I missed them, and not being able to see. I never once gave a thought to the days when I believed that bulbs were starburst patterns of color, because that was what all light looked like to me.

It must have been close to summer by this time. As I sat with the dunce cap on, I can remember the sun pouring through the classroom window hot upon my back, as the rest of the class dutifully entoned their Hail Marys for my soul, and I played secret games with the distorted rainbows of light, until Sister noticed and made me stop blinking my eyes so fast.

How I Became a Poet

"Wherever the bird with no feet flew she found trees with no limbs."

When the strongest words for what I have to offer come out of me sounding like words I remember from my mother's mouth, then I either have to reassess the meaning of everything I have to say now, or re-examine the worth of her old words.

My mother had a special and secret relationship with words, taken for granted as language because it was always there. I did not speak until I was four. When I was three, the dazzling world of strange lights and fascinating shapes which I inhabited resolved itself in mundane definitions, and I learned another nature of things as seen through eyeglasses. This perception of things was less colorful and confusing but much more comfortable than the one native to my nearsighted and unevenly focused eyes.

I remember trundling along Lenox Avenue with my mother, on our way to school to pick up Phyllis and Helen for lunch. It was late spring because my legs felt light and real, unencumbered by bulky snowpants. I dawdled along the fence around the public playground, inside of which grew one stunted plane tree. Enthralled, I stared up at the sudden revelation of each single and particular leaf of green, precisely shaped and laced about with unmixed light. Before my glasses, I had known trees as tall brown pillars ending in fat puffy swirls of paling greens, much like the pictures of them I perused in my sisters' storybooks from which I learned so much of my visual world.

But out of my mother's mouth a world of comment came cascading when she felt at ease or in her element, full of picaresque constructions and surreal scenes.

We were never dressed too lightly, but rather "in next kin to nothing." *Neck skin to nothing?* Impassable and impossible distances were measured by the distance "from Hog to Kick 'em Jenny." *Hog? Kick 'em Jenny?* Who knew until I was sane and grown a poet with a mouthful of stars, that these were two little reefs in the Grenadines, between Grenada and Carriacou.

The euphemisms of body were equally puzzling, if no less colorful. A mild reprimand was accompanied not by a slap on the behind, but a "smack on the backass," or on the "bamsy." You sat on your "bam-bam," but anything between your hipbones and upper thighs was consigned to the "lower-region," a word I always imagined to have french origins, as in "Don't forget to wash your *l'oregión* before you go to bed." For more clinical and precise descriptions, there was always "between your legs"—whispered.

The sensual content of life was masked and cryptic, but attended in well-coded phrases. Somehow all the cousins knew that Uncle Cyril couldn't lift heavy things because of his "bam-bam-coo," and the lowered voice in which this hernia was spoken of warned us that it had something to do with "down there." And on the infrequent but magical occasions when mother performed her delicious laying on of hands for a crick in the neck or a pulled muscle, she didn't massage your backbone, she "raised your zandalee."

I never caught cold, but "got co-hum, co-hum," and then everything turned "cro-bo-so," topsy-turvy, or at least, a bit askew.

I am a reflection of my mother's secret poetry as well as of her hidden angers.

Sitting between my mother's spread legs, her strong knees gripping my shoulders tightly like some well-attended drum, my head in her lap, while she brushed and combed and oiled and braided. I feel my mother's strong, rough hands all up in my unruly hair, while I'm squirming around on a low stool or on a folded towel on the floor, my rebellious shoulders hunched and jerking against the inexorable sharp-toothed comb. After each springy portion is combed and braided, she pats it tenderly and proceeds to the next.

I hear the interjection of *sotto voce* admonitions that punctuated whatever discussion she and my father were having.

"Hold your back up, now! Deenie, keep still! Put your head so!" Scratch, scratch. "When last you wash your hair? Look the dandruff!" Scratch, scratch, the comb's truth setting my own teeth on edge. Yet, these were some of the moments I missed most sorely when our real wars began.

I remember the warm mother smell caught between her legs, and the intimacy of our physical touching nestled inside of the anxiety/pain like a nutmeg nestled inside its covering of mace.

The radio, the scratching comb, the smell of petroleum jelly, the grip of her knees and my stinging scalp all fall into—*the rhythms of a litany, the rituals of Black women combing their daughters' hair.*

Saturday morning. The one morning of the week my mother does not leap from bed to prepare me and my sisters for school or church. I wake in the cot in their bedroom, knowing only it is one of those lucky days when she is still in bed, and alone. My father is in the kitchen. The sound of pots and the slightly off-smell of frying bacon mixes with the smell of percolating Bokar coffee.

The click of her wedding ring against the wooden headboard. She is awake. I get up and go over and crawl into my mother's bed. Her smile. Her glycerine-flannel smell. The warmth. She reclines upon her back and side, one arm extended, the other flung across her forehead. A hot-water bottle wrapped in body-temperature flannel, which she used to quiet her gall-bladder pains during the night. Her large soft breasts beneath the buttoned flannel of her nightgown. Below, the rounded swell of her stomach, silent and inviting touch.

I crawl against her, playing with the enflanneled, warm, rubber bag, pummeling it, tossing it, sliding it down the roundness of her stomach to the warm sheet between the bend' of her elbow and the curve of her waist below her breasts, flopping sideward inside the printed cloth. Under the covers, the morning smells soft and sunny and full of promise.

I frolic with the liquid-filled water bottle, patting and rubbing its firm giving softness. I shake it slowly, rocking it back and forth, lost in sudden tenderness, at the same time gently rubbing against my mother's quiet body. Warm milky smells of morning surround us.

Feeling the smooth deep firmness of her breasts against my shoulders, my pajama'd back, sometimes, more daringly, against my ears and the sides of my cheeks. Tossing, tumbling, the soft gurgle of the water within its rubber casing. Sometimes the thin sound of her ring against the bedstead as she moves her hand up over my head. Her arm comes down across me, holding me to her for a moment, then quiets my frisking.

"All right, now."

I nuzzle against her sweetness, pretending not to hear.

"All right, now, I said; stop it. It's time to get up from this bed. Look lively, and mind you spill that water."

Before I can say anything she is gone in a great deliberate heave. The purposeful whip of her chenille robe over her warm flannel gown and the bed already growing cold beside me.

"Wherever the bird with no feet flew she found trees with no limbs."

4 When 1 was around the age of four or five, I would have given anything I had in the world except my mother, in order to have had a friend or a little sister. She would be someone I could talk to and play with, someone close enough in age to me that I would not have to be afraid of her, nor she of me. We would share our secrets with each other.

Even though I had two older sisters, I grew up feeling like an only child, since they were quite close to each other in age, and quite far away from me. Actually, I grew up feeling like an only planet, or some isolated world in a hostile, or at best, unfriend-ly, firmament. The fact that I was clothed, sheltered, and fed better than many other children in Harlem in those Depression years was not a fact that impressed itself too often upon my child's consciousness.

Most of my childhood fantasies revolved around how I might acquire this little female person for my companion. I concen-trated upon magical means, having gathered early on that my family had no intention of satisfying this particular need of mine. The Lorde family was not going to expand any more.

The idea of having children was a pretty scary one, anyway, full of secret indiscretions peeked at darkly through the corner of an eye, as my mother and my aunts did whenever they passed a woman on the street who had one of those big, pushed-out-in-front, blouses that always intrigued me so. I wondered what great wrong these women had done, that this big blouse was a badge of, obvious as the dunce cap I sometimes had to wear in the corner at school.

Adoption was also out of the question. You could get a kitten from the corner grocery-store man, but not a sister. Like ocean cruises and boarding schools and upper berths in trains, it was not for us. Rich people, like Mr. Rochester in the movie *Jane Eyre*, lonely in their great tree-lined estates, adopted children, but not us.

Being the youngest in a West Indian family had many privileges but no rights. And since my mother was determined not to "spoil" me, even those privileges were largely illusory. I knew, therefore, that if my family were to acquire another little person voluntarily, that little person would most probably be a boy, and would most decidedly belong to my mother, and not to me.

I really believed, however, that my magical endeavors, done often enough, in the right way, and in the right places, letter-perfect and with a clean soul, would finally bring me a little sister. And I did mean little. I frequently imagined my little sister and I having fascinating conversations together while she sat cradled in the cupped palm of my hand. There she was, curled up and carefully shielded from the inquisitive eyes of the rest of the world, and my family in particular.

When I was three and a half and had gotten my first eyeglasses, I stopped tripping over my feet. But I still walked with my head down, all the time, counting the lines on the squares in the pavement of every street which I traveled, hanging onto the hand of my mother or one of my sisters. I had decided that if I could step on all the horizontal lines for one day, my little person would appear like a dream made real, waiting for me in my bed by the time I got home. But I always messed up, or skipped one, or someone pulled my arm at a crucial moment. And she never appeared.

Sometimes on Saturdays in winter, my mother made the three of us a little clay out of flour and water and Diamond Crystal Shaker Salt. I always fashioned tiny little figures out of my share of the mixture. I would beg or swipe a little vanilla extract from my mother's shelf in the kitchen, where she kept her wonderful spices and herbs and extracts, and mix that with the clay. Sometimes I dabbed the figures on either side of the head behind the ears as I had seen my mother do with her glycerine and rosewater when she got dressed to go out.

I loved the way the rich, dark brown vanilla scented the flour-clay; it reminded me of my mother's hands when she made peanut brittle and eggnog at holidays. But most of all, I loved the live color it would bring to the pasty-white clay.

I knew for sure that real live people came in many different shades of beige and brown and cream and reddish tan, but nobody alive ever came in that pasty-white shade of flour and salt and water, even if they were called white. So the vanilla was essential if my little person was to be real. But the coloring didn't help either. No matter how many intricate rituals and incantations and spells I performed, no matter how many Hail Marys and Our Fathers I said, no matter what I promised god in return, the vanilla-tinted clay would slowly shrivel up and harden, turn gradually brittle and sour, and then crumble into a grainy flour dust. No matter how hard I prayed or schemed, the figures would never come alive. They never turned around in the cupped palm of my hand, to smile up at me and say "Hi."

I found my first playmate when I was around four years old. It lasted for about ten minutes.

It was a high winter noontime. My mother had bundled me up in my thick one-piece woolen snowsuit and cap and bulky scarf. Once she had inserted me into all this arctic gear, pulled rubber galoshes up over my shoes and wrapped yet another thick scarf around the whole as if to keep the mass intact, she planted me out upon the stoop of the apartment building while she dressed herself hurriedly. Although my mother never liked to have me out of her sight for any period of time, she did this to keep me from catching my death of cold from becoming overheated and then going outdoors.

After many weighty warnings to me not to move from that spot, dire descriptions of what would happen to me if I did, and how I was to yell if any strangers spoke to me, my mother disappeared down the few feet of hallway back to our apartment to get her coat and hat, and to check all the windows of the house to make sure that they were locked.

I loved these few minutes of freedom, and treasured them secretly. They were the only times I ever got to be outside without my mother urging me along on my short stubby little legs that could never run fast enough to keep up with her purposeful strides. I sat quietly where she had put me on the slated top of the stone banisters of the stoop. My arms stuck out a little from my sides over the bulk of my clothing, my feet were heavy and awkward with sturdy shoes and galoshes, and my neck was stiffly encased in the woolen cap and wrapped scarf.

The sun shone with a winter milkiness onto the sidewalks across the street, and onto the few banks of dirty soot-covered snow that lined the sidewalks near the gutter's edge. I could see up to the corner of Lenox Avenue, about three houses away. At the corner near the building line, the Father Divine man ran his Peace Brother Peace shoe repair business from a ramshackled wooden kiosk heated by a small round stove. From the roof of the kiosk, a thin strand of smoke drifted upward. The smoke was the only sign of life and there was nobody on the street that I could see. I wished the street was warm and beautiful and busy, and that we were having cantaloupe for lunch instead of the hot homemade pea soup that was simmering on the back of the stove awaiting our return.

I had almost made a boat of newspaper just before I had to start being dressed to go out, and I wondered if my bits of newspaper would still be on the kitchen table when we got back, or was my mother even now sweeping them away into the garbage bag? Would I be able to rescue them before lunch or would there be nasty wet orange-peelings and coffee grounds all over them?

Suddenly I realized that there was a little creature standing on a step in the entryway of the main doors, looking at me with bright eyes and a big smile. It was a little girl. She was right away the most beautiful little girl I had ever seen alive in my life.

My lifelong dream of a doll-baby come to life had in fact come true. Here she stood before me now, smiling and pretty in an unbelievable wine-red velvet coat with a wide, wide skirt that flared out over dainty little lisle-stockinged legs. Her feet were clad in a pair of totally impractical, black patent-leather mary-jane shoes, whose silver buckles glinted merrily in the drab noon light.

Her reddish-brown hair was not braided in four plaits like mine, but framed her little pointy-chinned face, tight and curly. On her head sat a wine-colored velvet beret that matched her coat, and on the very top of that sat a big white fur pompom.

Even with decades of fashion between us now, and the dulling of time, it was the most beautiful outfit I had ever seen in my not quite five years of clothes-watching.

Her honey-brown skin had a ruddy glow that echoed the tones of her hair, and her eyes seemed to match both in a funny way that reminded me of my mother's eyes, the way, although light in themselves, they flashed alight in the sun.

I had no idea how old she was.

"What's your name? Mine's Toni."

The name called up a picture book I was just finished reading, and the image came out *boy*. But this delectable creature in front of me was most certainly a girl, and I wanted her for my very own—my very own what, I did not know—but for my very own self. I started to image in my head where I could keep her. Maybe I could tuck her up in the folds under my pillow, pet her during the night when everybody else was asleep, and I was fighting off nightmares of the devil riding me. Of course, I'd have to be careful that she didn't get squeezed into the cot in the morning, when my mother folded up my bed, covered it with an old piece of flowered cretonne bedspread and shoved the whole thing tidily into a corner behind the bedroom door. No, that certainly wouldn't work. My mother would most assuredly find her when, in my mother's way, she plumped up my pillows.

While I was trying to image a safe place to keep her by a rapid succession of pictures in my mind's eye, Toni had advanced towards me, and was now standing between my outspread snowsuited legs, her dark-bright fire-lit eyes on a level with my own. With my woolen mittens dangling down from cords which emerged from the cuffs at each of my wrists, I reached out my hands and lightly rubbed the soft velvet shoulders of her frock-coat up and down.

From around her neck hung a fluffy white fur muff that matched the white fur ball on the top of her hat. I touched her muff, too, and then raised my hand up to feel the fur pompom. The soft silky warmth of the fur made my fingers tingle in a way that the cold had not, and I pinched and fingered it until Toni finally shook her head free of my hand.

I began to finger the small shiny gold buttons on the front of her coat. I unbuttoned the first two of them at the top, just so I could button them back up again, pretending I was her mother.

"You cold?" I was looking at her pink and beige ears, now slowly turning rosy from the cold. From each delicate lobe hung a tiny gold loop.

"No," she said, moving even closer between my knees. "Let's play."

I stuck both of my hands into the holes of her furry muff, and she giggled delightedly as my cold fingers closed around her warm ones inside the quilted dark spaces of the fur. She pulled one hand out past mine and opened it in front of my face to reveal two peppermint lifesavers, sticky now from the heat of her palm. "Want one?"

I took one hand out of her muff, and never taking my eyes off her face, popped one of the striped candy rings into my mouth. My mouth was dry. I closed it around the candy and sucked, feeling the peppermint juice run down my throat, burning and sweet almost to the point of harshness. For years and years afterward, I always thought of peppermint lifesavers as the candy in Toni's muff.

She was beginning to get impatient. "Play with me, please?" Toni took a step backward, smiling, and I was terrified suddenly that she might disappear or run away, and the sunlight would surely vanish with her from 142nd Street. My mother had warned me not to move from that spot where she had planted me. But there was no question in my mind; I could not bear to lose Toni.

I reached out and pulled her back gently towards me, sitting her down crosswise upon my knees. She felt so light through the padding of my snowsuit that I thought she could blow away and I would not feel the difference between her being there and not being there.

I put my arms around her soft red velvet coat, and clasping my two hands together, I slowly rocked her back and forth the way I did with my sisters' big Coca-Cola doll that had eyes that opened and closed and that came down from the closet shelf every year around Christmas time. Our old cat Minnie the Moocher did not feel much lighter sitting on my lap.

She turned her face around to me with another one of her delighted laughs that sounded like the ice cubes in my father's nightly drink. I could feel the creeping warmth of her, slowly spreading all along the front of my body through the many layers of clothing, and as she turned her head to speak to me the damp warmth of her breath fogged up my spectacles a little in the crisp winter air.

I started to sweat inside my snowsuit as I usually did, despite the cold. I wanted to take off her coat and see what she had on underneath it. I wanted to take off all of her clothes, and touch her live little brown body and make sure she was real. My heart was bursting with a love and happiness for which I had no words. I unbuttoned the top buttons of her coat again.

"No, don't do that! My grandma won't like it. You can rock me some more." She cuddled down again into my arms.

I put my arms back around her shoulders. Was she really a little girl or a doll come alive? There was only one way I knew for sure of telling. I turned her over and put her across my knees. The light seemed to change around us on the stoop. I looked over once at the doorway leading into the hall, half-afraid of who might be standing there.

I raised up the back of Toni's wine-red velvet coat, and the many folds of her full-skirted green eyelet dress underneath. I lifted up the petticoats under that, until I could see her white cotton knickers, each leg of which ended in an embroidered gathering right above the elastic garters that held up her stockings.

Beads of sweat were running down my chest to be caught at my waist by the tight band of my snowsuit. Ordinarily I hated sweating inside my snowsuit because it felt like roaches were crawling down the front of me.

Toni laughed again and said something that I could not hear. She squirmed around comfortably on my knees and turned her head, her sweet face looking sideways up into mine.

"Grandma forgot my leggings at my house."

I reached up under the welter of dress and petticoats and took hold of the waistband of her knickers. Was her bottom going to be real and warm or turn out to be hard rubber, molded into a little crease like the ultimately disappointing Coca-Cola doll?

My hands were shaking with excitement. I hesitated a moment too long. As I was about to pull down Toni's panties I heard the main door open and out of the front hallway hurried my mother, adjusting the brim of her hat as she stepped out onto the stoop.

I felt caught in the middle of an embarrassing and terrible act from which there could be no hiding. Frozen, I sat motionless as Toni, looking up and seeing my mother, slid nonchalantly off my lap, smoothing down her skirts as she did so.

My mother stepped over to the two of us. I flinched, expecting instant retribution at her capable hands. But evidently the enormity of my intentions had escaped my mother's notice. Perhaps she did not care that I was about to usurp that secret prerogative belonging only to mothers about to spank, or to nurses with thermometers.

Taking me by the elbow, my mother pulled me awkwardly to my feet.

I stood for a moment like a wool-encased snow-girl, my arms stuck out a little from my body and my legs spread slightly apart. Ignoring Toni, my mother started down the steps to the street. "Hurry now," she said, "you don't want to be late."

I looked back over my shoulder. The bright-eyed vision in the wine-red coat stood at the top of the stoop, and pulled one hand out of her white rabbit-fur muff.

"You want the other candy?" she called. I shook my head frantically. We were never supposed to take candy from anybody and certainly not strangers.

My mother urged me on down the steps. "Watch where you're stepping, now."

"Can you come out and play tomorrow?" Toni called after me.

Tomorrow. Tomorrow. Tomorrow. My mother was already one step below, and her firm hand on my elbow kept me from falling as I almost missed a step. Maybe tomorrow...

Once on the street pavement, my mother resumed hold of my hand and sailed forth determinedly. My short legs in their bulky wrappings and galoshes chugged along, trying to keep up with her. Even when she was not in a hurry, my mother walked with a long and purposeful stride, her toes always pointed slightly outward in a ladylike fashion.

"You can't tarry, now," she said. "You know it's almost noon." Tomorrow, tomorrow, tomorrow.

"What a shame, to let such a skinny little thing like that out in this weather with no snowsuit or a stitch of leggings on her legs. That's how among-you children catch your death of cold."

So I hadn't dreamed her. She had seen Toni too. (What kind of name anyway was that for a girl?) Maybe tomorrow...

"Can I have a red coat like hers, Mommy?"

My mother looked down at me as we stood waiting for the street light to change.

"How many times I tell you not to call me Mommy on the street?" The light changed, and we hurried forward.

I thought about my question very carefully as I scurried along, wanting to get it exactly right this time. Finally, I had it.

"Will you buy me a red coat, please, Mother?" I kept my eyes on the treacherous ground to avoid tripping over my galoshed feet, and the words must have been muffled or lost in the scarf around my neck. In any case, my mother hurried on in silence, apparently not hearing. Tomorrow tomorrow tomorrow.

We had our split-pea soup, and hurriedly retraced our steps back to my sisters' school. But that day, my mother and I did not return directly home. Crossing over to the other side of Lenox Avenue, we caught the Number 4 bus down to 125th Street, where we went marketing at Weissbecker's for the weekend chicken.

My heart sank into hopelessness as I stood waiting, kicking my feet in the sawdust that covered the market's floor. I should have known. I had wanted too much for her to be real. I had wanted to see her again too much for it to ever happen.

The market was too warm. My sweaty skin itched in places I couldn't possibly scratch. If we were marketing today, that meant tomorrow would turn out to be Saturday. My sisters did not go to school on Saturday, which meant we couldn't go pick them up for lunch, which meant I would spend all day in the house because my mother had to clean and cook and we were never allowed out alone to play on the stoop.

The weekend was an eternity past which I could not see.

The following Monday I waited again on the stoop. I sat by myself, bundled up as usual, and nobody came except my mother.

I don't know how long I looked for Toni every day at noontime, sitting on the stoop. Eventually, her image receded into that place from which all my dreams are made.

5 Until this day, the essence of sorrow and sadness like a Picasso painting still-lifed and forever living, is the forlorn and remembered sight of a discarded silk stocking brick-caught and hanging against the rain-windy side of the tenement building wall opposite our kitchen window from which I hung, suspended by one hand, screaming at my elder sister who had been left in charge of the three of us while my mother went out marketing.

What our interactions had been before is lost, but my mother came home just in time to pull me back inside the dark kitchen,

saving me from a one-story drop into the air shaft below. I
don't remember the terror and fury, but I remember the whipping that both my sister and I got. More than that, I remember
the sadness and the deprivation and the loneliness of that discarded, torn, and brick-caught silk stocking, broken and hanging
against the wall in the tenement rain.

I was always very jealous of my two older sisters, because
they were older and therefore more privileged, and because they
had each other for a friend. They could talk to one another
without censure or punishment, or so I thought.

As far as I was concerned, Phyllis and Helen led a magical and
charmed existence down the hall in their room. It was tiny but
complete, with privacy and a place to be away from the eternal
parental eye which was my lot, having only the public parts of
the house to play in. I was never alone, nor far from my mother's
watchful eye. The bathroom door was the only door in the
house that I was ever allowed to close behind me, and even that
would be opened with an inquiry if I tarried too long on the
toilet.

The first time I ever slept anywhere else besides in my parents'
bedroom was a milestone in my journey to this house of myself.
When I was four and five, my family went to the Connecticut
shore for a week's vacation during the summer. This was much
grander than a day's outing to Rockaway Beach or Coney Island,
and much more exciting.

First of all, we got to sleep in a house that was not ours, and
Daddy was with us during the day. Then there were strange new
foods to sample, like blue soft-shelled crab, which my father ordered for his lunch and would sometimes persuade my mother to
let me have a taste of. We children were not allowed such alien
fare, but on Fridays we did have fried shrimp and little batter
cakes with pieces of clam in them. They were good, and very
different from my mother's codfish-and-potato fishcakes which
were our favorite Friday dinner back home.

A shimmering glare of silver coats every beach in my mind's
eye. Glistening childhood summers that sparkled like the thick
glass spectacles I could not wear because of the dilating drops in
my eyes.

The dilating drops were used by the Medical Center eye doctors to examine the progress of my eyes, and since the effects
seem to have lasted for weeks, my memories of those early summers are of constantly squinting against the piercing agony of
direct sunlight, while stumbling over objects that I could not
see, since everything was dazzled by light.

The crabshells in the sand were distinguished from the clam-shells, not by shape, but by the different feel of them beneath my brown toes. Delicate crabshells crumpled up like glasspaper around my heels, while the tough little clamshells crunched a hard and sturdy sound from under the balls of my fat little feet.

An old beached boat, abandoned on its side, lay in the sand above high tide down the beach a little from the hotel, and there my mother sat, day after day, in her light cotton dresses. Her ankles were properly crossed and her arms folded as she watched my two sisters and I play at the water's edge. Her eyes would be very soft and peaceful as she gazed over the water, and I knew she was thinking of "home."

Once my daddy picked me up and carried me into the water, as I squealed with delight and fear at being so high up. He dropped me into the ocean, holding onto my arms, and I re-member, as he raised me up, screaming in outrage at the burning taste of saltwater in my nostrils that made me want to fight or cry.

The first year there I slept in a cot in my parents' room, as usual, and I always went to bed before anyone else. Just as at home, the watery colors of twilight came in to terrify me, shin-ing greenly through the buff-colored window-shades which were like closed eyes above my bed. I hated the twilight color and go-ing to bed early, far from the comfortingly familiar voices of my parents, downstairs on the porch of this hotel which belong-ed to my father's real-estate buddy who was giving us a good deal for the week.

Those yellow-green window-shade twilights were the color of loneliness for me, and that has never left me. Everything else about that first summer week in Connecticut is lost to me, ex-cept the two photographs which show me, as usual, discontent and squinting up against the sun.

The second year we were even poorer, or maybe my father's real-estate friend had raised his prices. For whatever reason, the five of us shared one bedroom, and there was no space for an extra cot. The room had three windows in it, and two double beds that sagged ever so slightly in the middle of their white chenille-spread-covered expanses. My sisters and I shared one of these beds.

I was still put to bed earlier than my sisters, who were allow-ed to stay up and listen to "I Love a Mystery" on the old upright cabinet radio that sat in the living room downstairs near the porch window. Its soft tones would drift out across the porch to the cretonne-covered rocking chairs lined up in a row in the soft-salty back-street shore-resort night.

I didn't mind the twilights so much that year. We had a back room and it got darker earlier, so it was always night by the time I went to bed. Unterrified by the twilight green, I had no trouble at all falling asleep.

My mother supervised the brushing of my teeth, and the saying of my prayers, and then after assuring herself that all was in order, she kissed me goodnight, and turned out the dim, un-shaded bulb.

The door closed. I lay awake, rigid with excitement, waiting for "I Love a Mystery" to be over, and for my sisters to come and get into bed beside me. I made bargains with god to keep me awake. I bit my lips and pinched the soft fleshy parts of my palms with my fingernails, all to keep myself from falling asleep.

After an eternity of about thirty minutes, during which I re-viewed the entire contents of my day, including what I should and shouldn't have done that I didn't or did do, I heard my sis-ters' footsteps in the hallway. The door to our room opened and they stepped into the darkness.

"Hey, Audre. You still wake?" That was Helen, four years older than me and the closest to me in age.

I was torn with indecision. What should I do? If I didn't an-swer, she might tickle my toes, and if I did answer, what should I say?

"Say, you wake?"

"No," I whispered in a squeaky little voice I thought consis-tent with a sleeping state.

"Sure enough, see, she still wake." I heard Helen's disgusted whisper to Phyllis, followed by the sharp intake of her breath as she sucked her teeth. "Look, her eyes wide open still."

The bed creaked on one side of me. "What you still doin' up, staring like a ninny? On the way in, you know, I told the boogie-man come bite your head off, and he comin' just now to get you good."

I felt the bed sag under the weight of both of their bodies, one on either side of me. My mother had decreed that I should sleep in the middle, to keep me from falling out of bed, as well as to separate my two sisters. I was so enchanted with the idea of sharing a bed with them that I couldn't have cared less. Helen reached over and gave me a little preliminary pinch.

"Ouch!" I rubbed my tender upper arm, now sore from her strong little piano-trained fingers. "Oh, I'm goin' to tell Mommy

how you pinching me and you goin' to get a whipping sure
enough." And then, triumphantly, I played my hole card. "And
too besides, I'm goin' to tell her what among-you doing in bed
every night!"

"Go ahead, ninny, run your mouth. You goin' to run it once
too often 'til it drop off your face and then just see how it's
goin' to gobble up you toes!" Helen sucked her teeth again, but
moved her hand away.

"Oh, just go to sleep now, Audre." That was Phyllis, my
eldest sister, who was always the peacemaker, the placid, reasonable, removed one. But I knew perfectly well what I had
pinched my palms to stay awake for, and I was waiting, barely
able to contain myself.

For that summer, in that hot back room of a resort slum, I
had finally found out what my sisters did at home at night in
that little room they shared at the end of the hall, that enticing
little room which I was never allowed to enter except by an invitation that never came.

They told each other stories. They told each other stories in
endless installments, making up the episodes as they went
along, from fantasies engendered by the radio adventure shows
to which we were all addicted in those days.

There was "Buck Rogers," and "I Love a Mystery," "Jack
Armstrong, All-American Boy," "The Green Hornet," and
"Quiet Please." There was "The FBI in Peace and War," "Mr.
District Attorney," "The Lone Ranger," and my all-time favorite, "The Shadow," whose power to cloud men's minds so they
could not see him was something I did not stop lusting for until
quite recently.

I thought that the very idea of telling stories and not getting
whipped for telling untrue was the most marvelous thing I could
think of, and every night that week I begged to be allowed to
listen, not realizing that they couldn't stop me. Phyllis didn't
mind so long as I kept my mouth shut, but by bedtime Helen
had had enough of a pesky little sister and my endless stream of
questions. And her stories were always far and away the best,
filled with tough little girls who masqueraded in boys' clothing
and always foiled the criminals, managing to save the day. Phyllis's hero was a sweet strong boy of few words named George
Vaginius.

"Please, Phyllis?" I wheedled. There was a long moment of
quiet, with Helen sucking her teeth ominously, then Phyllis,
whispering, "All right. Who' turn it is tonight?"

"I'm not saying a word 'til she asleep!" That was Helen, determined.

"Please Phyllis, please let me listen?"

"No! No such thing!" Helen was adamant. "I know you too well in the dark to have to shine a light on you!"

"Please, Phyllis, I promise I be quiet." I could feel Helen swelling up beside me like a bullfrog, but I persisted, not realizing or caring that my appeal to Phyllis's authority as the elder sister only infuriated Helen even more.

Phyllis was not only softhearted, but very practical, with the pragmatic approach of an eleven-year-old West Indian woman.

"Now you promise you never goin' to tell?"

I felt like I was being inducted into the most secret of societies.

"Cross my heart." Catholic girls never hoped to die.

Helen was obviously not convinced. I stifled a squeak as she nipped me again with her fingers, this time on the thigh.

"I'm getting tired of all this, you know. So if you ever so much as breathe a *word* about my stories, Sandman's comin' after you the very same minute to pluck out you eyes like a mackerel for soup." And Helen smacked her lips suggestively, giving way with a parting shot.

I could just see those little white rubbery eyeballs swimming about in the bottom of the Friday night fish stew, and I shuddered.

"I promise, Helen, cross my heart. I don't say a word to nobody, and I'll be so quiet, you'll see." I put both of my hands up across my mouth in the darkness, jittering with anticipation.

It was Helen's turn to begin.

"Where were we, now? Oh yes, so me and Buck had just fetched back the sky-horse when Doc. . ."

I could not resist. Down came my hands.

"No, no, Helen, not yet. Don't you remember? Doc hadn't gotten there yet, because. . ." I didn't want to miss a single thing.

Helen's little brown fingers shot across the bedclothes and gave me such a nip on the buttocks that I screeched in pain. Her voice was high and indignant and full of helpless fury.

"You see that? You see that? What I tell you, Phyllis?" She was almost wailing in fury. "I knew it! She can't keep that miserable tongue in she mouth one minute. Sure enough, I told you so, didn't I? Didn't I? And now too besides she want to steal me story!"

"Sh-h-h-h! The two-a-you! Mommy's comin' back here just now, and among-you two goin' to make us all catch hell!"

But Helen wasn't going to play any more. I felt her flop over on her side with her disgruntled back towards me, and then I could feel our bed shaking with her angry sobs of rage, muffled in the sweaty pillow.

I could have kicked myself. "I truly sorry, Helen," I ventured. And I really was, because I realized that my big mouth had done me out of a night's installment, and probably of all the installments for the rest of the week. I also knew that Mother would never let me out of her sight the next day long enough for me to catch up to my sisters, as they ran off down the beach to complete their tale in secret.

"Honest, I didn't mean to, Helen." I tried one last time, reaching over to touch her. But Helen jerked her body sharply backward and her butt caught me in the stomach. I heard her still outraged warning hissed through clenched teeth.

"And don't you dare pat me!" I had been on the receiving end of her fingers often enough to know when to leave well enough alone.

So I turned over on my stomach, said goodnight to Phyllis, and finally went to sleep, too.

The next morning, I woke up before either Phyllis or Helen. I lay in the middle of the bed, being careful not to touch either one of them. Staring up at the ceiling, I listened to my father snoring, in the next bed, and to the sound of my mother's wedding ring hitting the headboard in her sleep, as she flung her arm across her eyes against the morning light. I relished the quiet, the new smells of strange bedclothes and sea-salty air, and the frank beams of yellow sunlight pouring through the high windows like a promise of endless day.

Right then and there, before anybody else woke up, I decided to make up a story of my own.

6 In the Harlem summers of my earliest days, I walked between my two sisters while they plotted the overthrow of universes, in the casual make-believe language of comic books. For those comic books, the other reigning and possessive passion of our summer days besides the library, we walked for miles uphill. With determination and

great resolve, we trudged up Sugar Hill, 145th Street from Lenox to Amsterdam, to trade in old comic books at the used comic-book store up on Amsterdam Avenue in Washington Heights, which was an all-white section of town then, in those days before the war, and which is where my mother now lives.

The store was run by a fat white man with watery eyes and a stomach that hung over his belt like badly made jello. He tore the covers off the leftover comic books and sold the books at half-price, or exchanged them for other old comics in good condition, one for two. There were rows and rows and rows of table bins with garish, frontless comics in them, and as soon as my sisters took off down one of the rows for their favorites, Buck Rogers and Captain Marvel, I started searching for pictures of Bugs Bunny. The old man followed me down the aisle, puffing his evil cigar.

I tried to run back to my sisters, but it was too late. His bulk took up the whole row, and I was painfully aware that I was not supposed to have left their sides, anyway.

"Lemme help you up, sweetheart, you can see better." And I felt his slabby fingers like sausages grab my ribs and hoist me through a sickening arc of cigar fumes to the edge of the bins full of Bugs Bunny and Porky Pig comics. I seized whichever was nearest and squirmed to be put down, frantic for the feeling of the floor under my feet once more, and sickened by the squishy touch of his soft belly against the small of my back.

His nasty fingers moved furtively up and down my body, now trapped between his pressing bulges and the rim of the bin. By the time he loosened his grip and allowed me to slide down to the blessed floor, I felt dirtied and afraid, as if I had just taken part in some filthy rite.

I soon learned I could avoid him by staying close to my sisters. If I ran out the other end of the row he would not follow, but then when my sisters finally tallied up their transactions, there would be no extra one tossed in, "for the little sweetheart." The slabby fingers and the nauseating hoist were the price I paid for a torn and faceless copy of an old Bugs Bunny comic. For years I had nightmares of being hoisted up to the ceiling and having no way of getting down again.

It was a day's journey up the hill for us, three little brown girls, one not even yet able to read. But it was a summer outing, and better than sitting at home until our mother came back from the office or from marketing. We were never allowed to go out and simply play in the street. It was a day's journey there

and back again, across the two flat crosstown blocks to Eighth
Avenue where the Father Divine shoe repair booth stood, and
then up the endless hills, block after crosstown block.

Sometimes, when my mother announced to my father after
dinner our planned journey the next day, they would slip into
patois for a brief consultation. By searching their faces carefully,
I could tell they were discussing whether or not they could afford to spare the few cents necessary to finance the expedition.

At other times, we were commissioned by our father to drop
off his shoes at the Father Divine booth to be half-soled. That
would also include a shoeshine, an allowable extravagance because it only cost three cents and a Peace, Brother, Peace saluta-
tion.

Right after breakfast was cleared away, my mother left to go
down to the office and we walked with her as far as the corner.
Then the three of us turned left to 145th Street, past the Lido
Bowling Palace, a few bars and some indeterminate candy-
grocery stores whose largest turnover was in little white slips
with numbers scrawled upon them.

Three plump little Black girls, dimpled knees scrubbed and
oiled to a shine, hair tightly braided and tied with threads. Our
seersucker sunsuits, mother-made, were not yet an embarrassment to my budding older sister.

We trudged up the hill past the Stardust Lounge, Micky's
Hair-Styling—Hot and Cold Press, the Harlem Bop Lounge, the
Dream Café, the Freedom Barber Shop, and the Optimo Cigar
Store which seemed to decorate every important street corner
of those years. There was the Aunt May Eat Shoppe, and Sadie's
Ladies and Children's Wear. There was Lum's Chop Suey Bar,
and the Shiloh Baptist Mission Church painted white with colored storefront windows, the Record Store with its big radio
chained outside setting a beat to the warming morning sidewalk. And on the corner of Seventh Avenue as we waited for
the green light arm in arm, the yeasty and suggestively mysterious smell issuing from the cool dark beyond the swinging half-
doors of the Noon Saloon.

We started up the hill, which was really six hills. Standing up
at the bottom on Eighth Avenue and looking upward in the
bright sunlight seemed like forever. Vertical trolley tracks dis-
sected the hills. The sidewalks were ribbons of pavement and
people. Halfway up the hill on the right side, between Bradhurst
and Edgecombe Avenues, was the broad expanse of tufted
green, surrounded by a high wrought-iron fence, that was Colo-

nial Park. It was not a public park, or at least it was not free. Since we never had the ten cents admission price, we had never been inside.

My arm was sore from being pulled along, but that was the price I had to pay if I dared fall behind. Just as taking me along was the price my literate, comic-book-reading sisters had to pay if they wanted to go out at all. I was always much too out of breath to complain.

We crossed over the busy thoroughfare of 145th Street, all holding hands. We paused halfway up the hills at Bradhurst, to press our faces against the wrought-iron bars around Colonial Park. I could barely hear the splashing of cool bright water and the liquid laughter rising up from the half-hidden private swimming pool. But even those faint sounds of coolness drifted greenly toward our dry mouths. By that time it seemed as if we had been walking forever. The sun beat down without mercy straight out of the sky over Colonial Park. There was no shade anywhere. But beside the park, the air was somewhat cooler. We hung around for a while even though there were no benches outside. The busy life of the Harlem thoroughfare swept along past us.

Despite Mother's cautionings not to tarry, we lingered near the green pool's fresh smell. The bags of comic books were jealously guarded in the hands of each of my sisters, and in my sweaty hands I clutched a bag of saltines and three bananas for a snack. Our lunch was prepared and waiting at home.

We each had a saltine cracker, leaning against the railing of the park. My sister Helen fussed at me because I had mashed up all the crackers by swinging the bag back and forth in time to my trot. We brushed off the crumbs with the napkin in the bag, and then continued our journey up the seemingly endless hills.

Finally we reached the crest of Amsterdam Avenue. On the clearest days, I could stand on tiptoe and look westward, barely sighting along the buildings across Broadway to Riverside Drive. Behind the drive's sharp dip of trees was the faint, almost imagined, line of water that was the Hudson River. For years, whenever I heard the song "America the Beautiful," I would think of those moments standing on the crest of Amsterdam Avenue. In my mind, the phrase "from sea to shining sea" was visualized as from the East to the Hudson Rivers.

As we waited for the light to change on the corner of Amsterdam and 145th, I turned around and looked back down the long narrow valley of 145th Street. My eyes took in the blocks teeming with cars and horse-drawn wagons and people, straight across and down the hill all the way past Colonial Park and Father Divine and the drugstore on Lenox Avenue to the bridge across the Harlem River leading to the Bronx.

I shook with a sudden spasm of terror. Suppose I fell down at that crucial point? I could roll down hill after successive hill all the way back across Lenox Avenue, and if I happened to miss the bridge I could roll right on into the water. Everyone would jump out of my pathway on the way down the hills, just like the people did in the picture book *Johnny Cake.* They would jump aside to keep from being knocked over and crushed by the screaming little fat girl on her slide down to the Harlem River waters.

No one would catch me or hold me or save me, and eventually I would float slowly out to sea past the Armory at 142nd Street and the water's edge, where my father drilled regularly on week-ends with the Black Home Guard. I would be carried out to the ocean on that treacherous current that flowed through the Harlem River from a mythic place called the "Spitting Devil" which our father had cautioned us about; this current which had claimed so many of our classmates every summer before the Harlem River Drive was finally built, cutting off access to the free cooling waters of the river for all those hot and dusty little Black children with no dime to buy the doors open into the green coolness of the Colonial Park pool and no sisters to take them comic-book trading.

7 War came to our house on the radio one Sunday afternoon after church, sometime between "Olivio, the Boy Yodeler," and the Moylan Sisters. It was Pearl Harbor Sunday.

"The Japanese have bombed Pearl Harbor," my father announced gravely, as he came in from showing a house to a prospective buyer, making a beeline for the radio.

"Where's that?" Helen asked, looking up from trying to fit her cat Cleo into a dress she had just made for the animal.

"That must be why we can't get Olivio," Phyllis said, with a disappointed sigh. "I *thought* something was the matter because he always comes on this time."

And my mother left the parlor to check out her store of coffee and sugar under the sink in the kitchen.

I sat on the floor with my back against the wooden cabinet radio, *The Blue Fairy Book* in my lap. I loved to read and listen to the radio at the same time, feeling the vibrations of sound through my back like an activating background to the pictures that streamed through my head, spun by the fairy tales. I looked up, momentarily confused and disoriented as I usually was when I stopped reading suddenly. Had trolls really attacked a harbor where some hidden treasure of pearls was buried?

I could tell something real and terrible had happened from the smell in the living-room air, and from the tight grave lowering of my father's voice as he searched back and forth over the radio dials for Gabriel Heatter or H. V. Kaltenborn or some other one of his favorite news commentators. They were his constant links with the outside world, second only to the *New York Times*. And I could tell something real and terrible must have happened because neither "The Lone Ranger" nor "The Shadow" nor "This Is Your FBI" came on that night.

Instead, in newscast after newscast, grave and excited voices were talking of death and destruction and casualties and burning ships and brave men and war. I finally put down my fairy tales to listen more intently, captivated and frightened by the high drama swirling around me, and for once wise enough to keep my mouth shut. But my parents were too engrossed in the reports to think of banishing me to the kitchen. Even supper was later than usual that night.

My mother said something in patois and my father answered. Watching their eyes I could tell they were talking about the office and money. My mother got up and went back to the kitchen.

"Bee, it's time to eat," my mother called, finally, reappearing at the parlor door. "There's nothing we can do about this."

"You said it, Lin. But war is here." My father reached over and clicked off the radio, and we all went into the kitchen to supper.

A few days later, after school, all the students were lined up in the auditorium, class by class, and the nuns issued us little cream-colored bone discs that were engraved in blue ink with name, address, age, and something called *blood type*. Each one of us was to wear this disc around the neck on a long nickel chain with no catch, and this was never never to be taken off for the duration, under pain of mortal sin, or worse.

That phrase, *for the duration*, began to assume a tangible life and energy all its own, like *infinity*, or *forever*.

The nuns told us that gas masks were coming later, and we should all pray that we did not have to do like the poor little english children did—leave their parents and be sent away into the countryside for safety. In my secret heart of hearts I thought that was a very exciting prospect, and hoped it might come to pass. I bent my head with the others, but could not bring myself to pray that it wouldn't happen.

Then we said another ten Our Fathers and ten Hail Marys for the souls of the brave young men who had lost their lives at Pearl Harbor the Sunday before, and then five more of each for the starving children in Europe.

When we had finished praying, we all stood up, and Mother Josepha showed us how to cross our arms over our chests and touch the opposite shoulder, the safest position in case we fell while running. Then we practiced how to run to the basement of the church through a connecting passageway during an air-raid drill. We practiced air-raid drills until we could do them absolutely silently and quickly. I began to be impressed with the seriousness of it all, as this went on for what felt like hours, while our mothers sat and waited in the auditorium. It was almost twilight by the time we were finally on our way home through the December cold, and the streets looked odd and eerie with the streetlamps dimmed and already capped on top, and the store windows shrouded in the blackout.

The following spring, all the mothers were asked to come to school on some regular basis to help watch the skies for enemy aircraft that might have slipped by our shore defenses. Mothers all over New York City were doing the same thing from the roofs of schoolhouses. Because of the careful censorship of the news, I don't think any of us, including our parents, realized how real a threat offshore shelling was, for there actually were german submarines in Long Island Sound. All we knew was that, perched as it was on the east coast facing Europe, New York City was a prime target for bombing.

Even simple conversation became suspect. *Silence was golden*, didn't all the posters say so? Despite the fact that I had no secrets at all to tell, I always felt a pang of self-righteous pleasure whenever I passed the corner lamp post at 140th Street and

Lenox Avenue. From it hung a brightly colored sign of a white man with his fingers to his lips. Beneath his half-turned face in big block letters it warned: A SLIP OF THE LIP MAY SINK A SHIP! I felt my silences socially and patriotically endorsed.

But meanwhile, life went on almost as usual, and it was hard at seven to distinguish between this real-life drama and the ones I was addicted to on the radio.

The mothers at St. Mark's watched for enemy planes from a roof culvert that adjoined the third grade classroom and was reached through a doorway in the front of our room. We had spelling right before lunch in the third grade, and my mother's turn to watch was from 11:00 A.M. to 12 noon.

I bent over my spelling book in the warm spring light, my stomach grumbling and anxious for lunch. Just outside the window, I could see my mother standing in her dowdy dark woolen suit and her severe cuban-heeled oxfords, a rakishly brimmed but no-nonsense hat shading her hawk-grey eyes. Her arms were folded across her ample chest as she frowned up at the sky intently from under the brim of her hat, daring any enemy plane to appear.

I was bursting with pride that this important woman was my mother. She was the only mother in my class who watched for airplanes, and was also involved with the mysterious process of giving out ration books from an official-looking table set up in the back of the school auditorium, on a special day set aside for that purpose. And, she was the only mother I knew who sat behind another table every Election Day in the lobby of the infamous public school, checking off voters in huge magic books, and guarding the magical, grey-curtained voting booths. Even though she was the only mother I knew who never wore lipstick, not even for Mass on Sundays, still, she was also the only mother I knew who "went to business" every day.

I was very proud of her, but sometimes, just sometimes, I wished she would be like all the other mothers, one waiting for me at home with milk and home-baked cookies and a frilly apron, like the blonde smiling mother in *Dick and Jane*.

On catholic holidays or half-days when I was off from school, I loved to go down to the office with my mother and sit behind my father's oaken desk, in his great wooden swivel chair, watching my mother write out rent receipts, or interview prospective tenants, or argue imperiously with the coal delivery man over whether the coal should be dumped on the sidewalk or into the coal bin under the street.

During the war years, I remember days of standing beside my
mother in front of the huge plate glass windows that swiveled
inward, now taped up against the cold. We waited anxiously, watching up Lenox Avenue for the first glimpse of the
Public Fuel coal truck that might bring whatever poor-grade
coal was left from the "war-effort" to take the chill off the
rooms in those dreary rooming houses that she and Daddy managed. Sometimes my father would join us; more often he was
either showing a house or out on some real-estate business, or
doing some minor repair work in one of the rundown houses.
As labor demands increased and the war went on, my father was
in the office less and less, because he had taken a night job as a
maintenance man in a war plant out in Queens which made
aluminum fittings for airplanes. He worked the night shift, and
then came to the office early in the morning straight from the
war plant. He did whatever repairs or work was needed, checking
for leaks in the houses' plumbing in summer and frozen pipes in
the winter. Then if he did not have another appointment to
show a house, he went upstairs to a vacant room and caught a
few hours sleep, while my mother came to the office and took
care of business. If he had a real-estate appointment, he went
upstairs to the room to shave and wash and change his clothes
and then went out again, returning to the office in the afternoon to sleep for a few hours.

At noontime when my mother brought us back home for
lunch, she busily reheated and packed up a hot meal for my
father. It usually consisted of leftovers from supper the night
before, or some delicacy that she had prepared earlier that
morning. She packed the food into bottles and wrapped towels
around them to keep it warm, and after she dropped us off at
school, she would continue on her way back to the office and
either wake my father up, or await his return.

She did the books, dealt with problems, sewed sheets and
pillowcases on the Singer sewing machine kept in the back
room, and made up rooms upstairs. If the woman who had been
hired to clean was absent that day, my mother cleaned whatever
rooms were vacant. It was soon time to fetch us home from
school, ten blocks away.

Somedays, when time and need permitted or demanded, she
walked to the market on 125th Street to try and find a piece of
meat for supper, or some fresh fish and vegetables from the
West Indian markets along the way. After marketing, she caught
the bus back uptown to meet us at school, her arms heavy with

shopping bags. On those days, her face was drawn and tired and her eyes particularly fierce as she stepped off the bus at the corner of 138th Street where the three of us stood, silently waiting and watching for her. I would try to read and decipher the expression on my mother's face as soon as the bus stopped and she slowly descended the steps, shopping bags banging the sides of her legs. The look on her face would tell me what the tenor of our seven-block walk home would be like. A tight drawn mouth often meant a whipping for one of us, usually me, whether or not we helped her carry the packages.

Once in the house, discipline and reprimands all had to be postponed until supper was prepared and put on the stove to cook. Then the bad reports that had been given to my sisters about me that day at school would be trotted out and examined, and my mother's heavy-handed household justice would ensue.

At other times, for particularly wicked and sinful infractions, the ominous verdict would be "Wait until your father comes home." My father never hit us. There was a myth abroad among the relatives that Uncle Lorde was so strong if he ever laid a hand upon you he might kill you. But his very presence at the administering of punishment made that whipping somehow official and therefore all the more terrifying and terrible. Probably the postponement and dread expectation accomplished the same effect.

Whether it was true or not about my father's killing power I do not know. He was a very large, strong man, and his six-foot-four-inch frame in the beach pictures of that period do not show much fat. His eyes were small but piercing, and when he set his mammoth jaw and dropped his voice to the hoarse, intense low that signified he meant business, he was very scary.

I remember one light-hearted evening before the war when my father returned home from the office. I was sitting on my mother's lap while she brushed my hair. My father picked us up together and swung us over his head, laughing and calling us his "excess baggage." I remember being delighted and thrilled at his attention, as well as terrified by the familiar surroundings suddenly turning *cro-bo-so*.

During the war, my father was almost never at home in the evenings, except on weekends, so punishment, by and large, became much more immediate.

As the war lengthened, more and more money came into circulation among Black people, and my father's real-estate business got better and better. After the race riots of 1943, the area

around Lenox Avenue and 142nd Street became known as the
"gutbucket" of Harlem. My family moved "up the hill," the
same long series of hills that my sisters and I used to traverse on
summer days to trade comic books.

8 As a child, the most horrible condition I could
contemplate was being wrong and being discovered. Mistakes could mean exposure, maybe
even annihilation. In my mother's house, there was no room in
which to make errors, no room to be wrong.

I grew Black as my need for life, for affirmation, for love, for
sharing—copying from my mother what was in her, unfulfilled.
I grew Black as *Seboulisa*, who I was to find in the cool mud
halls of Abomey several lifetimes later—and, as alone. My mother's words teaching me all manner of wily and diversionary defenses learned from the white man's tongue, from out of the
mouth of her father. She had had to use these defenses, and had
survived by them, and had also died by them a little, at the
same time. All the colors change and become each other,
merge and separate, flow into rainbows and nooses.

I lie beside my sisters in the darkness, who pass me in the
street unacknowledged and unadmitted. How much of this is
the pretense of self-rejection that became an immovable protective mask, how much the programmed hate that we were fed to
keep ourselves a part, apart?

One day (I remember I was still in the second grade) my
mother was out marketing, and my sisters were talking about
someone being *Colored*. In my six-year-old way, I jumped at
this chance to find out what it was all about.

"What does *Colored* mean?" I asked. To my amazement,
neither one of my sisters was quite sure.

"Well," Phyllis said. "The nuns are white, and the Short-Neck
Store-Man is white, and Father Mulvoy is white and we're Colored."

"And what's Mommy? Is she white or Colored?"

"I don't know," answered Phyllis impatiently.

"Well," I said, "If anybody asks me what I am, I'm going to
tell them I'm white same as Mommy."

"Ohhhhhhhhhh, girl, you better not do that," they both chorused in horror.

"Why not?" I asked, more confused than ever. But neither of them could tell me why.

That was the first and only time my sisters and I discussed race as a reality in my house, or at any rate as it applied to ourselves.

Our new apartment was on 152nd Street between Amsterdam Avenue and Broadway in what was called Washington Heights, and already known as a "changing" neighborhood, meaning one where Black people could begin to find overpriced apartments out of the depressed and decaying core of Harlem.

The apartment house that we moved into was owned by a small landlord. We moved at the end of the summer, and I began school that year in a new catholic school which was right across the street from our house.

Two weeks after we moved into the new apartment, our landlord hanged himself in the basement. The *Daily News* reported that the suicide was caused by his despondency over the fact that he finally had to rent to Negroes. I was the first Black student in St. Catherine's School, and all the white kids in my sixth grade class knew about the landlord who had hanged himself in the basement because of me and my family. He had been Jewish; I was Black. That made us both fair game for the cruel curiosity of my pre-adolescent classmates.

Ann Archdeacon, red-headed darling of the nuns and of Monsignor Brady, was the first one to ask me what I knew about the landlord's death. As usual, my parents had discussed the whole matter in patois, and I only read the comics in the daily paper.

"I don't know anything about it," I said, standing in the schoolyard at lunchtime, twisting my front braids and looking around for some friendly face. Ann Archdeacon snickered, and the rest of the group that had gathered around us to hear roared with laughter, until Sister Blanche waddled over to see what was going on.

If the Sisters of the Blessed Sacrament at St. Mark's School had been patronizing, at least their racism was couched in the terms of their mission. At St. Catherine's School, the Sisters of Charity were downright hostile. Their racism was unadorned, unexcused, and particularly painful because I was unprepared for it. I got no help at home. The children in my class made fun of my braids, so Sister Victoire, the principal, sent a note home to my mother asking her to comb my hair in a more "becoming" fashion, since I was too old, she said, to wear "pigtails."

All the girls wore blue gabardine uniforms that by springtime were a little musty, despite frequent drycleanings. I would come in from recess to find notes in my desk saying "You Stink." I showed them to Sister Blanche. She told me that she felt it was her christian duty to tell me that Colored people *did* smell different from white people, but it was cruel of the children to write nasty notes because I couldn't help it, and if I would remain out in the yard the next day after the rest of the class came in after lunchtime, she would talk to them about being nicer to me!

The head of the parish and the school was Monsignor John J. Brady, who told my mother when she registered me that he had never expected to have to take Colored kids into his school. His favorite pastime was holding Ann Archdeacon or Ilene Crimmons on his lap, while he played with their blonde and red curls with one hand, and slid the other hand up the back of their blue gabardine uniforms. I did not care about his lechery, but I did care that he kept me in every Wednesday afternoon after school to memorize latin nouns.

The other children in my class were given a cursory quiz to test their general acquaintance with the words, and then let go early, since it was the early release day for religious instruction.

I came to loathe Wednesday afternoons, sitting by myself in the classroom trying to memorize the singular and plural of a long list of latin nouns, and their genders. Every half-hour or so, Father Brady would look in from the rectory, and ask to hear the words. If I so much as hesitated over any word or its plural, or its gender, or said it out of place on the list, he would spin on his black-robed heel and disappear for another half-hour or so. Although early dismissal was at 2:00 P.M., some Wednesdays I didn't get home until after four o'clock. Sometimes on Wednesday nights I would dream of the white, acrid-smelling mimeograph sheet: *agricola, agricolae,* fem., farmer. Three years later when I began Hunter High School and had to take latin in earnest, I had built up such a block to everything about it that I failed my first two terms of it.

When I complained at home about my treatment at school, my mother would get angry with me.

"What do you care what they say about you, anyway? Do they put bread on your plate? You go to school to learn, so learn and leave the rest alone. You don't need friends." I did not see her helplessness, nor her pain.

I was the smartest girl in the class, which did nothing to contribute to my popularity. But the Sisters of the Blessed Sacrament had taught me well, and I was way ahead in math and mental arithmetic.

In the spring of the sixth grade, Sister Blanche announced that we were going to hold elections for two class presidents, one boy and one girl. Anyone could run, she said, and we would vote on Friday of that week. The voting should be according to merit and effort and class spirit, she added, but the most important thing would be marks.

Of course, Ann Archdeacon was nominated immediately. She was not only the most popular girl in the school, she was the prettiest. Ilene Crimmons was also nominated, her blonde curls and favored status with the Monsignor guaranteed that.

I lent Jim Moriarty ten cents, stolen from my father's pocket at lunchtime, so Jim nominated me. A titter went through the class, but I ignored it. I was in seventh heaven. I knew I was the smartest girl in the class. I had to win.

That afternoon when my mother came home from the office, I told her about the election, and how I was going to run, and win. She was furious.

"What in hell are you doing getting yourself involved with so much foolishness? You don't have better sense in your head than that? What-the-france do you need with election? We send you to school to work, not to prance about with president-this election-that. Get down the rice, girl, and stop talking your foolishness." We started preparing the food.

"But I just might win, Mommy. Sister Blanche said it should go to the smartest girl in the class." I wanted her to see how important it was to me.

"Don't bother me with that nonsense. I don't want to hear any more about it. And don't come in here on Friday with a long face, and any 'I didn't win, Mommy,' because I don't want to hear that, either. Your father and I have enough trouble to keep among-you in school, never mind election."

I dropped the subject.

The week was a very long and exciting one for me. The only way I could get attention from my classmates in the sixth grade was by having money, and thanks to carefully planned forays into my father's pants pockets every night that week, I made sure I had plenty. Every day at noon, I dashed across the street, gobbled down whatever food my mother had left for my lunch, and headed for the schoolyard.

Sometimes when I came home for lunch my father was asleep in my parents' bedroom before he returned to work. I now had my very own room, and my two sisters shared another. The day before the election, I tiptoed through the house to the closed french doors of my parents' bedroom, and through a crack in the portières peeked in upon my sleeping father. The doors seemed to shake with his heavy snoring. I watched his mouth open and close a little with each snore, stentorian rattles erupting below his nuzzled moustache. The covers thrown partially back, to reveal his hands in sleep tucked into the top of his drawstring pajamas. He was lying on his side toward me, and the front of his pajama pants had fallen open. I could see only shadows of the vulnerable secrets shading the gap in his clothing, but I was suddenly shaken by this so-human image of him, and the idea that I could spy upon him and he not be aware of it, even in his sleep. I stepped back and closed the door quickly, embarrassed and ashamed of my own curiosity, but wishing his pajamas had gapped more so that I could finally know what exactly was the mysterious secret men carried between their legs.

When I was ten, a little boy on the rooftop had taken off my glasses, and so seeing little, all I could remember of that encounter, when I remembered it at all, was a long thin pencil-like thing that I knew couldn't have any relationship to my father.

Before I closed the door, though, I slipped my hand around the door-curtains to where Daddy's suit hung. I separated a dollar bill from the thin roll which he carried in his pants pocket. Then I retreated back into the kitchen, washed my plate and glass, and hurried back to school. I had electioneering to do.

I knew better than to say another word to my mother about the presidency, but that week was filled with fantasies of how I would break the news to her on Friday when she came home.

"Oh, Mommy, by the way, can I stay later at school on Monday for a presidents' meeting?" Or "Mother, would you please sign this note saying it is all right for me to accept the presidency?" Or maybe even, "Mother, could I have a little get-together here to celebrate the election?"

On Friday, I tied a ribbon around the steel barrette that held my unruly mass of hair tightly at the nape of my neck. Elections were to be held in the afternoon, and when I got home for lunch, for the first time in my life, I was too excited to eat. I buried the can of Campbell's soup that my mother had left out for me way behind the other cans in the pantry and hoped she had not counted how many were left.

We filed out of the schoolyard and up the stairs to the sixth grade room. The walls were still lined with bits of green from the recent St. Patrick's Day decorations. Sister Blanche passed out little pieces of blank paper for our ballots.

The first rude awakening came when she announced that the boy chosen would be president, but the girl would only be vice-president. I thought this was monstrously unfair. Why not the other way around? Since we could not, as she explained, have two presidents, why not a girl president and a boy vice-president? It doesn't really matter, I said to myself. I can live with being vice-president.

I voted for myself. The ballots were collected and passed to the front of the room and duly counted. James O'Connor won for the boys. Ann Archdeacon won for the girls. Ilene Crimmons came in second. I got four votes, one of which was mine. I was in shock. We all clapped for the winners, and Ann Archdeacon turned around in her seat and smiled her shit-eating smile at me. "Too bad you lost." I smiled back. I wanted to break her face off.

I was too much my mother's daughter to let anyone think it mattered. But I felt I had been destroyed. How could this have happened? I was the smartest girl in the class. I had not been elected vice-president. It was as simple as that. But something was escaping me. Something was terribly wrong. It wasn't fair.

A sweet little girl named Helen Ramsey had decided it was her christian duty to befriend me, and she had once lent me her sled during the winter. She lived next to the church, and after school, that day, she invited me to her house for a cup of cocoa. I ran away without answering, dashing across the street and into the safety of my house. I ran up the stairs, my bookbag banging against my legs. I pulled out the key pinned to my uniform pocket and unlocked the door to our apartment. The house was warm and dark and empty and quiet. I did not stop running until I got to my room at the front of the house, where I flung my books and my coat in a corner and collapsed upon my convertible couch-bed, shrieking with fury and disappointment. Finally, in the privacy of my room, I could shed the tears that had been burning my eyes for two hours, and I wept and wept.

I had wanted other things before that I had not gotten. So much so, that I had come to believe if I really wanted something badly enough, the very act of my wanting it was an assurance that I would not get it. Was this what had happened with the election? Had I wanted it too much? Was this what my mother was always talking about? Why she had been so angry? Because wanting meant I would not get? But somehow this felt different. This was the first time that I had wanted something so badly, the getting of which I was sure I could control. The election was supposed to have gone to the smartest girl in the class, and I was clearly the smartest. That was something I had done, on my own, that should have guaranteed me the election. The smartest, not the most popular. That was me. But it hadn't happened. My mother had been right. I hadn't won the election. My mother had been right.

This thought hurt me almost as much as the loss of the election, and when I felt it fully I shrieked with renewed vigor. I luxuriated in my grief in the empty house in a way I could never have done if anyone were home.

All the way up front and buried in my tears, kneeling with my face in the cushions of my couch, I did not hear the key in the lock, nor the main door open. The first thing I knew, there was my mother standing in the doorway of my room, a frown of concern in her voice.

"What happened, what happened? What's wrong with you? What's this racket going on here?"

I turned my wet face up to her from the couch. I wanted a little comfort in my pain, and getting up, I started moving toward her.

"I lost the election, Mommy," I cried, forgetting her warnings. "I'm the smartest girl in class, Sister Blanche says so, and they chose Ann Archdeacon instead!" The unfairness of it all flooded over me again and my voice cracked into fresh sobs.

Through my tears, I saw my mother's face stiffen with rage. Her eyebrows drew together as her hand came up, still holding her handbag. I stopped in my tracks as her first blow caught me full on the side of my head. My mother was no weakling, and I backed away, my ears ringing. The whole world seemed to be going insane. It was only then I remembered our earlier conversations.

"See, the bird forgets, but the trap doesn't! I warned you! What you think you doing coming into this house wailing about election? If I told you once I have told you a hundred times, don't chase yourself behind these people, haven't I? What kind of ninny raise up here to think those good-for-nothing white piss-jets would pass over some little jacabat girl to elect you

anything?" Smack! "What did I say to you just now?" She
cuffed me again, this time on my shoulders, as I huddled to escape her rain of furious blows, and the edges of her pocketbook.

"Sure enough, didn't I tell you not to come in here bringing
down tears over some worthless fool election?" Smack! "What
the hell you think we send you to school for?" Smack! "Don't
run yourself behind other people's business, you'll do better.
Dry up, now, dry up!" Smack! She pulled me to my feet from
where I had sunk back onto the couch.

"Is cry you want to cry? I'll give you something hard to cry
on!" And she cuffed me again, this time more lightly. "Now get
yourself up from there and stop acting like some stupid fool,
worrying yourself about these people's business that doesn't
concern you. Get-the-france out of here and wipe up your face.
Start acting like a human being!" ~uh

Pushing me ahead of her, my mother marched back through
the parlor and into the kitchen. "I come in here tired from the
street and here you, acting like the world is ending. I thought
sure enough some terrible thing happened to you, come to find
out it's only election. Now help me put away this foodstuff."

I was relieved to hear her tone mollify, as I wiped my eyes.
But I still gave her heavy hands a wide berth.

"It's just that it's not fair, Mother. That's all I was crying
about," I said, opening the brown paper bags on the table. To
admit I had been hurt would somehow put me in the wrong for
feeling pain. "It wasn't the election I cared about so much really, just that it was all so unfair."

"Fair, fair, what's fair, you think? Is fair you want, look in
god's face." My mother was busily dropping onions into the
bin. She paused, and turning around, held my puffy face up,
her hand beneath my chin. Her eyes so sharp and furious before, now just looked tired and sad.

"Child, why you worry your head so much over fair or not
fair? Just do what is for you to do and let the rest take care of
themselves." She smoothed straggles of hair back from my face,
and I felt the anger gone from her fingers. "Look, you hair all
mess-up behind from rolling around with foolishness. Go wash
your face and hands and come help me dress this fish for supper."

9 Except for political matters, my father was a man of few words. But he carried on extensive conversations with himself in the bathroom every morning.

During the last years of the war, my father could be found more often away from home than not, or at best, sleeping a few hours before going back out to his night job at the war plant.

My mother would rush home from the office, market, fuss with us a little, and fix supper. Phyllis, Helen, or I would have put on the rice or potatoes already, and maybe my mother had seasoned some meat earlier in the day and left it on the stove with a note for one of us to turn on the fire low under the pot when we came home. Or perhaps there would be something left on purpose from last night's supper ("Leave some of that for your father's dinner tomorrow!"). On those afternoons, I didn't wait for my mother to come home. Instead, I packed the food up myself and took off downtown on the bus, headed for my father's office.

I heated each separate portion until it was piping hot. Carefully, I packed the hot rice and savory bits of meat stew or spicy chicken and gravy into scoured milk bottles which we saved for that purpose. I packed the vegetables separately in their own bottle, with a little pat of butter if we could get it, or margarine, on top. I wrapped each bottle in layers of newspapers, and then in an old towel, to keep the food warm. Placing them in a shopping bag together with the shirt and sweater that my mother had left for me to take to my father, I set off by bus down to the office, heavy with a sense of mission and accomplishment.

The bus from Washington Heights ran downtown and across 125th Street. I got off at Lenox Avenue, and walked the three blocks up to the office, past bars and grocery stores and small groups of people in lively conversation on the street.

Sometimes when I arrived, my father was downstairs in the office already, poring over receipt books or taxes or bills. Sometimes he was still asleep in a room upstairs, and the janitor had to go up and knock on the room door to waken him. I was never allowed to go upstairs, nor to enter the room where my father slept. I always wondered what mysteries occurred "upstairs," and what it was up there my parents never wanted me to see. I think it was that same vulnerability that had so shocked and embarrassed me the day I peered into their bedroom at home. His ordinary humanity.

When my father came downstairs, I kissed him hello, and he went into the back of the office to wash his face and hands preparatory to eating. I spread out the meal carefully, on a special desk in the back room. If anyone came in to see my father while he was eating, I wrote out a receipt, proudly, or relayed the message to him in the back room. For my father, eating was too human a pastime to allow just anyone to see him at it.

If no one came in, I sat quietly in the back room and watched him eat. He was meticulously neat, placing his bones in even rows on the paper towel beside his plate. Sometimes my father looked up and saw me watching him, and he reached out and gave me a morsel of meat or a taste of rice and gravy from his plate.

Other times I sat with my book, quietly reading, but secretly waiting and hoping for this special treat. Even if I had already just eaten the same food, or even if it was some dish I did not particularly like, these tastes of my father's food from his plate in the back room of his office had an enchantment to them that was delicious and magical, and precious. They form the fondest and closest memories I have of warm moments shared with my father. There were not many.

When my father was finished with his meal, I rinsed out the bottles, and washed his dish and silverware. I placed them back upon the shelf especially cleared for them, and covered them with the cloth napkin that was kept there for that purpose, to protect them from the dust of the back room. I carefully re-packed the bottles into the shopping bag, and took the nickel carfare that my father gave me for the bus trip back. I kissed him goodbye and headed for home.

Sometimes no more than two or three sentences passed between us during the whole time we were together in the office. But I remember those evenings, particularly in the springtime, as very special and satisfying times.

10

The first time I went to Washington, D.C. was on the edge of the summer when I was supposed to stop being a child. At least that's what they said to us all at graduation from the eighth grade. My sister Phyllis graduated at the same time from high school. I don't know what she was supposed to stop being. But as graduation presents for us both, the whole family took a Fourth of July trip to Washington, D.C., the fabled and famous capital of our country.

It was the first time I'd ever been on a railroad train during the day. When I was little, and we used to go the Connecticut shore, we always went at night on the milk train, because it was cheaper.

Preparations were in the air around our house before school was even over. We packed for a week. There were two very large suitcases that my father carried, and a box filled with food. In fact, my first trip to Washington was a mobile feast; I started eating as soon as we were comfortably ensconced in our seats, and did not stop until somewhere after Philadelphia. I remember it was Philadelphia because I was disappointed not to have passed by the Liberty Bell.

My mother had roasted two chickens and cut them up into dainty bite-size pieces. She packed slices of brown bread and butter and green pepper and carrot sticks. There were little violently yellow iced cakes with scalloped edges called "marigolds," that came from Cushman's Bakery. There was a spice bun and rock-cakes from Newton's, the West Indian bakery across Lenox Avenue from St. Mark's School, and iced tea in a wrapped mayonnaise jar. There were sweet pickles for us and dill pickles for my father, and peaches with the fuzz still on them, individually wrapped to keep them from bruising. And, for neatness, there were piles of napkins and a little tin box with a washcloth dampened with rosewater and glycerine for wiping sticky mouths.

I wanted to eat in the dining car because I had read all about them, but my mother reminded me for the umpteenth time that dining car food always cost too much money and besides, you never could tell whose hands had been playing all over that food, nor where those same hands had been just before. My mother never mentioned that Black people were not allowed into railroad dining cars headed south in 1947. As usual, whatever my mother did not like and could not change, she ignored. Perhaps it would go away, deprived of her attention.

I learned later that Phyllis's high school senior class trip had been to Washington, but the nuns had given her back her deposit in private, explaining to her that the class, all of whom were white, except Phyllis, would be staying in a hotel where Phyllis "would not be happy," meaning, Daddy explained to her, also in private, that they did not rent rooms to Negroes. "We will take among-you to Washington, ourselves," my father had avowed, "and not just for an overnight in some measly fleabag hotel."

American racism was a new and crushing reality that my parents had to deal with every day of their lives once they came to this country. They handled it as a private woe. My mother and father believed that they could best protect their children from the realities of race in america and the fact of american racism by never giving them name, much less discussing their nature. We were told we must never trust white people, but *why* was never explained, nor the nature of their ill will. Like so many other vital pieces of information in my childhood, I was supposed to know without being told. It always seemed like a very strange injunction coming from my mother, who looked so much like one of those people we were never supposed to trust. But something always warned me not to ask my mother why she wasn't white, and why Auntie Lillah and Auntie Etta weren't, even though they were all that same problematic color so different from my father and me, even from my sisters, who were somewhere in-between.

In Washington, D. C. we had one large room with two double beds and an extra cot for me. It was a back-street hotel that belonged to a friend of my father's who was in real estate, and I spent the whole next day after Mass squinting up at the Lincoln Memorial where Marian Anderson had sung after the D.A.R. refused to allow her to sing in their auditorium because she was Black. Or because she was "Colored," my father said as he told us the story. Except that what he probably said was "Negro," because for his times, my father was quite progressive.

I was squinting because I was in that silent agony that characterized all of my childhood summers, from the time school let out in June to the end of July, brought about by my dilated and vulnerable eyes exposed to the summer brightness.

I viewed Julys through an agonizing corolla of dazzling whiteness and I always hated the Fourth of July, even before I came to realize the travesty such a celebration was for Black people in this country.

My parents did not approve of sunglasses, nor of their expense.

I spent the afternoon squinting up at monuments to freedom and past presidencies and democracy, and wondering why the light and heat were both so much stronger in Washington, D. C. than back home in New York City. Even the pavement on the streets was a shade lighter in color than back home.

Late that Washington afternoon my family and I walked back down Pennsylvania Avenue. We were a proper caravan, mother bright and father brown, the three of us girls step-standards in-between. Moved by our historical surroundings and the heat of the early evening, my father decreed yet another treat. He had a great sense of history, a flair for the quietly dramatic and the sense of specialness of an occasion and a trip.

"Shall we stop and have a little something to cool off, Lin?"

Two blocks away from our hotel, the family stopped for a dish of vanilla ice cream at a Breyer's ice cream and soda fountain. Indoors, the soda fountain was dim and fan-cooled, deliciously relieving to my scorched eyes.

Corded and crisp and pinafored, the five of us seated ourselves one by one at the counter. There was I between my mother and father, and my two sisters on the other side of my mother. We settled ourselves along the white mottled marble counter, and when the waitress spoke at first no one understood what she was saying, and so the five of us just sat there.

The waitress moved along the line of us closer to my father and spoke again. "I said I kin give you to take out, but you can't eat here. Sorry." Then she dropped her eyes looking very embarrassed, and suddenly we heard what it was she was saying all at the same time, loud and clear.

Straight-backed and indignant, one by one, my family and I got down from the counter stools and turned around and marched out of the store, quiet and outraged, as if we had never been Black before. No one would answer my emphatic questions with anything other than a guilty silence. "But we hadn't done anything!" This wasn't right or fair! Hadn't I written poems about Bataan and freedom and democracy for all?

My parents wouldn't speak of this injustice, not because they had contributed to it, but because they felt they should have anticipated it and avoided it. This made me even angrier. My fury was not going to be acknowledged by a like fury. Even my two sisters copied my parents' pretense that nothing unusual and anti-american had occurred. I was left to write my angry letter to the president of the united states all by myself, although my father did promise I could type it out on the office type-writer next week, after I showed it to him in my copybook diary.

The waitress was white, and the counter was white, and the ice cream I never ate in Washington, D. C. that summer I left childhood was white, and the white heat and the white pavement and the white stone monuments of my first Washington sum-mer made me sick to my stomach for the whole rest of that trip and it wasn't much of a graduation present after all.

11 When I was growing up in my mother's house, there were spices you grated and spices you pounded, and whenever you pounded spice and garlic or other herbs, you used a mortar. Every West Indian woman worth her salt had her own mortar. Now if you lost or broke your mortar, you could, of course, buy another one in the market over on Park Avenue, under the bridge, but those were usually Puerto Rican mortars, and even though they were made out of wood and worked exactly the same way, somehow they were never really as good as West Indian mortars. Now where the best mortars came from I was never really sure, but I knew it must be in the vicinity of that amorphous and mys-tically perfect place called "home." And whatever came from "home" was bound to be special.

My mother's mortar was an elaborate affair, quite at vari-ance with most of her other possessions, and certainly with her projected public view of herself. It stood, solid and elegant, on a shelf in the kitchen cabinet for as long as I can remember, and I loved it dearly.

The mortar was of a foreign fragrant wood, too dark for cher-ry and too red for walnut. To my child eyes, the outside was carved in an intricate and most enticing manner. There were rounded plums and oval indeterminate fruit, some long and fluted like a banana, others ovular and end-swollen like a ripe alligator pear. In between these were smaller rounded shapes like cherries, lying in batches against and around each other.

I loved to finger the hard roundness of the carved fruit, and the always surprising termination of the shapes as the carvings stopped at the rim and the bowl sloped abruptly downward, smoothly oval but suddenly businesslike. The heavy sturdiness of this useful wooden object always made me feel secure and somehow full; as if it conjured up from all the many different flavors pounded into the inside wall, visions of delicious feasts both once enjoyed and still to come.

The pestle was long and tapering, fashioned from the same mysterious rose-deep wood, and fitted into the hand almost casually, familiarly. The actual shape reminded me of a summer crook-necked squash uncurled and slightly twisted. It could also have been an avocado, with the neck of the alligator pear elongated and the whole made efficient for pounding, without ever losing the apparent soft firmness and the character of the fruit which the wood suggested. It was slightly bigger at the grinding end than most pestles, and the widened curved end fitted into the bowl of the mortar easily. Long use and years of impact and grinding within the bowl's worn hollow had softened the very surface of the wooden pestle, until a thin layer of split fibers coated the rounded end like a layer of velvet. A layer of the same velvety mashed wood lined the bottom inside the sloping bowl.

My mother did not particularly like to pound spice, and she looked upon the advent of powdered everything as a cook's boon. But there were some certain dishes that called for a particular savory blending of garlic, raw onion, and pepper, and souse was one of them.

For our mother's souse, it didn't matter what kind of meat was used. You could have hearts, or beefends, or even chicken backs and gizzards when we were really poor. It was the pounded-up saucy blend of herb and spice rubbed into the meat before it was left to stand so for a few hours before cooking that made that dish so special and unforgettable. But my mother had some very firm ideas about what she liked best to cook and about which were her favorite dishes, and souse was definitely not one of either.

On the very infrequent occasions that my mother would allow one of us three girls to choose a meal—as opposed to helping to prepare it, which was a daily routine—on those occasions my sisters would usually choose one of those proscribed dishes so dear to our hearts remembered from our relatives' tables, contraband, and so very rare in our house. They might ask for hot dogs, perhaps, smothered in ketchup sauce, or with crusty Boston-baked beans; or american chicken, breaded first and fried crispy the way the southern people did it; or creamed something-or-other that one of my sisters had tasted at school;

what-have-you croquettes or anything fritters; or once even a daring outrageous request for slices of fresh watermelon, hawked from the back of a rickety wooden pickup truck with the southern road-dust still on her slatted sides, from which a young bony Black man with a turned-around baseball cap on his head would hang and half-yell, half-yodel—"Wahr—deeeeeee-mayyyyyyy-lawnnnnnnnn."

There were many american dishes I longed for too, but on the one or two occasions a year that I got to choose a meal, I would always ask for souse. That way, I knew that I would get to use my mother's mortar, and this in itself was more treat for me than any of the forbidden foods. Besides, if I really wanted hot dogs or anything croquettes badly enough, I could steal some money from my father's pocket and buy them in the school lunch.

"Mother, let's have souse," I'd say, and never even stop to think about it. The anticipated taste of the soft spicy meat had become inseparable in my mind from the tactile pleasures of using my mother's mortar.

"But what makes you think anybody can find time to mash up all that stuff?" My mother would cut her hawk-grey eyes at me from beneath their heavy black brows. "Among-you children never stop to think," and she'd turn back to whatever it was she had been doing. If she had just come from the office with my father, she might be checking the day's receipts, or she might be washing the endless piles of dirty linen that always seemed to issue from rooming-houses.

"Oh, I'll pound the garlic, Mommy!" would be my next line in the script written by some ancient and secret hand, and off I'd go to the cabinet to get down the heavy wooden mortar and pestle.

I took a head of garlic out from the garlic bottle in the icebox, and breaking off ten or twelve cloves from the head, I carefully peeled away the tissue lavender skin, slicing each stripped peg in half lengthwise. I dropped them piece by piece into the capacious waiting bowl of the mortar. Taking a slice from a small onion, I put the rest aside to be used later over the meat, and cutting the slice into quarters, I tossed it into the mortar also. Next came the coarsely ground fresh black pepper, and then a lavish blanketing cover of salt over the whole. Last, if we had any, a few leaves from the top of a head of celery. My mother sometimes added a slice of green pepper, but I did not

like the texture of the pepper-skin under the pestle, and preferred to add it along with the sliced onion later on, leaving it
all to sit over the seasoned and resting meat.

After all the ingredients were in the bowl of the mortar, I
fetched the pestle and placing it into the bowl, slowly rotated
the shaft a few times, working it gently down through all the
ingredients to mix them. Only then would I lift the pestle, and
with one hand firmly pressed around the carved side of the mortar caressing the wooden fruit with my aromatic fingers, I thrust
sharply downward, feeling the shifting salt and the hard little
pellets of garlic right up through the shaft of the wooden pestle.
Up again, down, around, and up—so the rhythm began.

The *thud push rub rotate up* repeated over and over. The
muted thump of the pestle on the bed of grinding spice as the
salt and pepper absorbed the slowly yielding juices of the garlic
and celery leaves.

Thud push rub rotate up. The mingling fragrances rising from
the bowl of the mortar.

Thud push rub rotate up. The feeling of the pestle held between my curving fingers, and the mortar's outside rounding
like fruit into my palm as I steadied it against my body.

All these transported me into a world of scent and rhythm
and movement and sound that grew more and more exciting as
the ingredients liquefied.

Sometimes my mother would look over at me with that
amused annoyance which passed for tenderness.

"What you think you making there, garlic soup? Enough, go
get the meat now." And I would fetch the lamb hearts, for instance, from the icebox and begin to prepare them. Cutting
away the hardened veins at the top of the smooth firm muscles,
I divided each oval heart into four wedge-shaped pieces, and
taking a bit of the spicy mash from the mortar with my fingertips, I rubbed each piece with the savory mix, the pungent smell
of garlic and onion and celery enveloping the kitchen.

The last day I ever pounded seasoning for souse was in the
summer of my fifteenth year. It had been a fairly unpleasant
summer for me. I had just finished my first year in high school.
Instead of being able to visit my newly found friends, all of
whom lived in other parts of the city, I had had to accompany
my mother on a round of doctors with whom she would have
long whispered conversations. Only a matter of utmost importance could have kept her away from the office for so many
mornings in a row. But my mother was concerned because I

was fourteen and a half years old and had not yet menstruated. I had breasts but no period, and she was afraid there was something "wrong" with me. Yet, since she had never discussed this mysterious business of menstruation with me, I was certainly not supposed to know what all this whispering was about, even though it concerned my own body.

Of course, I knew as much as I could have possibly found out in those days from the hard-to-get books on the "closed shelf" behind the librarian's desk at the public library, where I had brought a forged note from home in order to be allowed to read them, sitting under the watchful eye of the librarian at a special desk reserved for that purpose.

Although not terribly informative, they were fascinating books, and used words like *menses* and *ovulation* and *vagina*.

But four years before, I had had to find out if I was going to become pregnant, because a boy from school much bigger than me had invited me up to the roof on my way home from the library and then threatened to break my glasses if I didn't let him stick his "thing" between my legs. And at that time I knew only that being pregnant had something to do with sex, and sex had something to do with that thin pencil-like "thing" and was in general nasty and not to be talked about by nice people, and I was afraid my mother might find out and what would she do to me then? I was not supposed to be looking at the mailboxes in the hallway of that house anyway, even though Doris was a girl in my class at St. Mark's who lived in that house and I was always so lonely in the summer, particularly that summer when I was ten.

So after I got home I washed myself up and lied about why I was late getting home from the library and got a whipping for being late. That must have been a hard summer for my parents at the office too, because that was the summer that I got a whipping for something or other almost every day between the Fourth of July and Labor Day.

When I wasn't getting whippings, I hid out at the library on 135th Street, and forged notes from my mother to get books from the "closed shelf," and read about sex and having babies, and waited to become pregnant. None of the books were very clear to me about the relationship between having your period and having a baby, but they were all very clear about the relationship between penises and getting pregnant. Or maybe the confusion was all in my own mind, because I had always been a very fast but not a very careful reader.

So four years later, in my fifteenth year, I was a very scared
little girl, still half-afraid that one of that endless stream of doctors would look up into my body and discover my four-year-
old shame and say to my mother, "Aha! So that's what's wrong!
Your daughter is about to become pregnant!"

On the other hand, if I let Mother know that I knew what
was happening and what these medical safaris were all about, I
would have to answer her questions about how and wherefore I
knew, since she hadn't told me, divulging in the process the
whole horrible and self-incriminating story of forbidden books
and forged library notes and rooftops and stairwell conversations.

It was a year after the rooftop incident, when we had moved
farther uptown. The kids at St. Catherine's seemed to know a
lot more about sex than at St. Mark's. In the eighth grade, I had
stolen money and bought my classmate Adeline a pack of cigarettes and she had confirmed my bookish suspicions about how
babies were made. My response to her graphic descriptions had
been to think to myself, *there obviously must be another way
that Adeline doesn't know about, because my parents have children and I know they never did anything like that!* But the
basic principles were all there, and sure enough they were the
same as I had gathered from *The Young People's Family Book.*

So in my fifteenth summer, on examining table after examining table, I kept my legs open and my mouth shut, and when I
saw blood on my pants one hot July afternoon, I rinsed them
out secretly in the bathroom and put them back on wet because
I didn't know how to break the news to my mother that both
her worries and mine were finally over. (All this time I had at
least understood that having your period was a sign you were
not pregnant.)

What then happened felt like a piece of an old and elaborate
dance between my mother and me. She discovers finally, through
a stain on the toilet seat left there on purpose by me as a mute
announcement, what has taken place; she scolds, "Why didn't
you tell me about all of this, now? It's nothing to get upset over,
you are a woman, not a child anymore. Now you go over to the
drugstore and ask the man for. . ."

I was just relieved the whole damn thing was over with. It's
difficult to talk about double messages without having a twin
tongue. Nightmarish evocations and restrictions were being
verbalized by my mother:

"This means from now on you better watch your step and not be so friendly with every Tom, Dick, and Harry. . ." (which must have meant my staying late after school to talk with my girlfriends, because I did not even know any boys); and, "Now remember, too, after you wrap up your soiled napkins in newspaper, don't leave them hanging around on the bathroom floor where your father has to see them, not that it's anything shameful but all the same, remember. . ."

Along with all of these admonitions, there was something else coming from my mother that I could not define. It was the lurking of that amused/annoyed brow-furrowed half-smile of hers that made me feel—all her nagging words to the contrary— that something very good and satisfactory and pleasing to her had just happened, and that we were both pretending otherwise for some very wise and secret reasons. I would come to understand these reasons later, as a reward, if I handled myself properly. Then, at the end of it all, my mother thrust the box of Kotex at me (I had fetched it in its plain wrapper back from the drugstore, along with a sanitary belt), saying to me,

"But look now what time it is already, I wonder what we're going to eat for supper tonight?" She waited. At first I didn't understand, but I quickly picked up the cue. I had seen the beefends in the icebox that morning.

"Mommy, please let's have some souse—I'll pound the garlic." I dropped the box onto a kitchen chair and started to wash my hands in anticipation.

"Well, go put your business away first. What did I tell you about leaving that lying around?" She wiped her hands from the washtub where she had been working and handed the plain wrapped box of Kotex back to me.

"I have to go out, I forgot to pick up tea at the store. Now make sure you rub the meat good."

When I came back into the kitchen, my mother had left. I moved toward the kitchen cabinet to fetch down the mortar and pestle. My body felt new and special and unfamiliar and suspect all at the same time.

I could feel bands of tension sweeping across my body back and forth, like lunar winds across the moon's face. I felt the slight rubbing bulge of the cotton pad between my legs, and I smelled the delicate breadfruit smell rising up from the front of my print blouse that was my own womansmell, warm, shameful, but secretly utterly delicious.

Years afterward when I was grown, whenever I thought about the way I smelled that day, I would have a fantasy of my mother, her hands wiped dry from the washing, and her apron untied and laid neatly away, looking down upon me lying on the couch, and then slowly, thoroughly, our touching and caressing each other's most secret places.

I took the mortar down, and smashed the cloves of garlic with the edge of its underside, to loosen the thin papery skins in a hurry. I sliced them and flung them into the mortar's bowl along with some black pepper and celery leaves. The white salt poured in, covering the garlic and black pepper and pale chartreuse celery fronds like a snowfall. I tossed in the onion and some bits of green pepper and reached for the pestle.

It slipped through my fingers and clattered to the floor, rolling around in a semicircle back and forth, until I bent to retrieve it. I grabbed the head of the wooden stick and straightened up, my ears ringing faintly. Without even wiping it, I plunged the pestle into the bowl, feeling the blanket of salt give way, and the broken cloves of garlic just beneath. The downward thrust of the wooden pestle slowed upon contact, rotated back and forth slowly, and then gently altered its rhythm to include an up and down beat. Back and forth, round, up and down, back, forth, round, round, up and down. . . . There was a heavy fullness at the root of me that was exciting and dangerous.

As I continued to pound the spice, a vital connection seemed to establish itself between the muscles of my fingers curved tightly around the smooth pestle in its insistent downward motion, and the molten core of my body whose source emanated from a new ripe fullness just beneath the pit of my stomach. That invisible thread, taut and sensitive as a clitoris exposed, stretched through my curled fingers up my round brown arm into the moist reality of my armpits, whose warm sharp odor with a strange new overlay mixed with the ripe garlic smells from the mortar and the general sweat-heavy aromas of high summer.

The thread ran over my ribs and along my spine, tingling and singing, into a basin that was poised between my hips, now pressed against the low kitchen counter before which I stood, pounding spice. And within that basin was a tiding ocean of blood beginning to be made real and available to me for strength and information.

The jarring shocks of the velvet-lined pestle, striking the bed of spice, traveled up an invisible pathway along the thread into the center of me, and the harshness of the repeated impacts became increasingly more unbearable. The tidal basin suspended between my hips shuddered at each repetition of the strokes which now felt like assaults. Without my volition my downward thrusts of the pestle grew gentler and gentler, until its velvety surface seemed almost to caress the liquefying mash at the bottom of the mortar.

The whole rhythm of my movements softened and elongated, until, dreamlike, I stood, one hand tightly curved around the carved mortar, steadying it against the middle of my body; while my other hand, around the pestle, rubbed and pressed the moistening spice into readiness with a sweeping circular movement.

I hummed tunelessly to myself as I worked in the warm kitchen, thinking with relief about how simple my life would be now that I had become a woman. The catalogue of dire menstruation-warnings from my mother passed out of my head. My body felt strong and full and open, yet captivated by the gentle motions of the pestle, and the rich smells filling the kitchen, and the fullness of the young summer heat.

I heard my mother's key in the lock.

She swept into the kitchen briskly, like a ship under full sail. There were tiny beads of sweat over her upper lip, and vertical creases between her brows.

"You mean to tell me no meat is ready?" My mother dropped her parcel of tea onto the table, and looking over my shoulder, sucked her teeth loudly in weary disgust. "What do you call yourself doing, now? You have all night to stand up there playing with the food? I go all the way to the store and back already and still you can't mash up a few pieces of garlic to season some meat? But you know how to do the thing better than this! Why you vex me so?"

She took the mortar and pestle out of my hands and started to grind vigorously. And there were still bits of garlic left at the bottom of the bowl.

"Now you do, so!" She brought the pestle down inside the bowl of the mortar with dispatch, crushing the last of the garlic. I heard the thump of wood brought down heavily upon wood, and I felt the harsh impact throughout my body, as if something had broken inside of me. Thump, thump, went the pestle, purposefully, up and down in the old familiar way.

"It was getting mashed, Mother," I dared to protest, turning away to the icebox. "I'll fetch the meat." I was surprised at my own brazenness in answering back.

But something in my voice interrupted my mother's efficient motions. She ignored my implied contradiction, itself an act of rebellion strictly forbidden in our house. The thumping stopped.

"What's wrong with you, now? Are you sick? You want to go to your bed?"

"No, I'm all right, Mother."

But I felt her strong fingers on my upper arm, turning me around, her other hand under my chin as she peered into my face. Her voice softened.

"Is it your period making you so slow-down today?" She gave my chin a little shake, as I looked up into her hooded grey eyes, now becoming almost gentle. The kitchen felt suddenly oppressively hot and still, and I felt myself beginning to shake all over.

Tears I did not understand started from my eyes, as I realized that my old enjoyment of the bone-jarring way I had been taught to pound spice would feel different to me from now on, and also that in my mother's kitchen there was only one right way to do anything. Perhaps my life had not become so simple, after all.

My mother stepped away from the counter and put her heavy arm around my shoulders. I could smell the warm herness rising from between her arm and her body, mixed with the smell of glycerine and rosewater, and the scent of her thick bun of hair.

"I'll finish up the food for supper." She smiled at me, and there was a tenderness in her voice and an absence of annoyance that was welcome, although unfamiliar.

"You come inside now and lie down on the couch and I'll make you a hot cup of tea."

Her arm across my shoulders was warm and slightly damp. I rested my head upon her shoulder, and realized with a shock of pleasure and surprise that I was almost as tall as my mother, as she led me into the cool darkened parlor.

12 At home, my mother said, "Remember to be sisters in the presence of strangers." She meant white people, like the woman who tried to make me get up and give her my seat on the Number 4 bus, and who smelled like cleaning fluid. At St. Catherine's, they said, "Be sisters in the presence of strangers," and they meant non-catholics. In high school, the girls said, "Be sisters in the presence of strangers," and they meant men. My friends said, "Be sisters in the presence of strangers," and they meant the squares.

But in high school, my real sisters were strangers; my teachers were racists; and my friends were that color I was never supposed to trust.

In high school, my best friends were "The Branded," as our sisterhood of rebels sometimes called ourselves. We never talked about those differences that separated us, only the ones that united us against the *others*. My friends and I talked about who studied german or french, who liked poetry or doing "the twist," who went out with boys, and who was "progressive." We even talked about our position as women in a world supposed to be run by men.

But we never ever talked about what it meant and felt like to be Black and white, and the effects that had on our being friends. Of course, everybody with any sense deplored racial discrimination, theoretically and without discussion. We could conquer it by ignoring it.

I had grown up in such an isolated world that it was hard for me to recognize difference as anything other than a threat, because it usually was. (The first time I saw my sister Helen in the tub naked I was almost fourteen, and I thought she was a witch because her nipples were pale pink against her light brown breasts, not deeply purple like mine.) But sometimes, I was close to crazy with believing that there was some secret thing wrong with me personally that formed an invisible barrier between me and the rest of my friends, who were white. What was it that kept people from inviting me to their houses, their parties, their summer homes for a weekend? Was it that their mothers did not like them to have friends, the way my mother didn't? Did their mothers caution them about never trusting outsiders? But they visited each other. There was something here that I was missing. Since the only place I couldn't see clearly was behind my own eyes, obviously the trouble was with me. I had no words for racism.

On the deepest level, I probably knew then what I know now. But it was not serviceable to my child's mind to understand, and I needed too much to remain a child for a little bit more.

We were The Branded, the Lunatic Fringe, proud of our outrageousness and our madness, our bizarre-colored inks and quill pens. We learned how to mock the straight set, and how to cultivate our group paranoia into an instinct for self-protection that always stopped our shenanigans just short of expulsion. We wrote obscure poetry and cherished our strangeness as the spoils of default, and in the process we learned that pain and rejection hurt, but that they weren't fatal, and that they could be useful since they couldn't be avoided. We learned that not feeling at all was worse than hurting. At that time, suffering was clearly what we did best. We became The Branded because we learned how to make a virtue out of it.

How meager the sustenance was I gained from the four years I spent in high school; yet, how important that sustenance was to my survival. Remembering that time is like watching old pictures of myself in a prison camp picking edible scraps out of the garbage heap, and knowing that without that garbage I might have starved to death. The overwhelming racism of so many of the faculty, including the ones upon whom I had my worst schoolgirl crushes. How little I settled for in the way of human contact, compared to what I was conscious of wanting.

It was in high school that I came to believe that I was different from my white classmates, not because I was Black, but because I was me.

For four years, Hunter High School was a lifeline. No matter what it was in reality, I got something there I needed. For the first time I met young women my own age, Black and white, who spoke a language I could usually understand and reply within. I met girls with whom I could share feelings and dreams and ideas without fear. I found adults who tolerated my feelings and ideas without punishment for insolence, and even a few who respected and admired them.

Writing poetry became an ordinary effort, not a secret and rebellious vice. The other girls at Hunter who wrote poetry did not invite me to their homes, either, but they did elect me literary editor of the school arts magazine.

By my sophomore year in high school, I was in open battle on every other front in my life except school. Relationships with my family had come to resemble nothing so much as a West Indian version of the Second World War. Every conversation with my parents, particularly with my mother, was like a playback of the Battle of the Bulge in Black panorama with stereophonic sound. Blitzkrieg became my favorite symbol for home. I fantasized all my dealings with them against a backdrop of Joan of Arc at Rheims or the Revolutionary War.

I cleaned my flintlocks nightly, and poured my lead-mold bullets after midnight when everybody else in my family was asleep. I had discovered a new world called voluntary aloneness. After midnight was the only time it was possible in my family's house. At any other time, a closed door was still considered an insult. My mother viewed any act of separation from her as an indictment of her authority. I was allowed to shut my door to my room only while I was doing my homework and not for a moment longer. My room opened into the living room, and an hour after dinner I could hear my mother calling me.

"What's that door still closed about? You not finished your homework still?"

I came to the door of my room. "I'm still studying, Mother, I have a geometry test tomorrow."

"You can't bring the book and study out here? Look your sister working on the couch."

A request for privacy was treated like an outright act of insolence for which the punishment was swift and painful. In my junior year, I was grateful for the advent of television into our house. It gave me an excuse to retreat into my room and close my door for an acceptable reason.

When I finally went to bed, scenes of violence and mayhem peopled my nightmares like black and white pepper. Frequently I woke to find my pillowcase red and stiffened by gushing nosebleeds during the night, or damp and saturated with the acrid smell of tears and the sweat of terror.

I unzipped my pillow-covering and washed it by hand surreptitiously every weekend when I changed my bedlinen. I hung it on the back of the radiator in my room to dry. That pillow-covering became a heavy, unbleached muslin record of all the nightly blitzes of my emotional war. Secretly, I rather enjoyed the rank and pungent smells of my pillowcase, even the yeasty yellow stains that were left after my blood was washed away. Unsightly as they were, the stains, like the smells, were evidence of something living, and I so often felt that I had died and wakened up in a hell called home.

I memorized Edna St. Vincent Millay's poem "Renascence," all eight pages. I said it to myself often. The words were so

beautiful they made me happy to hear, but it was the sadness
and the pain and the renewal that gave me hope.

> For east and west will pinch the heart
> that cannot keep them pushed apart
> and he whose soul is flat, the sky
> will cave in on him, by and by.

My mother responded to these changes in me as if I were a foreign hostile.

I tried confiding in a guidance counselor at school. She was
also the head of the english department, who kept telling me
that I could do much better work if I tried, and that I could
really be a credit to my people.

"Are you having trouble at home, dear?"

How did she know? Maybe she could help, after all. I poured
my heart out to her. I told her all my unhappiness. I told her
about my mother's strictness and meanness and unfairness at
home, and how she didn't love me because I was bad and I was
fat, not neat and well-behaved like my two older sisters. I told
Mrs. Flouton I wanted to leave home when I was eighteen, or go
away to school, but my mother didn't want me to.

The sounds of traffic outside the window on Lexington Avenue grew louder. It was 3:30. Mrs. Flouton looked at her watch.

"We'll have to stop now, dear. Why don't you ask your mother to drop in to see me tomorrow? I'm sure we can fix this little
problem."

I didn't know which problem she meant, but her condescend-
ing smile was sweet, and it felt good for once to have a grown-
up on my side.

Next day, my mother left the office early and came to Hunter.
The night before I had told her Mrs. Flouton wanted to see her.
She fixed me with a piercing look from out of the corner
of her tired eyes.

"Don't tell me you making trouble again in this school, too?"

"No, Mother, it's just about going to college." Somebody on
my side. I sat outside the guidance room door while my mother
was inside talking to Mrs. Flouton.

The door opened. My mother sailed out of the office and
headed for the school exit without so much as a look at me.
Oh boy. Was I going to be allowed to go away to school if I
could get a scholarship?

I caught up with my mother at the door leading to the street.

"What did Mrs. Flouton say, Mother? Can I go away to college?"

Just before the street, my mother finally turned to me, and I saw with a shock that her eyes were red. She had been crying. There was no fury in her voice, only heavy, awful pain. All she said to me before she turned away was, "How could you say those things about your mother to that white woman?"

Mrs. Flouton had repeated all of my words to my mother, with a ghoulish satisfaction of detail. Whether it was because she saw my mother as an uppity Black woman refusing her help, or both of us as a sociological experiment not involving human feeling, confidentiality, or common sense, I will never know. This was the same guidance counselor who gave me an aptitude test a year later and told me I should consider becoming a dental technician because I had scored very high on science and manual dexterity.

At home, it all seemed very simple and very sad to me. If my parents loved me I wouldn't annoy them so much. Since they didn't love me they deserved to be annoyed as much as possible within the bounds of my own self-preservation. Sometimes when my mother was not screaming at me, I caught her observing me with frightened and painful eyes. But my heart ached and ached for something I could not name.

13

In my first year at Hunter, there were three other Black girls in my term, although not in my class. One of them was very proper, and she avoided all The Branded with great care. The other two girls came from the same school in Queens and they hung together in self-protection.

In the middle of my freshman year, two more Black girls came to Hunter. One was sister to Yvonne Grenidge, who had dated my cousin Gerry. This brought my totally separate worlds of school and home threateningly close together. I was accustomed to thinking of them as separate planets.

The other girl was Gennie.

Gennie was the beginning of a double life for me at Hunter; actually, it was a triple life. There was The Branded, with whom I held seances and raised the ghosts of Byron and Keats. There was Maxine, my shy piano-playing Jewish friend with whom I roamed the locker rooms after curfew, and who later had a nervous breakdown because she was afraid she was dying of leprosy. And there was Gennie.

Each part of my school life was separate from the other, with no connection except through me. None of the other people involved would have anything at all to do with each other. Maxine thought The Branded were too dangerous, and Gennie too flamboyant. The Branded thought Maxine was a mama's baby, and Gennie, a snob. Gennie thought they were all bores, and said so loudly at any provocation.

"You surely do hang around with some funny people. They act like they think the stars are their garters." I laughed as she stuffed her toeshoes with lambswool and tied them around her ankles. Gennie was always either coming from or going to dance class.

I shared classes and lunchtime with The Branded, some lunches and after-school time with Maxine, and study periods, and every other chance I could get, with Gennie. She was the only one I saw on weekends.

Suddenly life became an exciting game of how much time I could spend with the people I wanted to spend it with. We learned to appreciate each other's softness behind the lockers, calling it all different kinds of names and games—from touch tag, to how-does-that-feel, to I-can-hit-harder-than-you. Until Gennie said to me one day, "Is that the only way you know how to make friends?" and right then and there I began to learn other ways.

I learned how to feel first and ask questions afterward. I learned how to cherish first the facade and then the fact of being an outlaw.

That spring term, Gennie and I did things that I thought made The Branded look like kindergarten kids. We smoked in the bathrooms and on the street. We played hookey from school and forged notes for each other in our mothers' handwriting. We hid out at Gennie's house and toasted marshmallows in her mother's bed. We stole nickels from our mothers' purses and roamed Fifth Avenue singing union songs. We played sexy games with the Latino boys up in the bluffs of granite above Morningside Park. And, we did a lot of talking. The Berlin Airlift was just beginning, and the state of Israel represented a newly born hope for human dignity. Our budding political consciousness had already soured us on Coca-Cola democracy.

Gennie had been trained in classical ballet. I never saw her dance except privately, for me. In the beginning of our junior year she left Hunter so she could have more time to dance, she said. Actually it was because she hated to do schoolwork. Our friendship, then, became less connected with school.

Gennie was the first person in my life that I was ever conscious of loving.

She was my first true friend.

The summer of 1948 was a time of powerful change all over the world. Gennie and I felt ourselves a part of it, as did most of the girls at Hunter High. We envied the girls who were Jewish, and who already were making plans to go to Israel and work on a kibbutz in the new nation. The mild-mannered skinny little man in the white sheet had prevailed, and India was finally free, but they had killed him for it. There was no longer any doubt in anybody's mind that China would soon be Red China, and three cheers for the communists. My revolutionary fervor that had begun with a white waitress refusing to serve my family ice cream in the nation's capital was becoming a clearer and clearer position, a lens through which to view the world.

We had huddled under schooldesks for air-raid drills, and had shaken with terror at the idea of a whole city instantly destroyed by a bomb of atoms. We had danced in the streets and listened to the horns of the fire engines and tugboats in the river the day the War was over. For us in 1948, Peace was a very real and vivid issue. Thousands of american boys had died to make the world safe for democracy, even though my family and I couldn't be served ice cream in Washington, D. C. But we were going to change all that, Gennie and I, in our full skirts and ballet slippers, the New Look.

There was a wind blowing all over the world, and we were a part of it.

Gennie lived with her mother in a one-bedroom kitchenette apartment on 119th Street between Eighth and Morningside Avenues. Gennie had the bedroom, and her mother, Louisa, slept on a wide couch in the living room.

Louisa went to work every day. I woke Gennie up whatever time I came over, cutting summer school, and we spent the next few hours deciding what she would wear, and who we were going to be for the world on that particular day. If we did not have something suitable, we stitched and pinned

an assortment of wide skirts and kerchiefs into place. Since
Gennie was slimmer than I, we often had to alter things on the
spot to fit me, but always in such a way that it could be easily
restored.

We took hours and hours attiring each other, sometimes
changing entire outfits at the last minute to become two different people, complimenting each other always. We blossomed
forth, finally, after hours of tacking and pinning and last-minute
ironing-board decisions.

That summer all of New York, including its museums and
parks and avenues, was our backyard. What we wanted and
couldn't afford, we stole money from our mothers for.

Bandits, Gypsies, Foreigners of all degree, Witches, Whores,
and Mexican Princesses—there were appropriate costumes for
every role, and appropriate places in the city to go to play them
all out. There were always things to do to match whomever we
decided to be.

When we decided to be workers, we wore loose pants and
packed our shoe-dyed lunchboxes, and tied red bandannas
around our throats. We rode up and down Fifth Avenue on the
old open double-decker omnibuses, shouting and singing union
songs at the tops of our lungs.

Solidarity foreverrrrr, the Union makes us strong!
When the unions' inspiration through the workers' blood
shall run. . .

When we decided to be hussies we wore tight skirts and high
heels that hurt, and followed handsome respectable-looking
lawyer types down Fifth and Park Avenues, making what we
thought were salacious worldly comments about their anatomies,
in loud voices.

"What a beautiful behind he has."

"I bet he sleeps bare-angle." That was a Hunter euphenism
for naked.

"He's pretending not to hear us, foolish boy."

"No, he's just too embarrassed to turn around."

When we were African we wrapped our heads in gaily printed
skirts and talked our own made-up language in the subway on
our way down to the Village. When we were Mexican, we wore
full skirts and peasant blouses and huaraches and ate tacos,
which we bought at a little stall in front of Fred Leighton's on
MacDougal Street. Once, we exchanged the word "fucker" for

"mother" in a whole day's conversation, and got put off the
Number 5 bus by an irate driver.

Sometimes we roamed through the Village in dirndl skirts
and cinch-belts, with flowers in our hair, taking turns strumming
Gennie's guitar and singing songs which we adapted from Pablo
Neruda's early poems.

> All you red yankees are sons of a shrim
> Born of a bottle, a bottle of rum.

Sometimes we made up our own:

> Drinking gin goddam drinking gin, drinking gin
>   goddam drinking gin,
> If you won't drink gin with me, goddam
> You'll drink no gin with no dam man
> Drinking gin goddam drinking gin. . .

to the most monotonous plunking beat.

In the Village, we met Gennie's friend, Jean, who was a dancer also. She was dark and beautiful and lived around the corner
from Gennie and went to the High School of Music and Art.
Jean was engaged to a white boy named Alf, who had left school
and gone to Mexico to paint with Diego Rivera. Sometimes I accompanied them to one of their dance classes at the New Dance
Group on 59th Street.

But mostly, Gennie and I went out into the city by ourselves.
By tacit agreement, we usually didn't see each other on weekends that summer because of our families. Weekends became
endlessly dull bridges between Friday and Monday. The whole
summer was made up of glorious and exciting days with Genevieve, and evenings of war at home, commencing with my
mother's, "Where have you been all day, and why aren't your
clothes done?" Or my room cleaned, or the kitchen floor washed, or the milk bought.

We sallied forth in the afternoon sun to launch our joint assault upon the city. On the days when we had no money for
carfare downtown, we went to Central Park to watch the bears.
Sometimes we just held hands and walked through the streets of
Harlem around her house. They seemed so much more alive to
me than the streets of Washington Heights where I lived. They
reminded me of the streets around where I grew up, on 142nd
Street.

We bought and ate icies which were scraped up from a block
of ice and packed into a little paper cup and then liberally covered with brilliant sticky syrups kept in a rainbow of bottles
lined up on either side of the ice. They were sold from rickety
homemade wooden wagons with bright umbrellas shielding the
ice, which was always slowly melting under an indifferently
clean old turkish towel.

These chilly cups of shaved ice were the most deliciously
cooling confection in the world, made more so by the vehemence
with which both of our mothers had forbidden them to us. Icies
were suspected by many Black mothers of spreading polio
through Harlem, and they were to be shunned, along with public swimming pools. Eventually, the icie-carts were banned from
the streets by Mayor La Guardia. Wherever we were, as the
shadows of late afternoon began to grow long, we began to
wind our way homeward. We both knew that there was only so
much we could presume before our freedom would be cut off,
and we tried to keep this side of that line. Sometimes we goofed
and overstepped some ignored rule, and then Gennie would be
decked for a few days. For me at home, punishment was always
much more swift and direct and short, and many days that summer my arms and back were sore from whatever handy weapon
my mother could lay her hands on to hit me with.

When Gennie was decked, I would go over to her house for
the day. We sat and talked and drank coffee at the kitchen table,
or lay naked on her mother's sofa bed in the living room and listened to the radio and drank Champale, which the cornerstore
man gave Gennie on credit because he thought it was for her
mother. Sometimes we visited her grandmother who lived upstairs, and she would let us play her Nat King Cole records.

> Dance Ballerina dance
> and do your pirouettes
> in rhythm with your aching heart

Gennie's mother had raised Genevieve alone from the time
she was an infant. Her father had left Louisa before Genevieve
was born. I liked Mrs. Thompson. She was young, and pretty,
and very reasonable, I thought, compared to my mother. She
had been to college and that made her somehow even more acceptable in my eyes. She and Gennie could talk to each other in
a way not possible between my mother and me. Louisa seemed
very modern. Genevieve and she shared many of the same interests, and the same clothes, and I thought how exciting it must

be to have a mother who wore and liked the same kinds of clothes you did.

That summer, Genevieve met her father, Phillip Thompson, for the first time. She fell completely under his charming net. He was a quick and bitter man of much wit and little love, who preyed upon whatever admiration he could find. (Genevieve was fifteen when she first met her father. She was two months short of sixteen when she died.)

Frequently, Gennie visited Phillip and Ella, the woman with whom he lived. She and Louisa began to fight more and more often over Gennie's seeing her father. Louisa had worked fifteen years by herself to provide Gennie with a home and food and clothes and schooling. Now suddenly Phillip appeared, handsome and irresponsible, to sweep Gennie off her feet. Louisa Thompson was not a woman to bite her tongue.

By the middle of the summer, and with Phillip's prodding, Gennie decided she wanted to go and live with him and Ella. Louisa was beside herself, and very emphatic in her "no." It was then that Gennie began telling me, and anybody else who would listen, that she was going to kill herself at the end of the summer.

I both did and didn't believe her. She wasn't pushy about it. Gennie wouldn't mention committing suicide for days and days at a time, and I would believe that she had forgotten about it, or changed her mind in the quick and decisive way she often did. Then on the bus she'd make a casual comment or reference to something we were planning to do in terms of the time element, or how much time there was left before she was going to die.

It gave me a very eerie feeling, and I didn't want to think about it. Gennie spoke about killing herself as an irreversible and already finished decision, as if there were no more questions and I had only to accept it with the finality that I accepted approaching winter. A piece of me always screamed inside no, no, no, and one day coming home from Washington Square Park I said to her, "But Gennie, what about all of us who love you?" meaning me and Jean and all her other friends whom I did not know but always imagined. Gennie gave her familiar arrogant toss of her two long black braids. She beetled her thick eyebrows over great dark eyes and said, in her most imperious manner:

"Well, I guess you will all just have to take care of yourselves, now won't you?" And it suddenly seemed like a very foolish thing to have said, and I had no answer for her.

The day Gennie picked for dying was the last day of August. It was a damp rainy Saturday, and I lay on the couch of my family's darkened living room hugging a pillow and praying to god not to let Genevieve die. I had not talked to god in a very long time, and did not really believe in it anymore. But I was willing to grasp at any straw. I felt powerless to do anything else.

I promised not to steal my Sunday church collection money, and to go back to confession after so many years.

It was the Saturday before Labor Day, and the summer was over. All summer long, Gennie had said she was going to cut her wrists when the summer was over.

And, that is exactly what she did.

Her grandmother found her, smoking a blood-stained cigarette in a bathtub full of warm and already reddened water.

We didn't see each other for two weeks, but we talked daily on the phone. Gennie said she was annoyed at herself for botching the job, but satisfied at the outcome. Louisa had agreed to let her go and live with Phil and Ella.

I was just grateful she was still alive. I started going back to Mass on Sundays for a while, and found an out-of-the-way church on the East side and went to confession.

Autumn came very quickly. Gennie and I saw less of each other since we were at different schools. I told her I missed her over the phone. Life over at Phil and Ella's was very different, I sensed, from living with Louisa, but Gennie didn't like to talk about it much. Sometimes I'd visit her there, and we sat on the daybed in Phil and Ella's room and drank Champale and ate marshmallows toasted on a pencil with a match. You have to keep blowing the flame around the candy.

But there was an uneasy feeling about that house for me, and Gennie always seemed different around there, probably because I heard Ella always listening outside the closed door from where she was sweeping or dusting. It seemed Ella was always cleaning house, with carpet slippers on and a rag around her head, humming the same little tune over and over and over and over under her breath.

We could never go over to my house because my parents didn't allow visitors when they were not home. They didn't approve of friends in general, and they did not care much for Gennie because my mother thought she was too "loud." So we usually made dates to meet at Columbus Circle or in Washington Square Park, and for a while the golden leaves near each fountain hid the harshness of the confused and alien colors that were sweeping up over our paths.

Without Gennie, Hunter was another set of worlds. Mostly, that autumn, it was Maxine and her music and her acne treatments and her desperate crush on the chairwoman of the music department. It matched my own on the latest addition to the english faculty who wore suits and flats and had a most charming malocclusion. And it was our getting into constant trouble for hanging out in the lockers after school.

We never really knew what we were being accused of doing down there. We just knew that we weren't supposed to be there, and that it was the only place where we could be totally alone, meaning without our mothers. Neither one of us ever wanted to go home to the family wars. The lockers were a private world for Maxine and me. Sometimes, when we roamed through the locker room, we crossed the private worlds of other fugitives from the warlight, whispering animatedly two by two in the aisles of lockers, as we ran by.

I played gallant swain and stepped boldly and fearlessly upon the hard swift waterbugs that seemed to ride back and forth on horseback. They were a very common sight, surrounded by frozen and screaming girls. I became the offical waterbug killer of the locker room society, and that served to make me braver. Once I even killed a sleek four-inch american cockroach. It was years before I ever admitted how terrified of them I was, also. It was too important to me to seem fearless and in charge and brave, an applauded champion killer of waterbugs.

Maybe that is all any bravery is, a stronger fear of not being brave.

Gennie and I had a fight over something or the other at the end of January. We didn't talk or see each other again for two weeks. She called me on my birthday, and we saw each other a few days later, on Washington's Birthday. We held hands in Central Park Zoo and watched the monkeys. The mandrill looked at us with great sad eyes and we agreed with him that whether we were angry or not we'd never go that long without talking again, because friendship was too important and besides, neither one of us could remember what we'd argued about.

Afterward, we went to her house. It started to snow and we lay on the couch with Gennie's head on my tummy, and we

toasted marshmallows and smoked cigarettes. That bedroom
was the only private room in the house. Gennie slept on a couch
in the living room, except when her uncle came, and then she
slept on the floor. She said she hated not having anywhere permanent to sleep, or keep her clothes.

It was the middle of March when Gennie came to my house
one night. She called and said she had to talk to me and could
she come over. My mother gave a grudging permission. I said we
had to study for a geometry midterm. It was almost nine
o'clock when Gennie came in. No hour to be visiting on a
school night, my mother observed acidly as she acknowledged
Gennie's greeting.

We went into my room and shut the door. Gennie looked
terrible. There were circles under her eyes, and long ugly
scratches on both sides of her face. Her usually neat long braids
were disheveled and mussed. All she would tell me was that she
and her father had had a fight and she didn't have any place to
sleep and she didn't want to talk about it anymore. She asked
if she could spend the night at my house. I knew that was impossible. My parents would never allow it, and they would want
to know why. I was torn, but I knew I had pushed them as far
as I could with the visit.

"Can't you go stay with Louisa?" I said. What father would
scratch up his daughter like that? "Don't go back there, please
Gennie."

Gennie looked at me as if I couldn't understand anything,
but her voice wasn't as impatient as usual. She looked tired. "I
can't go back there, she doesn't have room for me anymore.
She's fixed over the bedroom and everything, and besides she
said I had to choose and I did. She said if I went to Phillip's I
couldn't come back. And now Ella's gone down south to see her
mother, and my father and Uncle Leddie are drinking all the
time. And when Phillip drinks he doesn't know what. . . ."

It looked like Gennie was going to cry and suddenly I was
terribly scared. I heard my mother in the living room, warning,
in a raised voice:

"It's nine-thirty P.M. in the night, are you children finished?
You sure it's study you studying this time of night?"

"Gennie, why don't you at least call your mother?" I was
pleading with her. She would have to go soon. In another minute my mother was going to come in, storming nicely.

Gennie stood up with a sudden dash of her old spirit. "I said no already, didn't I? I can't talk to my mother about Phil. He's crazy sometimes." She fingered the scratches on her face. "All right, I'm going. Look, I'll meet you at Hunter after your exams on Friday, okay? What time are you done?" She was pulling on her coat.

"Twelve o'clock. What are you going to do, Gennie?" I was worried by the way she looked. I was also relieved that she was going. I could already anticipate the scene between my mother and me as soon as Gennie left.

"Never mind about me. I'm going over to Jean's house. Good luck with your midterms. I'll see you on Friday near the 68th Street entrance at noon." I walked her to the front door, and we ran the gauntlet of the living room together.

"How'd'do, Genevieve," my father said, sternly, and returned his eyes to his newspaper. He did not get involved in these matters unless I gave my mother a hard time.

"Good night, dear," my mother said, sweetly. "Your father doesn't mind you traveling by yourself so late at night?"

"No, ma'am. I'm just taking a bus straight to my mother's house," Gennie lied, smoothly, giving my mother one of her most radiant smiles.

"Well, it's very late." My mother gave the slightest of her reproachful hums. "You get home safely, now, and say good-night to your mother for me." I saw my mother shrewdly eyeing Gennie's scratched face, and I hurried her into the hallway.

"Bye, Gennie. Please be careful."

"Don't be silly, I don't need to be careful, I just need some sleep." I locked the door behind her.

When I came back into the living room, I was surprised to find that my mother was more worried than angry.

"What's wrong with your friend, now?" My mother peered at me closely from on top of her spectacles.

"Nothing's wrong, Mother. I needed some of her geometry notes."

"You have all day long to get work in school. You come home here and all of a sudden you need geometry notes this time of night? Huh!" My mother was not convinced. "Come give me your bed linen if you want it to go to the wash tomorrow." She got up, laying her sewing aside, and followed me across to my room.

My mother's intuitions had fastened upon something; she did not examine what. She could not question her perceptions;

I could not utilize the concern in her voice. How dare she follow me into my room like a peremptory reminder that no place in this house was sacrosanct from her!

My mother smelled trouble, but her concern was misplaced; it was not I who was in danger.

She poked at my soiled clothes for a moment, abstractedly, snatching up a torn slip on one finger. "You don't have anything better to put on besides this piece of rags-knit you call slip? You going to be walking the streets pretty soon one-hand-before one-hand-behind?" She tossed the garment aside as I gathered up the rest of my laundry.

"Listen, my darling child, let me tell you something for your own good. Don't get mix-up with this girl and her parents' business, you hear? What kind of jackabat woman. . . and to let her go off with that good-for-nothing call himself father. . ." My mother had met Phil Thompson once on 125th Street when we were shopping for school clothes. Gennie had introduced him proudly, and he had been his most superficial and debonair self.

She took the laundry out of my hands. "Well, anyway. Look. I don't want you hanging around till all hours of the night with that girl. Whatever she doing she buying trouble to feed it. You mark my words. I wouldn't be a bit surprise if she bring a stomach. . ." I could feel rage like a thin curtain rising over my vision.

"Mother, there's nothing wrong with Genevieve and she's not like that." I tried to keep the outrage out of my voice. But how could she say something like that about Gennie? And she didn't even know her. Just because we were friends.

"Don't let me hear that tone of voice to your mother, young woman," my father warned ominously from the living room.

Real or fancied insolence to my mother was the cardinal sin, and it always brought my father out of his pose of neutral observer to the war between my mother and me. My father was about to become involved, and that was the last thing I needed.

One of my sisters was typing a report. The staccato sound from the room which they shared came through the french doors which separated it from the living room. I wondered if Gennie had gotten down to Jean's yet. If I got into a fight with them now I might have to come straight home after all my exams this week. I swallowed my fury and it lay like a rotten egg halfway between my stomach and my throat. I could taste the sour in my mouth.

"I didn't mean to use any tone, Daddy. I'm sorry, Mother."
I stepped back out into the living room. "Goodnight."

I kissed each one of them dutifully and retreated back into
the relative safety of my room.

> We did not weep for the thing that was once a child
> did not weep for the thing that had been a child
> did not weep for the thing that had been
> nor for the deep dark silences
> that ate of the so-young flesh.
> But we wept at the sight of two men standing alone
> flat on the sky, alone,
> shoveling earth as a blanket
> to keep the young blood down.
> For we saw ourselves in the dark warm mother-blanket
> saw ourselves deep in the earth's breast-swelling—
> no longer young—
> and knew ourselves for the first time
> dead and alone.
> We did not weep for the thing—weep for the thing—
> we did not weep for the thing that was
> once a child.

May 22, 1949

14 *Things I never did with Genevieve: Let our bodies touch and tell the passions that we felt. Go to a Village gay bar, or any bar anywhere. Smoke reefer. Derail the freight that took circus animals to Florida. Take a course in international obscenities. Learn Swahili. See Martha Graham's dance troupe. Visit Pearl Primus. Ask her to take us away with her to Africa next time. Write THE BOOK. Make love.*

Louisa's voice on the phone at 3:30 P.M., tight and unbelieving.

"They found Gennie on the steps of the 110th Street Community Center this morning. She's taken rat poison. Arsenic. They don't expect her to live."

That wasn't true. Gennie was going to live. She'd fool all of us again. *Gennie, Gennie, please don't die, I love you.* Something will save her. Something. Maybe she's run away, maybe she's just run away again. Not to her relatives in Richmond this time. Oh no. Gennie'll think of someplace nobody'll think of looking, and then eventually she'll come sauntering in with a new outfit she got someone to buy her and that quick toss of her head, saying, "I was fine all the time."

"Where is she, Mrs. Thompson?"

"She's at Sydenham. Evidently she rode the subways all night, that's what she told the police, but nobody knows where she'd been before. She didn't go to school yesterday."

Cutting through Louisa's voice is the sound of the jukebox in Mike's Food Shoppe. Yesterday, after school, hearing Gennie's favorite song these days—the richly elongated tones of Sarah Vaughan's chocolate voice repeating over and over,

> I saw the harbor lights they only told me we were parting
> The same old harbor lights that once brought you to me
> I saw the harbor lights, how could I help the tears were starting,
> > were starting,
> > > were starting. . .

Mike came over and kicked the box. "Albanian magic," he grinned, and went back to his griddle. The hateful taste of black coffee and lemon in my mouth. *Gennie Gennie Gennie Gennie.*

"Can I see her, Mrs. Thompson? When are visiting hours?" Could I go see Gennie and still get back before my mother got home?

"You can come anytime, honey, but you better hurry."

Rifling my mother's old pocketbooks for ten cents carfare. My empty stomach churning. Louisa's tears as she greets me at the door of the emergency room, as she takes my hands.

"They're working on her again, honey. They won't even admit her up in the ward. They say she won't last 'til night."

The hospital bed in the glass cubicle behind the emergency room in Harlem Hospital. Her mother and grandmother and I clutching each other for comfort. Louisa smelling of Evening in Paris that always made me sneeze. My head an endless kaleidoscope of numb images, jumbled, repeated.

Speech class, the only class we ever had together.

> Jenny come tie my, Jenny come tie my, Jenny come
> tie my bonny cravat.

> I've tied it behind and I've tied it before
> and I've tied it so often, I'll tie it no more.

Miss Mason's monotonous voice drilling us through the exercise over and over. "Nice wide i's, now. Again, class." Gennie's grandmother, her insistent southern voice looking for meaning.

"She didn't talk about it this time. Nobody knew. If only she'd said something. I'da believed her this time. . ." The young white doctor, "You can go in now, but she's asleep."

Gennie Gennie Gennie I never saw you asleep before. You look just like you awake except your eyes are closed. Your brows still bend down in the middle like you frowning. What time is my mother coming home? Suppose I get on the same bus as she does coming uptown from the office? What shall I tell them when I get home?

My mother was home when I got in. An unwillingness to share any piece of my private world, even the pain, made me lie. I said Gennie was in the hospital because she had swallowed poison, by accident. Iodine, from the medicine chest.

"But what kind of house is that for a young girl to grow up in? How could she make such a mistake, poor thing? Wasn't her stepmother home?"

"I don't know, Mother. That's all her father told me." Under my mother's curious gaze I kept my face carefully blank.

Early early the next morning. Using my church collection for carfare. The hospital odor and the muted sound of the p.a. Nobody around, nobody to stop me. The hospital bed in the glass cubicle. *You can't just die like this, Gennie, we haven't had our summer yet. Don't you remember? You promised.* She can't die. Too much poison, they say. She stuffed rat poison into the gelatin capsules, ate them, one by one. We had bought two dozen capsules on Friday.

A crumpled flower on the hospital bed. Arsenic is a corrosive. She lingered, metallic-smelling foam at the corners of her mouth, blackened and wet. Her Gennie braids askew, unraveling. The last five inches of them revealed as a hairpiece. How could it be that I never knew? Gennie had plaited false hair into her braids. She was so proud of her long hair. Sometimes she wound them around her head like a crown. Now they were unraveling on the hospital pillow as she tossed her head from side to side, her eyes closed in the emptiness and quiet of the early Sunday morning hospital light. I took her hand.

"I'm supposed to be at church, Gennie, but I had to come see you." She smiled, her eyes still closed. She turned her head towards me. Her breath was foul and shallow.

"Don't die, Gennie. Do you still want to?"

"Of course, I do. Didn't I tell you I was going to?"

I bent close to her and touched her forehead. "Oh why, Gennie, why?" I whispered.

Her great black eyes flashed open. Her head moved on the pillow in a parody of her old arrogance. Her brows came down in the center. "Why what?" she snapped. "Now don't be silly. You know why."

But I did not know why. I scanned her face turned toward me, eyes closed again. The wrinkle-frown still between the thick brows. I did not know why. Only that for my beloved Gennie, pain had become enough of a reason not to stay. And our friendship had not been able to alter that. I remembered Gennie's favorite lines in one of my poems. I had found them doodled and scrawled along the margins of page after page of the notebooks which she had entrusted to my care in the movies that Friday afternoon.

> and in the brief moment that is today
> wild hope this dreamer jars
> for I have heard in whispers talk
> of life on other stars.

None of us had given her a good enough reason to stay here, not even me. I could not escape that. Was that the anger behind her great closed eyes? The skin of Gennie's cheek was hot and rough under my fingers.

Why what? You know why. Those were the last words Gennie ever said to me.

Don't go, Gennie, don't go. *I mustn't let her go. Two dozen empty capsules. Sitting through the movie twice. Standing on the corner waiting for the 14th Street bus. I should never have left her. But it was getting dark already. Scared of another whipping for getting home too late. Come home with me, Gennie. Not caring any more what my mother would say to that. Gennie, angry with me. Telling me to go away. I went.* Don't go, Gennie, don't go.

By Monday afternoon Genevieve was dead.

I called the hospital from Hunter. I walked out of the building and went home, leaving my books behind, wanting to be alone. My mother opened the door. She put one arm around me as I walked into the kitchen.

"Genevieve's dead, Mother." I sat down heavily at the table.

"Yes, I know. I called her father to see if there was anything we could do, and he told me." She was looking into my face.

"Why didn't you tell us it was suicide?"

I wanted to cry—even that little piece was gone.

"It's her father himself said so. Do you know anything about it? You can tell me, I'm your mother, after all. We won't say anything more about your lying this time. Did she talk to you about it?"

I put my head down on the table. From there I could see out the kitchen window, slightly open. The woman across the air shaft was fixing food.

"No."

"I'll fix you some tea. You mustn't be upset too much by all this, dear heart." My mother turned, rubbing the edge of the tea strainer dry, over and over again. "Look, my darling child, I know she was your friend and you feel bad, but this is what I been cautioning you about. Be careful who you go around with. Among-you children do things different in this place and you think we stupid. But this old head of mine, I know what I know. There was something totally wrong there from the start, you mark my words. That man call himself father was using that girl for I don't know what."

The merciless quality of my mother's fumbling insights turned her attempt at comfort into another assault. As if her harshness could confer invulnerability upon me. As if in the flames of truth as she saw it, I could eventually be forged into some pain-resistant replica of herself.

But all this was so beside the point. Across the darkening air shaft Mrs. Washer pulled down her window-shade. *Gennie was dead. Dead dead dead, a nickel a rabbit's head.*

When my father came home, he knew, too. "Next time, don't lie to us. Was your girlfriend in trouble?"

Days later, I sat on the low bench beside Louisa's window, newly opened after its end-of-winter untaping. It was an early spring afternoon. The season had begun unusually warm. The street outside was runny with old rain, the still slick pavement reflecting oily rainbows.

Louisa perched upon her window ledge. One high hip nudged against the wooden window frame, her stockinged leg moving back and forth ever so slightly. The other drooped down over the edge of the bench where I was sitting.

"You and Gene were such good friends." Louisa's tones were clipped and longing. "Matter of fact, she saw you more than. . ." she fingered the spirals of Gennie's notebook which I had just given her, keeping the diary for myself. Louisa's eyes were dry and desperately conversational. I suddenly remembered Gennie saying her mother had once been a schoolteacher down south and prided herself on proper speech. ". . . than she saw anybody else." Louisa finished abruptly. I savored this piece of information in silence. *Gennie's best friend.* "You looked enough alike to be sisters, people said." *Except Gennie was lighter and thinner and beautiful.*

Something about Louisa's eyes warned me and I stood up quickly. "I gotta go, Miz Thompson, my mother. . ." I reached for my coat on the couch. It had once been Louisa's daybed, the one where Gennie and I lay laughing and talking and smoking. When Gennie left, Louisa had redone the tiny apartment and taken over the bedroom. I suddenly saw again Gennie's scratched face and tired eyes as she snapped at me that night, "I can't go back, there's no room for me anymore. . . I can't talk to my mother about Phillip. . ."

I buttoned my coat hurriedly. "She's waiting for me to go marketing, because my sisters have a rehearsal at school." But swift-moving Louisa caught me, one hand on my arm, before I could open the door.

Louisa took off her rimless glasses and she did not look like anybody's mother at all. She looked too young, and too pretty, and too tired, and her red-rimmed eyes were full of tears and pleading. She was thirty-four years old and tomorrow we were going to bury her only child, a sixteen-year old suicide.

"You-all were best friends," insistent, less proper, her fingers tight through my coat sleeve. "Do *you* know why she did it?"

Louisa had a mole on her face beside her nose, almost exactly the same place as Gennie's had been. It was magnified by the tears rolling down her cheeks. I looked away, my hand still on the doorknob.

"No, ma'am." I looked up, again. I remembered my mother's words, resisting them, "That man call himself father was using that girl for I don't know what."

"I have to go now."

I opened the door, stepped over the floor-anchored metal rod upon which I had tripped so many times before, and closed the door behind me. I heard the metallic clang of the police lock rod as it slid back into place, mingled with the muffled sounds of Louisa's sobbing.

Gennie was buried in Woodlawn Cemetery on the first day of April. The *Amsterdam News* story about her death announced that she was not pregnant and so no reason for her suicide could be established. Nothing else.

The sound of dirt clods flying hollow against the white coffin. The sound of birds who knew death as no reason for silence. A black-clad man mouthing words in a foreign tongue. No hallowed ground for suicides. The sound of weeping women. The wind. The forward edge of spring. The sound of grass growing, flowers beginning to blossom, the branching of a far-off tree. Clods against the white coffin.

We drove away from the grave, down a winding hill. The last thing I saw of that place was two large gravemen with unshaven faces pulling the lowering straps from the grave. They tossed the still living flowers into a waiting bin, and shoveled earth into the grave. Two grave-hands, putting the finishing touches on a raw mound of earth, outlined against the suddenly grey and lowering April sky.

15

Two weeks after I graduated from high school, I moved out of my parents' home. I hadn't planned it that way; that's just the way it worked out. I went to stay with a friend of Jean's who had her own apartment on the Lower East Side, on Rivington Street.

I worked at Beth David hospital nights as a nurses' aide, and had an affair with a boy named Peter.

I met Peter at a Labor Youth League party in February and we made a date. He arrived to take me to the movies the next afternoon. It was Washington's Birthday, and both of my parents were home. My father answered the door, and would not let Peter into the house because he was white. That immediately catapulted what would have been a passing teenage fancy into a revolutionary cause célèbre.

The precipitating factors in my leaving home were some disparaging remarks my father made about Gennie, now dead almost two years, and a fight with my sister Helen. My mother threatened to call the police and I left. I went to work, returned home after my family was asleep, and packed. What I couldn't carry I dumped into a sheet and dragged down the street and left at the foot of the steps of the police station. I took my clothes, some books, and Gennie's guitar and went to Iris's house. The next day I hailed a man on the street with a pick-up truck and paid him five dollars to come uptown with me and get my bookcase out of my family's house. Nobody was home. I left a cryptic note on the kitchen table which read, "I am moving out. Since the causes are obvious, the results are well-known." I think I meant it the other way around, but I was very excited and very scared.

I was seventeen years old.

When I moved out of my mother's house, shaky and determined, I began to fashion some different relationship to this country of our sojourn. I began to seek some more fruitful return than simple bitterness from this place of my mother's exile, whose streets I came to learn better than my mother had ever learned them. But thanks to what she did know and could teach me, I survived in them better than I could have imagined. I made an adolescent's wild and powerful commitment to battling in my own full eye, closer to my own strength, which was after all not so very different from my mother's. And there I found other women who sustained me and from whom I learned other loving. How to cook the foods I had never tasted in my mother's house. How to drive a stick-shift car. How to loosen up and not be lost.

Their shapes join Linda and Gran'Ma Liz and Gran'Aunt Anni in my dreaming, where they dance with swords in their hands, stately forceful steps, to mark the time when they were all warriors.

In libation, I wet the ground to my old heads.

I spent the summer feeling free and in love, I thought. I was also hurting. No one had even tried to find me. I had forgotten at whose knee I learned my pride. Peter and I saw each other a lot, and slept together, since it was expected.

Sex seemed pretty dismal and frightening and a little demeaning, but Peter said I'd get used to it, and Iris said I'd get used to it, and Jean said I'd get used to it, and I used to wonder why it wasn't possible to just love each other and be warm and close and let the grunting go.

In September I moved to my own place out in Brighton Beach. The Branded and I had found the room at the beginning of the summer, but it was occupied. The landlady said it could be rented all winter for twenty-five dollars a month. Since I was only making a hundred dollars plus one meal a day at the hospital, I couldn't afford any more.

My landlady's name was Gussie Faber. Her brother offered to help me move my stuff from Iris's house. When it was all moved in and Mrs. Faber had gone upstairs, her brother closed the door to my room and said I was a nice girl and I wouldn't have to pay him for moving me if I'd just be quiet and stand still for a minute.

I thought it was all pretty stupid, and he got cum all over the back of my dungarees.

It was a single large room with the use of a community bath and a kitchen down the hall. I shared both of them with a permanent tenant, an old woman whose children paid rent for her not to live with them. At night she would talk to herself aloud, crying because her children were making her live with a schwartze. I could hear her through the common wall adjoining our very common kitchen. By day, she sat at the kitchen table and drank my soda while I was away at work and school.

When college started, Peter and I broke up. I hadn't known really why it had begun, and I didn't know why it ended. One day Peter just said we should probably stop seeing each other for a while, and I agreed, thinking that must be the thing to do.

The rest of the autumn was an agony of loneliness, long subway rides, and not enough sleep. I worked forty-four hours a week at the hospital and went to school for fifteen more. I traveled three hours a day to and from Brighton Beach. That left half-day Saturday and all day Sunday to cry over Peter's silence and to wonder if my mother was missing me. I couldn't study.

Near the end of November I simply stayed in bed for three days, and when I got up I found I had lost my job at the hospital.

Being out of work brought a lot of new and starkly instructive experiences. It meant pawning my typewriter, which gave me nightmares, and selling my blood, which gave me chills.

Coming out of the bloodbank on the Bowery and Houston Street, clutching my five dollars, I had an image of myself ad-

justing the transfusion tube over a patient while I worked at
Beth David. Into whose veins would my blood soon be flowing? And what would that person then become to me? What
kind of relationship was established by the selling of blood,
one to another?

Most of all, being out of work meant drinking hot water,
free in the college cafeteria, and the grinding annihilation of
employment agencies and the personnel clerks who grinned at
my presumption in applying for jobs as a medical receptionist,
and part-time at that. (I had ten dollars a week from a scholarship, most of which went towards my rent.)

Just before Christmas, I got a job through college, working
afternoons for a doctor. That provided me with money to get
my typewriter out of hock, and a little more time to be depressed. I took long walks along the winter beach. Coney Island
was a mile away, and now that the concessions were closed, the
boardwalk was a lovely quiet that matched my need. I could
not go to the movies, even though I loved the pictures, because
all around were people in couples and groups, and they under-
lined my solitary state until I felt my heart would break if I
were any more alone.

One night I couldn't sleep, I walked down to the beach. The
moon was full, and the tide was coming in. On the crest of every little wave, instead of whitecaps, was a fluorescent crown.
The joining line of sea and sky was veiled; angles of green flame
rode the night, line upon line, until the whole darkness was
alight with brilliant scallops of phosphorescence, moving rhyth-
mically in toward shore upon the waves.

Nothing I did could stop them, nor bring them back again.

That was the first Christmas I ever spent alone. I stayed in
bed all day long. I could hear the old lady next door vomiting
into her basin. I had put *nux vomica* into a bottle of my cream
soda.

That night, Peter called, and I saw him again during the next
week. We made arrangements to go away for the New Year's
Eve weekend to a furriers union camp. I was to meet him at the
Port Authority bus station after I finished work. I was excited;
I had never been to the camp before.

I brought my boots and my jeans and my knapsack to work
with me, together with a sleeping bag I had borrowed from Iris.
I changed in Dr. Sutter's back office, and arrived at the bus sta-

tion at 7:30. Peter was due at 8:00 and our bus left at 8:45. He never showed up.

By 9:30 I realized he wasn't going to show up. The bus station was warm and I just sat there for another hour or so, too stunned and tired to move. At last, I gathered up my belongings and started to trudge across town to the BMT subway. The holiday crowd was already beginning to form, and the festivities and horn-blowing to welcome in the New Year were already beginning. I walked through Times Square in my jeans and my jackboots and my lumber jacket, carrying my knapsack and sleeping bag, and the tears rolled down my face as I made my way through the crowds and the slush. I could not quite believe this was all happening to me.

He called me a few days later with an explanation and I hung up on him immediately, in self-protection. I wanted to pretend he had never existed and that I had never been someone who could be treated so. I would never let anyone treat me like that again.

Two weeks later I discovered I was pregnant.

I tried to recall half-remembered information garnered from other people's friends who had been "in trouble." The doctor in Pennsylvania who did good clean abortions very cheaply because his daughter had died on a kitchen table after he had refused to abort her. But sometimes the police grew suspicious, so he wasn't always working. A call through the grapevine found out that he wasn't.

Trapped. Something—anything—had to be done. No one else can take care of this. What am I going to do?

The doctor who gave me the results of my positive rabbit test was a friend of Jean's aunt, who had said he might "help." This help meant offering to get me into a home for unwed mothers out of the city run by a friend of his. "Anything else," he said, piously, "is illegal."

I was terrified by the stories I had heard in school and from my friends about the butchers and the abortion mills of the *Daily News*. Cheap kitchen table abortions. Jean's friend Francie had died on the way to the hospital just last year after trying to do it with the handle of a number 1 paintbrush.

These horrors were not just stories, nor infrequent. I had seen too many of the results of botched abortions on the bloody gurneys lining the hallways outside the emergency room.

Besides, I had no real contacts.

Through winter-dim streets, I walked to the subway from the doctor's office, knowing I could not have a baby and knowing it with a certainty that galvanized me far beyond anything I knew to do.

The girl in the Labor Youth League who had introduced me to Peter had had an abortion, but it had cost three hundred dollars. The guy had paid for it. I did not have three hundred dollars, and I had no way of getting three hundred dollars, and I swore her to secrecy telling her the baby wasn't Peter's. Whatever was going to be done I had to do. And fast.

Castor oil and a dozen bromo quinine pills didn't help.

Mustard baths gave me a rash, but didn't help either.

Neither did jumping off a table in an empty classroom at Hunter, and I almost broke my glasses.

Ann was a licensed practical nurse I knew from working the evening shift at Beth David Hospital. We used to flirt in the nurses' pantry after midnight when the head nurse was sneaking a doze in some vacant private room on the floor. Ann's husband was a soldier in Korea. She was thirty-one years old—and *knew her way around*, in her own words—beautiful and friendly, small, sturdy, and deeply Black. One night, while we were warming the alcohol and talcum for p.m. care backrubs, she pulled out her right breast to show me the dark mole which grew at the very line where her deep-purple aureola met the lighter chocolate brown of her skin, and which, she told me with a mellow laugh, "drove all the doctors crazy."

Ann had introduced me to amphetamine samples on those long sleepy night shifts, and we crashed afterward at her bright kitchenette apartment on Cathedral Parkway, drinking black coffee and gossiping until dawn about the strange habits of head nurses, among other things.

I called Ann at the hospital and met her after work one night. I told her I was pregnant.

"I thought you was gay!"

I heard the disappointed half-question in Ann's voice, and remembered suddenly our little scene in the nurses' pantry. But my experience with people who tried to label me was that they usually did it to either dismiss me or use me. I hadn't even acknowledged my own sexuality yet, much less made any choices about it. I let the remark lay where Jesus flang it.

I asked Ann to get me some ergotrate from the pharmacy, a drug which I had heard from nurses' talk could be used to encourage bleeding.

"Are you crazy?" she said in horror. "You can't mess around with that stuff, girl; it could kill you. It causes hemorrhaging. Let me see what I can find out for you."

Everybody knows somebody, Ann said. For her, it was the mother of another nurse in surgery. Very safe and clean, foolproof and cheap, she said. An induced miscarriage by Foley catheter. A homemade abortion. The narrow hard-rubber tube, used in post-operative cases to keep various body canals open, softened when sterilized. When passed through the cervix into the uterus while soft, it coiled, all fifteen inches, neatly into the womb. Once hardened, its angular turns ruptured the bloody lining and began the uterine contractions that eventually expelled the implanted fetus, along with the membrane. If it wasn't expelled too soon. If it did not also puncture the uterus.

The process took about fifteen hours and cost forty dollars, which was a week and a half's pay.

I walked over to Mrs. Muñoz' apartment after I had finished work at Dr. Sutter's office that afternoon. The January thaw was past, and even though it was only 1:00 P.M., the sun had no warmth. The winter grey of mid-February and the darker patches of dirty Upper-East-Side snow. Against my peacoat in the wind I carried a bag containing the fresh pair of rubber gloves and the new bright-red catheter Ann had taken from the hospital for me, and a sanitary pad. I had most of the contents of my last pay envelope, plus the five dollars Ann had lent me.

"Darling, take off your skirt and panties now while I boil this." Mrs. Muñoz took the catheter from the bag and poured boiling water from a kettle over it and into a shallow basin. I sat curled around myself on the edge of her broad bed, embarrassed by my half-nakedness before this stranger. She pulled on the thin rubber gloves, and setting the basin upon the table, looked over to where I was perched in the corner of the neat, shabby room.

"Lie down, lie down. You scared, huh?" She eyed me from under the clean white kerchief that completely covered her small head. I could not see her hair, and could not tell from her sharp featured, bright-eyed face how old she was, but she looked so young it surprised me that she could have a daughter old enough to be a nurse.

"You scared? Don't be scared, sweetheart," she said, picking up the basin with the edge of a towel and moving it onto the other edge of the bed.

"Now just lie back and put your legs up. Nothing to be scared of. Nothing to it—I would do it on my own daughter. Now if you was three, four months, say, it would be harder because it would take longer, see? But you not far gone. Don't worry. To-night, tomorrow, maybe, you hurt a little bit, like bad cramps. You get cramps?"

I nodded, mute, my teeth clenched against the pain. But her hands were busy between my legs as she looked intently at what she was doing.

"You take some aspirin, a little drink. Not too much though. When it's ready, the tube comes back down and the bleeding comes with it. Then, no more baby. Next time you take better care of yourself, darling."

By the time Mrs. Muñoz was finished talking she had skill-fully passed the long slender catheter through my cervix into my uterus. The pain had been acute but short. It lay coiled in-side of me like a cruel benefactor, soon to rupture the delicate lining and wash away my worries in blood.

Since to me all pain was beyond bearing, even this short bout seemed interminable.

"You see, now, that's all there is to it. That wasn't so bad, was it?" She patted my shuddering thigh reassuringly. "All over. Now get dressed. And wear the pad," she cautioned, as she pulled off the rubber gloves. "You start bleeding in a couple of hours, then you lie down. Here, you want the gloves back?"

I shook my head, and handed her the money. She thanked me. "That's a special price because you a friend of Anna's," she smiled, helping me on with my coat. "By this time tomorrow, it will be all over. If you have any trouble you call me. But no trouble, just a little cramps."

I stopped off on West 4th Street and bought a bottle of apri-cot brandy for eighty-nine cents. It was the day before my eigh-teenth birthday and I decided to celebrate my relief. Now all I had to do was hurt.

On the slow Saturday local back to my furnished room in Brighton Beach the cramps began, steadily increasing. Every-thing's going to be all right now, I kept saying to myself as I leaned over slightly on the subway seat, if I can just get through the next day. I can do it. She said it was safe. The worst is over, and if anything goes wrong I can always go to the hospital. I'll tell them I don't know her name, and I was blindfolded so I couldn't know where I was.

I wondered how bad the pain was going to get, and that terri-fied me more than anything else. I did not think about how I could die from hemorrhage, or a perforated uterus. The terror was only about the pain.

The subway car was almost empty.

Just last spring around that same time one Saturday morning, I woke up in my mother's house to the smell of bacon frying in the kitchen, and the abrupt realization as I opened my eyes that the dream I had been having of giving birth to a baby girl was in fact only a dream. I sat bolt upright in my bed, facing the little window onto the air shaft, and cried and cried and cried from disappointment until my mother came into the room to see what was wrong.

The train came up out of the tunnel over the bleak edge of south Brooklyn. The Coney Island parachute jump steeple and a huge grey gas storage tank were the only breaks in the leaden skyline.

I dared myself to feel any regrets.

That night about 8 P.M., I was lying curled tightly on my bed, trying to distract myself from the stabbing pains in my groin by deciding whether or not I wanted to dye my hair coal black.

I couldn't begin to think about the risks I was running. But another piece of me was being amazed at my own daring. I had done it. Even more than my leaving home, this action which was tearing my guts apart and from which I could die except I wasn't going to—this action was a kind of shift from safety towards self-preservation. It was a choice of pains. That's what living was all about. I clung to that and tried to feel only proud.

I had not given in. I had not been merely the eye on the ceiling until it was too late. They hadn't gotten me.

There was a tap on the alley door, and I looked out the window. My friend Blossom from school had gotten one of our old high school teachers to drive her out to see if I was "okay," and to bring me a bottle of peach brandy for my birthday. She was one of the people I had consulted, and she had wanted to have nothing to do with an abortion, saying I should have the baby. I didn't bother to tell her Black babies were not adopted. They were absorbed into families, abandoned, or "given up." But not adopted. Nonetheless I knew she was worried to have come all the way from Queens to Manhattan and then to Brighton Beach.

I was touched.

We only talked about inconsequential things. Never a word about what was going on inside of me. Now it was my secret; the only way I could handle it was alone. I sensed they were both grateful that I did.

"You sure you're going to be okay?" Bloss asked. I nodded.

Miss Burman suggested we go for a walk along the boardwalk in the crisp February darkness. There was no moon. The walk helped a little, and so did the brandy. But when we got back to my room, I couldn't concentrate on their conversation any more. I was too distracted by the rage gnawing at my belly.

"Do you want us to go?" Bloss asked with her characteristic bluntness. Miss Burman, sympathetic but austere, stood quietly in the doorway looking at my posters. I nodded at Bloss gratefully. Miss Burman lent me five dollars before she left.

The rest of the night was an agony of padding back and forth along the length of the hallway from my bedroom to the bathroom, doubled over in pain, watching clots of blood fall out of my body into the toilet and wondering if I was all right, after all. I had never seen such huge red blobs come from me before. They scared me. I was afraid I might be bleeding to death in that community bathroom in Brighton Beach in the middle of the night of my eighteenth birthday, with a crazy old lady down the hall muttering restlessly in her sleep. But I was going to be all right. Soon this was all going to be over, and I would be safe.

I watched one greyish mucous shape disappear in the bowl, wondering if that was the embryo.

By dawn, when I went to take some more aspirin, the catheter had worked its way out of my body. I was bleeding heavily, very heavily. But my experience in the OB wards told me that I was not hemorrhaging.

I washed the long stiff catheter and laid it away in a drawer, after examining it carefully. This implement of my salvation was a wicked red, but otherwise innocuous-looking.

I took an amphetamine in the thin morning sun and wondered if I should spend a quarter on some coffee and a danish. I remembered I was supposed to usher at a Hunter College concert that same afternoon, for which I was to be paid ten dollars, a large sum for an afternoon's work, and one that would enable me to repay my debts to Ann and Miss Burman.

I made myself some sweet milky coffee and took a hot bath, even though I was bleeding. After that, the pain dimmed gradually to a dull knocking gripe.

On a sudden whim, I got up and threw on some clothes and went out into the morning. I took the bus into Coney Island to an early-morning foodshop near Nathan's, and had myself a huge birthday breakfast, complete with french fries and an english muffin. I hadn't had a regular meal in a restaurant for a long time. It cost almost half of Miss Burman's five dollars, because it was kosher and expensive. And delicious.

Afterward, I returned home. I lay resting upon my bed, filled with a sense of well-being and relief from pain and terror that was almost euphoric. I really was all right.

As the morning slipped into afternoon, I realized that I was exhausted. But the thought of making ten dollars for one afternoon's work got me wearily up and back onto the weekend local train for the long trip to Hunter College.

By mid-afternoon my legs were quivering. I walked up and down the aisles dully, hardly hearing the string quartet. In the last part of the concert, I went into the ladies room to change my tampax and the pads I was wearing. In the stall, I was seized with a sudden wave of nausea that bent me double, and I promptly and with great force lost my $2.50-with-tip Coney Island breakfast, which I had never digested. Weakened and shivering, I sat on the stool, my head against the wall. A fit of renewed cramps swept through me so sharply that I moaned softly.

Miz Lewis, the Black ladies-room attendant who had known me from the bathrooms of Hunter High School, was in the back of the room in her cubby, and she had seen me come into the otherwise empty washroom.

"Is that you, Autray, moaning like that? You all right?" I saw her low-shoed feet stop outside my stall.

"Yes ma'am," I gasped through the door, cursing my luck to have walked into that particular bathroom. "It's just my period."

I steadied myself, and arranged my clothes. When I finally stepped out, bravely and with my head high, Miz Lewis was still standing outside, her arms folded.

She had always maintained a steady but impersonal interest in the lives of the few Black girls at the high school, and she was a familiar face which I was glad to see when I met her in the washroom of the college in the autumn. I told her I was going to the college now, and that I had left home. Miz Lewis had raised her eyebrows and pursed her lips, shaking her grey head. "You girls sure are somethin'!" she'd said.

In the uncompromising harshness of the fluorescent lights, Miz Lewis gazed at me intently through her proper gold spectacles, which perched upon her broad brown nose like round antennae.

"Girl, you sure you all right? Don't sound all right to me." She peered up into my face. "Sit down here a minute. You just started? You white like some other people's child."

I took her seat, gratefully. "I'm all right, Miz Lewis," I pro-
tested. "I just have bad cramps, that's all."

"Jus' cramps? That bad? Then why you come here like that
today for? You ought to be home in bed, the way your eyes
looking. You want some coffee, honey?" She offered me her
cup.

"Cause I need the money, Miz Lewis. I'll be all right; I really
will." I shook my head to the coffee, and stood up. Another
cramp slid up from my clenched thighs and rammed into the
small of my back, but I only rested my head against the edge of
the stalls. Then, taking a paper towel from the stack on the glass
shelf in front of me, I wet it and wiped the cold sweat from my
forehead. I wiped the rest of my face, and blotted my faded lipstick carefully. I grinned at my reflection in the mirror and at
Miz Lewis standing to the side behind me, her arms still folded
against her broad short-waisted bosom. She sucked her teeth
with a sharp intake of breath and sighed a long sigh.

"Chile, why don't you go on back home to your mama,
where you belong?"

I almost burst into tears. I felt like screaming, drowning out
her plaintive, kindly, old-woman's voice that kept pretending
everything was so simple.

"Don't you think she's worrying about you? Do she know
you in all this trouble?"

"I'm not in trouble, Miz Lewis. I just don't feel well because
of my period." Turning away, I crumpled up the used towel
and dropped it into the basket, and then sat down again, heavily.
My legs were shockingly weak.

"Yeah. Well." Miz Lewis sucked her teeth again, and put her
hand into her apron pocket. "Here," she said, pulling four dollars out of her purse. "You take these and get yourself a taxi
home." She knew I lived in Brooklyn. "And you go right home,
now. I'll cross your name off the list downstairs for you. And
you can pay me back when you get it."

I took the crumpled bills from her dark, work-wise hands.
"Thanks a lot, Miz Lewis," I said gratefully. I stood up again,
this time a little more steadily. "But don't you worry about
me, this won't last very long." I walked shakily to the door.

"And you put your feet up, and a cold compress on your
tummy, and you stay in bed for a few days, too," she called
after me, as I made my way to the elevators to the main floor.

I asked the cab to take me around to the alley entrance, instead of getting out on Brighton Beach Avenue. I was afraid my

legs might not take me where I wanted to go. I wondered if I had almost fainted.

Once indoors, I took three aspirin and slept for twenty-four hours.

When I awoke Monday afternoon, the bed-sheets were stained, but my bleeding had slowed to normal and the cramps were gone.

I wondered if I had gotten some bad food at the foodshop Sunday morning that had made me sick. Usually I never got upset stomachs, and prided myself on my cast-iron digestion. The following day I went back to school.

On Friday, after classes, before I went to work, I picked up my money for ushering. I sought out Miz Lewis in the auditorium washroom and paid her back her four dollars.

"Oh, thank you, Autray," she said, looking a little surprised. She folded the bills up neatly and tucked them back into the green snap-purse she kept in her uniform apron pocket. "How you feeling?"

"Fine, Miz Lewis," I said jauntily. "I told you I was going to be all right."

"You did not! You said you *was* all right and I knew you wasn't, so don't tell me none of that stuff, I don't want to hear." Miz Lewis eyed me balefully.

"You gon' back home to your mama, yet?"

16 My apartment on Spring Street was not exactly an enchanted palace, but it was my first real apartment and it was all my own. Iris's apartment on Rivington Street was a brief stopover after the trauma of declaring myself independent. The place in Brighton Beach was, after all, only a large furnished room with cooking privileges. But Spring Street was really my own, even though it was on a sublet from a friend of Jean's who was in Paris for a year. He had left a very complicated hi-fi hookup, a wooden rocking horse, and unbelievable filth encrusting everything in the kitchen. Otherwise, there wasn't much else except dirty linoleum in every room and ashes in a fireplace which was the only source of heat for the whole little three-room apartment. But the rent was only ten dollars a month.

I moved in two weeks after the abortion. Since I was physically fine and healthy, it didn't occur to me that I wasn't totally free from any aftermath of that grueling affair. But the months between that birthday weekend in February and the first stirring smells of spring in the air, as I took a train to Bennington for a weekend, are very much a blur. I was visiting Jill, one of The Branded.

I came home from school and my part-time job, to sometimes sit on the edge of my boxspring bed in the center room, still with my coat on, and would suddenly realize that it was the next morning, and I had not taken off my coat yet, much less put away the container of milk I had bought for the cat I had found to join me in my misery.

The house was the only thing I had that belonged to me, and the cat I got from the neighborhood grocery store, and two Javanese temple birds in a little cage that Martha and Judy had brought me as a housewarming gift. They were still seniors in high school, and had appeared one Sunday afternoon with the birds and a bottle of apricot brandy and four strong young willing arms. After we hung some curtains on the tall narrow windows of the front room, which faced the back windows of the tenement in front, the three of us sat on my couch before the fireplace, contemplating ripping off the cracking plaster above the fireplace to expose the beautiful old red brick of the firewall just beneath. We sat, listening to the indignant caw of the temple lovebirds, and Rachmaninoff on the record player, and drinking apricot brandy in the chill. Later that evening we built a fire in the fireplace, and I knocked over the bottle of brandy or Martha did, because she was always doing things like that and then apologizing profusely. So we all made a lark of it and fantasized about digging through the softwood boards to see if we could find clean wood for apricot-brandy-flavored toothpicks.

But that's the only day I can recall between moving in and the first of summer. Yet I went to school, and passed all my subjects that term. I also went uptown every Thursday night to meetings of the Harlem Writers Guild.

The apartment was very small, and it is shocking to think of any more than one person living there, but of course a whole family had once lived in these three tiny rooms. The building faced a narrow courtyard separating its three stories from the main tenement, which was six stories high.

In the front room was the fireplace, and the main door of the flat. The center room was even smaller, with no windows at all and just enough space for a double bed, a thin chest of drawers, and the door to the kitchen, which had a sink, stove, refrigerator, and bathtub. There was another door leading to the outside hall, but it was bolted shut. This kind of apartment was called a floor-through. There was no hot water at all in the building, which had six apartments in it, two on each floor. The toilets were in the outside halls, one to a story, every two apartments. Ralph, my next-door neighbor, and I put a padlock on ours to keep the Bowery bums from coming upstairs and using it.

I scrubbed the apartment as best as I could, not quite believing the dirt that the former owner had allowed to accumulate. I got rid of what was possible, and resolved to ignore what I couldn't erase. The kitchen was the worst, so I concentrated on making the two other rooms my own.

I moved in my bookcase and my books and records, my guitar and my portable typewriter, and it seemed like I was acquiring an awful lot of things, including a little electric space-heater.

The two big purchases were a boxspring and mattress on sale, with two plushy feather pillows. Sheets and pillow-cases I had from Brighton Beach. I also bought another woolen blanket on Orchard Street. It was a bright red and white Indian-design blanket, warm and fuzzy, and it seemed to heat up the cold, dark bedroom.

I could seldom bring myself to use the kitchen, except to boil water. It was mostly a place to store the refrigerator, in which I kept whatever little food I did not bring home already fixed. I do remember making chicken-foot stew for Jean and Alf one Saturday night. I got very thin, for me.

When summer came, The Branded descended upon Spring Street one weekend and scrubbed and scoured. After that, I cooked more often.

I tore down the plaster wall around and over the fireplace and hand-sanded the old brick until it was rich and smooth and even. I hung Gennie's guitar over the fireplace, a little to one side.

Summer came down with a vengeance into the tiny backyard tenement, and the two windows in the apartment gave no relief. I began to learn how to lay back and enjoy heat, how not to fight it, to open up my pores and let the heat in and the sweat out.

I used to sit in my underpants and a half-slip and type on a card-table in the living room, at 3:00 A.M. in the morning, with the sweat pouring down the front of me and between my breasts.

The lovebirds were now dead, and the cat had run away after he killed them. Writing was the only thing that made me feel like I was alive.

I never reread what I was writing. They were strange poems of death, destruction, and deep despair. When I went to the *Harlem Writers' Quarterly* meetings, I only read old poems from my high school days, a whole year before.

> I came from the valley
> laughing with blackness
> up between the   mouth of the mountains I rose
> weeping, cold
> hampered by the clinging souls of dead men
> shaken
> with reverberations of wasted minutes
> unborn years. . . . .
> . . . .
> I was the story of a phantom people
> I was the hope of lives never lived
> I was a thought-product of the emptiness of space
> and the space in the empty bread baskets
> I was the hand, reaching toward the sun
> the burnt crisp that sought relief. . . .
> . . . .
> And on the tree of mourning they hanged me
> the lost emotion of an angry people
> hanged me, forgetting how long I was
> in dying
> how deathlessly I stood
> forgetting how easily
> I could rise
> again.

April 20, 1952

17 When I found out that I had failed german and trig in summer school that year, it never occurred to me to think that it was because I had spent the summer wetnursing the girls of The Branded in my tiny tenement apartment.

It never occurred to me that it was because every evening when I came home from work, instead of doing the assignments for my classes the next day, I was serving us coffee and cinnamon ice cubes in powdered milk with dexedrine chasers. We were all poor and ravenous. We sat around on the tiny living-room floor with the now dead fireplace and the two tall windows open, trying to catch a breath of air as we sprawled on the mattress pulled out of the bedroom. Our only coverings were nylon half-slips pulled up over our breasts, sometimes with a sash tied around.

I told myself I had failed in summer school because I just could not learn german. Some people can, I decided, and some people can't; and I couldn't.

Besides, I was very bored and disappointed with Hunter College, which seemed to me like an extension of a catholic girls school and not at all like Hunter High School, peopled as it had been with our exciting and emotionally complicated lives. For most of the women I met in my freshman classes at Hunter College, an emotional complication meant cutting class to play bridge in the college cafeteria.

I was also beside myself with sexual frustration, given the presence of all the beautiful young women whom I was sheltering like a wounded banshee. The abortion had left me with an additional sadness about which I could not speak, certainly not to these girls who saw my house and my independence as a refuge, and seemed to think that I was settled and strong and dependable, which, of course, was exactly what I wanted them to think.

Whether or not they were sleeping with each other on my Bloom & Krup double boxspring with mattress while I was at school and work, I did not know. We joked about it often enough, but if they were, they did not tell me, and I never mentioned how enticing and frightening I found their strange blonde- and red- and chestnut-colored secrets that peeked out from beneath their pulled-up half-slips, in the hundred-degree heat of the small backyard apartment.

That summer I decided that I was definitely going to have an affair with a woman—in just those words. How I was going to accomplish that, I had no idea, or even what I meant by an affair. But I knew I meant more than cuddling under the covers and kissing in Marie's bed.

Marie, like me, had been on the fringes of The Branded in high school. She was short and round, with immense Mediter-

ranean eyes shining out of a heart-shaped face. We shared a passionate weakness for memorizing the same romantic ballads,
and for reciting Millay. Marie did not want to go to college, and
got a job after high school which gave her nominal independence, even though she still lived with her very strict Italian
family.

I went to dinner a few times at their house, the fall after I
left home. The food was plentiful and filling, served by Marie's
silently generous mother who did not approve of me at all,
mostly because I was Black, but also because I now lived alone.
No nice girl left her mother's house before she was married, unless she had become a whore, which in Mrs. Madrona's eyes was
synonymous with being Black anyway.

Sometimes I would sleep over, and get to share Marie's Castro
Convertible in the living room, because her brother had the second bedroom. We lay awake far into the night, snuggling under
the covers by the light of the votive candle on Our Lady's altar
in the corner, kissing and hugging and giggling in low tones so
her mother wouldn't hear us.

When the other members of The Branded came back from
their various ivy-league colleges in the late spring, we all had the
grand reunion/clean-up party at my apartment.

All except Marie. She had run away from home and moved
into the YWCA, and then married someone who sat down at her
table in the Waldorf Cafeteria. The same night. They drove into
Maryland and found a justice of the peace.

I opened my house to The Branded and they saw it as a second home. Since it was summer, none of us minded too much
that there was no heat or hot water in the apartment, although
not having a shower was a problem.

Sometimes my next-door neighbor and I would go to his
friend's apartment around the corner and have a hot shower.

There was a constant stream of young women in and out of
my apartment, most of them in varying periods and conditions
of distress. I particularly remember Bobbi, who lived around the
corner and had been a year behind us in high school. She was
now in her senior year, and was always being beaten by her
mother. Bobbi decided to run away to California even though
she had not yet finished school. In those days, that was an unusually bizarre and courageous thing to do, and she hid out at
my apartment until her plane left. We all thought she was very
daring, even if she was also very young and silly.

Luckily, Bobbi and her equally silly boyfriend had already left when the FBI came to my house looking for her.

This was 1952, the height of the McCarthy era, and I knew enough not to let them past my door. They stood outside, stupid and male and proper and blonde and only a little bit threatening in their buttoned-down shirts and striped ties. One had a crew cut, the other's hair was center-parted and slicked down.

All of my friends knew we were a menace to the status quo, and defined our rebellions as such. Scientists had broken the code of Linear B, enabling them to read ancient Minoan script. The day before the FBI agents stood in my doorway, Eva Perón had died in Argentina. But somehow *we* were a threat to the civilized world.

One day Marie came through my door with her new husband. I didn't like him at all, so although I was very fond of Marie I was glad to send them on their way. He had liquor on his breath and a nasty smile and some very bizarre sexual appetites that Marie whispered to me about while he was out buying more whiskey. My heart hurt to think of her with him, but she insisted he loved her. I couldn't understand how, but I took her word for it.

It was just as well, because two days later her mother showed up on my doorstep with a fresh contingent of FBI men, indistinguishable from the last. The economy was still in recession; there were few jobs around for veterans. White college students were obsessed with security and pensions, and there seemed to be a never-ending supply of slightly stupid-looking, slightly menacing, blonde, blue-eyed gumshoes available in 1952.

Marie's mother was hysterical and I knew Ralph, my friendly pacifist, slept during the day, so I let them inside the door this time. My cousin, Gerry, was asleep in the inner bedroom and his shoes and pants were in plain view on the couch. I could tell it didn't make a very good impression on either the FBI men or on Marie's momma. Young girls did not live alone unless they were whores, and here was the evidence slung across my couch. I paid no attention. It was obvious that the lump in my bed was a single one, and it didn't too much matter what Marie's mother called me.

Marie and Jim, her husband, were not in my house, and that was all the FBI legitimately could ask. I breathed a sigh of relief as I closed the door behind them. Before they left, they told me that Jim was wanted on a white-slavery charge in Texas, for transporting under-aged girls across state lines for purposes of prostitution.

I was so shaken up by this exchange that I woke Gerry up, and he persuaded me to go with him to an air-conditioned movie.

It was one of The Branded, Lori, who told me about the many jobs to be had in the factories of Stamford, Connecticut. The idea of leaving New York for a while, with its emotional complications, felt good to me, and the idea of plentiful jobs was particularly appealing. I had decided to leave college, since I couldn't learn german.

I put a combination padlock on the door of my apartment, giving the combination to The Branded, who would soon be returning to college. I packed my few clothes, some of my books and records, took my portable typewriter and moved to Stamford.

I had sixty-three dollars in my pocket.

I arrived in Stamford on the New Haven local on Thursday afternoon. I went to the Black Community Center whose address I had gotten from a previous visit the week before. From there, I got the address of someone who had a room to rent. I rented the room, which was a shockingly high eight dollars a week, stored my gear, and said goodbye to Martha, who had come up with me to help carry all my portable possessions. The next morning, I got a job at the ribbon factory where Lori had worked during the summer. I was to begin the following Monday morning.

My room was very tiny, and I shared the bathroom with two other women who also rented rooms in the private house. There were no cooking facilities, so I sneaked in a hotplate to warm up the cans of soup which became my standard evening meal.

That weekend I walked around Stamford, trying to get a feel of the place. I had never lived in a small town before, nor anywhere other than New York. The Liggett's Drugstore on Atlantic Avenue, the main thoroughfare, did not know what an egg cream was. They also called soda, pop. Walking down Atlantic Avenue to the railroad station and back, across the little bridge over the Rippowam River which separated East from West Main Street and the Black from the white communities, I marveled at the different scale life seemed to move on here.

On a Saturday afternoon, the streets seemed strangely un-crowded and unhurried. As I looked into the little dingy stores along the lower end of Atlantic near the station, I wondered why, if they had so much business, they all looked so poor and dull. I didn't realize for a few weeks why Saturday was not the shopping day that it was in New York.

I decided that weekend that I was going to work in Stamford, save money, and go to Mexico.

I could do that, I thought, by conserving on food, which would be no big thing since I couldn't cook in my room, any-way. I found a supermarket and bought five cans of Mooseabec sardines, a loaf of bread, and five cans of Campbell's pepperpot soup, my alltime favorite. I figured I was set for the week, a sandwich for lunch, and a can of soup for dinner. I would treat myself on the weekend, I decided, with franks or chicken-foot stew.

On Monday I started work, at 8:00 in the morning. I could walk to work in a half-hour from where I lived. I sat at a long table with other women, running a hand-cranked hanking ma-chine which made up ribbon into gaily turned hanks and clipped them with a tiny band of metal. The work was unbelievably boring, but the colors of the ribbons were bright and cheerful, and the table by lunchtime looked like a Christmas tree. This was September, but the factory was working on Christmas or-ders. It took me a while to get the hang of the machine, and how to turn neat hanks that were not returned by the foreman with a sneer. The woman I worked next to consoled me.

"Don't worry, honey. In three weeks he'll let you alone."

Stamford was a closed-shop town, and workers had to join the union within three weeks of beginning work. When I started, I was paid ninety cents an hour, which would increase to $1.15, the standard minimum wage, when I joined the union. My co-worker knew something I did not. It was standard procedure in most of the "software" factories to hire Black workers for three weeks, then fire them before they could join the union, and hire new workers. The work was not hard to learn. So three weeks later, I found myself with my first paycheck and no job.

That autumn I began to write poems again, after months of silence. My weekend nights became noisy with the limping clat-ter of my battered portable typewriter. The woman next door mildly suggested, when we passed on the outside stairs, that si-lence after midnight was the usual house rule for radios and typewriters. I folded up my blanket and used it as a pad to deaden the sound, as I worked away at the machine, perched upon my rickety table wedged in between my contraband hot-plate and the two neat stacks of Mooseabec sardines and Camp-bell's soup cans.

In the soft September evenings of this new place, it was as if Gennie had come alive again. I found myself on Saturday nights, walking through unfamiliar streets, explaining to Gennie in an undertone which streets were which, what the plant was like, and discussing with her the strange mannerisms of these non-New Yorkers.

> And you did not come back to April
> though spring was a powerful lure
> but bided your time in silence
> knowing the dead must endure.
>
> And you came not again to summer
> nor till the green oaks were leaving
> traces of blood in the autumn
> and there were hours for grieving.

Gennie was the only companion with whom I shared those first few weeks in Stamford, and sometimes, for days at a time, she was the only person to whom I spoke.

18 It was 10:00 A.M. on a crispy Monday morn-ing, and the West Main Community Center was almost empty. I stared straight ahead of me as I sat, waiting for Mrs. Kelly to finish. Starched and cocoa-brown, every iron-grey curl in place, she studied my application through gold-rimmed glasses. Across the lobby a printed white sign hung in front of the bronze name plaque on the wall. CRISPUS AT-TUCKS CENTER, the sign read. Some local dignitary, no doubt.

I turned as Mrs. Kelly sighed and looked up. "And what can we do for you today, young lady?" She smiled at me, her voice kindly and mama-soft, but I could tell from her eyes that she was remembering the strange new girl in town from New York who had come looking for a place to stay.

I smoothed the skirt of the shirtwaist dress I had worn to make a good impression. It was the only one I had, and I hunched my shoulders forward slightly, hoping Mrs. Kelly hadn't noticed how, like all cheap dresses, the bodice pulled too tightly across my breasts.

"I'm looking for work, Mrs. Kelly."

"And what kind of job are you looking for, dear?"

I leaned forward. "Well, really, I'd like to work as a medical receptionist."

"As a what, did you say?"

"A medical receptionist, ma'am. I've worked for two doctors before in New York."

Mrs. Kelly's arched eyebrows and averted eyes made me feel like I'd just belched without covering my mouth.

"Well, there was an opening for a ward maid up at Newton State Hospital last week, but I think that's already taken. And they usually like older women." She riffled absently through a file box on her desk and then turned back to me, her refined and motherly mouth slightly pursed. "You know, dear, there's not too much choice of jobs around here for Colored people, and especially not for Negro girls. Now if you could type. . ."

"No, ma'am, I can't," I said quickly. She closed her file with a snap.

"I tell you what, dear. Most of our unskilled people find some sort of work in the 'hardware' factories on the other side of town. Why don't you try some of the places over there? They don't register with us, but you can walk right in and ask if they're hiring. I'm sorry I can't help you." Mrs. Kelly pushed her chair back, stood, and gave a little tug to her fawn-grey tailored suit. "As soon as you learn how to type you come back and see us, now, you hear?"

I thanked her and left.

The following week, I got a job running a commercial X-ray machine.

Keystone Electronics was a relatively small factory as factories went in Stamford. It had a government contract to process and deliver quartz crystals used in radio and radar machinery. These small crystals were shipped from Brazil, cut at the plant and then ground, refined, and classified, according to how heavy an electrical charge they carried.

It was dirty work. The two floors of the plant rang with the whine of huge cutting and refining machines. Mud used by the

cutting crew was all over everything, cemented by the heavy oil
that the diamond-grit blades were mounted in. Thirty-two mud
saws were always running. The air was heavy and acrid with the
sickly fumes of carbon tetrachloride used to clean the crystals.
Entering the plant after 8:00 A.M. was like entering Dante's
Inferno. It was offensive to every sense, too cold and too hot,
gritty, noisy, ugly, sticky, stinking, and dangerous.

Men ran the cutting machines. Most local people would
not work under such conditions, so the cutting crew was com-
posed of Puerto Ricans who were recruited in New York City
and who commuted every morning up to Stamford on company-
paid tickets. Women read the crystals on a variety of X-ray
machines, or washed the thousands and thousands of crystals
processed daily in huge vats of carbon tetrachloride.

All the help in the plant, with the exception of the foreman
and forewomen, were Black or Puerto Rican, and all the women
were local, from the Stamford area.

Nobody mentioned that carbon tet destroys the liver and
causes cancer of the kidneys. Nobody mentioned that the X-ray
machines, when used unshielded, delivered doses of constant
low radiation far in excess of what was considered safe even in
those days. Keystone Electronics hired Black women and didn't
fire them after three weeks. We even got to join the union.

I was hired to run one of the two X-ray machines that read
the first cuttings of raw quartz. This enabled the cutters to align
their machines in such a way as to maximize the charge from
each rock. Two machines were therefore stationed directly outside of the cutting room, open to the noise and mud and grit
flying from the stone-cutters. These were the least desirable jobs
for women because of the working conditions, and because
there was no overtime or piecework bonuses to be made. The
other machine was run by a young woman named Virginia,
whom everybody called Ginger. I met her the first morning in
the luncheonette across the street from the plant where I stopped
to get coffee and a roll to celebrate my first day on the new job.

We worked from 8:00 A.M. to 4:30 P.M. with ten-minute
coffee breaks at 10:00 A.M. and 2:30 P.M., and a half-hour
lunch break at noon.

The cutting "boys" made the first cut through the thick
grease and mud of the machines, and then brought rough two-
inch slabs to Ginger or me to be read for an electrical charge before they set the axis of their machines. The reading was obtained by a small X-ray beam passed through the crystal. There was

a hood to be flipped to cover your fingers and prevent the X ray from touching you, but the second that it took to flip it down was often the difference between being yelled at for being too slow and a smooth-working relationship with the cutters.

The rock was then sliced along the axis that had been marked with an oil pencil. We read it again, and it was sliced into slabs. Ginger and I read these slabs, tossing them, thick with grime and mud, into the barrels next to our machines. Those slabs were then taken away, washed in huge trays of carbon tetra-chloride and cut into squares for the X-ray "reading room." This was a cleaner, quieter place to work, where the crystals were read one last time and stacked according to degree charge.

The women in the X-ray reading room made piecework bo-nuses over a large base expectation output, and these jobs were considered desirable. By cutting corners, saving time and not flipping the hood, it was possible to make a small weekly bonus.

After the first week, I wondered if I could stick it out. I thought that if I had to work under those conditions for the rest of my life I would slit my throat. Some mornings, I ques-tioned how I could get through eight hours of stink and dirt and din and boredom. At 8:00 A.M. I would set my mind for two hours, saying to myself, you can last two hours, and then there will be a coffee break. I'd read for ten minutes, and then I'd set myself for another two hours, thinking, now all right, you can last two hours until lunch. After lunch, when the ma-chines behind us kicked over, I felt a little refreshed after my sardine sandwich, but those two hours were the hardest of the day. It was a long time until the 2:30 break. But finally, I could tell myself, now you can make it for two more hours and then you'll be free.

Sometimes I stood waiting for the freight elevator in the ear-ly morning half-dark with the other workers, anxiously hoping it wouldn't stall and the time clock tick over into red. I tried to propel myself back out of the alley and toward home, because I knew I could not possibly go through another day like the day before. But the elevator came, and I got on with the others.

There were women who had worked at the plant for the en-tire ten years it had been open.

I would not get paid for three weeks, and my meager hoard of money was running dangerously low. (It was customary in factories in Stamford to hold back your first week's pay until you left your job, as a deposit, so to speak, on your space.) It

did not cover coffee breaks. Sometimes I would stay right at the
machines and read the book I brought. Ginger would bop off to
the relative cleanliness of the reading room to talk with the
other women. One day she clued me in.

"You better get your bottom off that chair in your breaks,
girl, before you get stuck to it. You can go crazy like that."

Those were my sentiments, exactly.

With different motivations in mind, my forewoman, Rose,
also advised me on my off-work habits. Pulling me aside at
lunchtime, and with an archly significant smile, she told me that
she thought I was a bright girl and could go places except I went
to the bathroom too much.

The cutters made piecework bonuses on their work, but
Ginger and I did not. One day the men had hassled me all morning, saying I was not giving them their readings fast enough, and
was holding up their cuttings. At 10:00 A.M. they trooped
downstairs for coffee, leaving their machines running. Under the
cover of the noise, I dropped my head over the nape of the
X-ray machine and burst into tears. At that point, Ginger appeared, having forgotten her change purse under the hamper
of her machine. She punched me gently on the arm.

"See that? What'd I tell ya? You can go nuts with all that
reading. What do ya take in your coffee? I'll buy you a cup."

"No, thank you." I wiped my eyes, ruffled to be caught crying.

"No, thank you." Ginger giggled, mimicking my tone. "You
sound just like a lady. C'mon, girl, *please* have some coffee. I
can't handle these motherfuckers by myself for the rest of the
day and they's out for blood this morning. Hurry up, what'll
you have?"

"Very light with sugar." I smiled in gratitude.

"Atta girl," she said, with her usual jocular laugh, and rolled
on down the narrow aisle separating our machines from the cutting-room din.

That's how Ginger and I became friends. That Thursday, she
invited me to drive downtown with her mother and her to cash
our checks.

It was my first paycheck from Keystone.

Since Thursday was payday, the shops on Atlantic Avenue
were lively and open late. Everybody turned out to market and
shop and cash checks and socialize downtown. People parked
on the main streets and chatted with the passersby, no matter
that tomorrow was a Friday workday to contend with.

Ginger told me she had spotted me in town the first Thursday I was there, before I even came to work at Keystone.

"That's right. Blue jeans and sneakers on Atlantic Avenue on Thursday night! I said to myself, who's this slick kitty from the city?"

I laughed at the idea that anyone could call me *slick*, and held my peace.

Ginger invited me home for dinner that Thursday night, and I realized, as I had a third helping of mashed potatoes, that I had almost forgotten what home-cooked food tasted like. I could see red-headed Cora, Ginger's youngish brash mother, looking at me half in amusement, half in annoyance. Ginger had four younger brothers at home, and Cora had a lot of hungry mouths to feed.

Sometimes Ginger would bring me a roll from home in the mornings; sometimes she would walk over to my house on Mill River Road in the evening after work and invite me out for a hamburger at the White Castle near the bridge, the only place in town open after 6:00, except on Thursdays.

Ginger had a battery-powered portable radio, a gift from her now-divorced husband, and before the weather turned cold, we would go out in the beautiful autumn evenings and sit by the embankment of the Rippowam River that faced my house, and listen to Fats Domino on WJRZ. His "Blueberry Hill" was tops on the hit parade through most of that fall, and Ginger had a special place in her heart for him anyway, since they looked so much alike. She even walked like Fats, with a swing-bopping step.

Ginger talked, and I listened. I soon discovered that if you keep your mouth shut, people are apt to believe you know everything, and they begin to feel freer and freer to tell you anything, anxious to show that they know something, too.

The old Ford swooped elegantly into the curb at the corner of Atlantic and Main, just the other side of the railroad tracks.

"End of the line, girls." CeCe, Ginger's brother, pulled loose the rope that held the front passenger door in place. Ginger and I clambered out into the autumn afternoon sun, bracing but not yet chill. Up and down Atlantic Avenue, schoolchildren were painting garish and ghostly murals in brilliant tempera and soap paint onto the windows and doors of the shops that had agreed to participate in the Halloween pageant and parade. Tomorrow was Halloween. The parade would wind through most of the downtown area, Ginger explained, and include most of the town's children.

"One big treat. The stores figure it'll save on tricks. They do it like that every year. Keeps the windows from being scratched and marked up. Watercolor's easier to wash off than house-paint. They don't do it in the city, do they?"

We walked into Gerber's Department Store looking for stockings for Ginger, because Cora insisted Ginger wear nylons to church on Sunday.

"I've never seen Halloween celebrated like that before."

"Well," Ginger drawled, fingering the nylons on display. "That's small-town stuff. There's a lot you haven't seen goes on here different from the big city. Like fo'instance, these stockings ain't shit. Let's go see at Grants'." We crossed the avenue and walked back up the other side of Main Street. From the record shop, snatches of Rosemary Clooney's voice singing *"Come on a my house, my house a come on,"* mixed with the Saturday afternoon traffic.

A tow-headed boy on a bike rolled past us, sucking a bright green pickle. The sharp smell of knife-clean dill and garlic pulled a rip-cord in my head, dropping me into the middle of Rivington Street, between Orchard and Delancey.

Bright Sunday morning on the Lower East Side of Manhattan, New York's eager and determined bargain-hunters searching through the sidewalk bins for good buys and old friends. On the corner of Orchard Street, the Pickle Man presided over wooden vats of assorted sizes and shades of green and succulent submarines, each hue denoting a different stage or flavor of pickle-ment. Half-submerged beneath the floating bits of garlic and peppercorns and twigs of dill, schools of pickles drifted like spiced fish waiting belly up for a bite. Nearby, sawhorse tables extended onto the sidewalk under a striped awning, holding flats of dried apricots, dark orange and mysteriously translucent. Beside them on the tables, long square wooden boxes half-open, waxed paper pulled back over the long slabs of halvah, ground sesame-paste candy. There were boxes of vanilla, smooth chocolate, and the crazy-quilt mixture of the two—my favorite, marble.

Over all, in the sharpening autumn air, the smells from Ratner's Dairy Restaurant drifting around the corner and over the rooftops, cheese blintzes and freshly baked onion rolls. They mingled with the heavier smells of the delicatessen next door, where all-beef garlic sausages and stuffed derma nestled along-

*side of the kasha knishes in the window-warmer. To the noses
on the busy street, religious and dietary separations did not
matter, and Sunday morning shopping on Rivington Street was
an orchestra of olfactory delights.*

I wondered where the boy had gotten a half-dill pickle in
Stamford, Connecticut.

"Do they sell pickles in Grants', Ginger?"

"What a great idea!" Ginger grinned as she took my arm.
"You like pickles, too? Big sour juicy ones, and the little—hey,
watch it!" Ginger yanked back on my arm as I glanced up the
avenue absently and stepped down into the street. "Speedy
Gonzales, you get tickets for jay-walking around here, and New
Yorkers get most of them. You don't have anything better to
do with your money?" She grinned again as the light changed.
"How'd you hear about the job at Keystone, anyway?"

"At the West Main Community Center."

"Good ole Crispus Attucks."

"What's that?" We turned the corner onto Main Street and
headed for Grants'.

"The center, stupid. It was just renamed in honor of a Negro,
so we shouldn't mind that they don't want us using the center
downtown."

"Who's it named for?"

"You mean you don't know who he is?" Ginger screwed her
face up, unbelieving. She cocked her head and wrinkled her
brow at me.

"I haven't been around here that long, you know," I counter-
ed, defensively.

"Well I'll be dipped. Slick kitty from the city! What kind of a
school was that you-all went to?" Her round, incredulous eyes
almost disappearing into the folds of her wrinkled-up face. "I
thought everybody knew about *him*. The first cat to die in the
Revolutionary War, in Concord, Massachusetts. A Black man,
name of Crispus Attucks. The shot heard 'round the world. Everybody knows that. They renamed our center after him." Ginger squeezed my arm again as we entered the store. "And they
got you the job at Keystone. I'm glad they did something useful,
after all."

Grants' didn't sell pickles except with sandwiches. But there
was a sale on nylons, three pair for $1.25, or fifty cents a pair.
The Korean War was already pushing prices back up, and this
was a good buy. Ginger tried to decide if she wanted to spend
that much.

"Come on, girl, get a pair with me," she urged. "They're real cheap, and your legs are going to get cold, even in pants."

"I hate nylons. I can't stand the way they feel on my legs." What I didn't say was that I couldn't stand the bleached-out color that the so-called neutral shade of all cheap nylons gave my legs. Ginger looked at me, pleadingly. And I relented. It wasn't her fault I was feeling so out of sorts all of a sudden, so disjointed. *Crispus Attucks.* Something had slipped out of place.

"Oh, buy them," I said. "You want them and you can always use them. 'Sides, your mother will never let them go to waste." I ran my fingers over the fine mesh of the display stockings hung from a T-rack on the counter. The dry slippery touch of nylon and silk filled me with distrust and suspicion. The effortlessness with which those materials passed through my fingers made me uneasy. They were illusive, confusing, not to be depended upon. The texture of wool and cotton with its resistance and unevenness, allowed, somehow, for more honesty, a more straightforward connection through touch.

Crispus Attucks.

Most of all, I hated the pungent, lifeless, and ungiving smell of nylon, its adamant refusal to become human or evocative in odor. Its harshness was never tampered by the smells of the wearer. No matter how long the clothing was worn, nor in what weather, a person dressed in nylon always approached my nose like a warrior approaching a tourney, clad in chain-mail.

I fingered the nylon, but my mind hammered elsewhere. *Crispus Attucks, Boston*?! Ginger *knew.* I prided myself on my collection of odds and ends of random information, more and less useful, gathered through avid curiosity and endless reading. I stored the garnered tidbits on the back-burner of consciousness, to be pulled forward on any appropriate occasion. I was used to being the one who knew some fact that everybody else in the conversation had not yet learned. It was not that I believed I knew EVERYTHING, just more than most people around me.

Ginger handed three pair of tissue-wrapped stockings to the woman behind the counter, and stood waiting for her change. I wondered where that half-dill pickle had come from.

Crispus Attucks. How was that possible? I had spent four years at Hunter High School, supposedly the best public high school in New York City, with the most academically advanced and intellectually accurate education available, for "preparing

young women for college and career." I had been taught by
some of the most highly considered historians in the country.
Yet, I never once heard the name mentioned of the first man to
fall in the american revolution, nor ever been told that he was a
Negro. What did that mean about the history I had learned?

Ginger's voice was a cheerful, soothing murmur over my
thoughts as she talked me part way up the hill back to my room
on Mill River Road.

"What's wrong with you today? Cat got your tongue?"

Before long, I was totally dependent upon Ginger for human
contact in Stamford, and her invitations to Sunday dinner represented the only real food I ever ate. She built up an incredible
mythology about me and what my life had been in New York,
and I did nothing to dissuade her. I told her that I had left
home when I was seventeen and gotten my own apartment, and
she thought that was very daring. She had gotten married when
she was twenty, in order to get out of her mother's house. Now
she was back, divorced, but with a certain amount of autonomy,
purchased by her weekly contributions to the family income.
Her mother worked as a bench-press operator at American Cyanimid, and her father was diabetic and blind. Her mother's
lover lived with them, along with her four younger brothers.

For some time, I had known that Ginger was flirting with
me, but had ignored it because I was at a loss as to how to handle the situation. As far as I knew, she was sweet and attractive
and warm and lovable, and straight as a die.

Ginger, on the other hand, was convinced that I had everything taped. She saw me as a citified little baby butch—bright,
knowledgeable, and secure enough to be a good listener *and*
to make the first move. She was sure that I was an old and accomplished hand at the seduction of young divorcées. But her
inviting glances and throaty chuckles were never enough to
tempt me, nor were the delicious tidbits she would sneak out
of Cora's kitchen and wrap up in handkerchiefs, persuading
Uncle Charlie to drive her over to Mill River Road in the truck
on his way to his night job. I remained determinedly oblivious
to all this for as long as possible.

Ginger, perfumed and delectable, perched on my desk chair
in the tiny second-floor room, watching incredulously as I sat
crosslegged on my bed, wolfing down her mother's goodies.

"I don't believe you're only eighteen. Come on, how old are
you, really?"

"I told you already." The chicken was crisp and delicious and totally preoccupying.

"When were you born?"

"Nineteen-thirty-four." Ginger calculated for a minute.

"I never met an eighteen-year-old like you before." Ginger spoke with the lofty advantage of her twenty-five years.

One weekend, Ginger stole a lobster claw for me. It was a make-up present that Charlie had bought for Cora's dinner, and when Cora found out she threatened to throw Ginger out of the house. Ginger decided then that this was all getting too costly. Long goodnight kisses on the back porch were definitely not enough; so she finally made her own move.

By the beginning of November, autumn was closing down. The trees were still incandescent colors, but the edge of winter was already in the air. The days were getting shorter and shorter, and this made me unhappy. There was very little time after work before sunset. If I went to the library, it was dark by the time I walked back to Mill River Road. Keystone was a daily trial that did not seem to get better nor easier, despite Ginger's warm-hearted attempts to cheer me up during our frightful days.

One Thursday after work, Ginger borrowed her brother's old beat-up Ford and we went downtown to cash our checks alone, without Cora, or Charlie, or any of the boys. It was still light when we were through, and I could tell Ginger had something on her mind. We drove around town for a while.

"What's up?" I asked.

"C'mon," Ginger said. "Let's go up on the hill."

Ginger was not much of a nature lover, but she had taken me to see her favorite spot, a wooded hill on the west edge of town where, hidden from view by the overgrown bushes and trees, we could sit on two old tree stumps left from long ago, smoking and listening to Fats Domino and watching the sun go down.

> I found ma' thrill-l-l-l-lll
> On Blueberreeeeee Hill——lllll.

We left the car and climbed to the top of the hill. The air was chill as we sat on the stumps to catch our breaths.

"Cold?"

"No," I said, pulling my ragged suede jacket, inherited from CeCe, around me.

"You ought to get a warm coat or something, winters around here ain't like in New York."

"I've got a coat, I just don't like to wear it, that's all."

Ginger cut her eyes at me. "Yeah, I know. Who you think you kidding? If it's money, I can lend you some till Christmas." She knew about the two-hundred-dollar phone bill The Branded had run up that summer at Spring Street, which I was now paying off.

"Hey, thanks, but I don't need a coat."

Ginger was walking back and forth now, puffing nervously on her Lucky Strike. I sat looking up at her. What was going on, and what was Ginger wanting me to say? I didn't want a coat, because I didn't mind the cold.

"You really think you're slick, huh?" Ginger turned to face me, regarding me with a slight smile and narrowed eyes, head up and to one side like a pigeon. Her voice was high and nervous.

"You always say that, Ginger, and I keep telling you it's not true. What are you talking about?"

"Slick kitty from the city. Well, kiddo, you don't have to keep your mouth shut around me, because I know all about you and your friends."

What was it that Ginger had discovered or invented in her own mind about me that I would now have to pretend to fulfill? Like the time I promptly downed two straight vodkas to fulfill her image of me as a hard-drinking New York Village girl.

"About me and my friends?" I was starting to get the drift of her conversation, and beginning to get acutely uncomfortable. Ginger butted her cigarette, took a deep breath, and moved a few steps closer.

"Look, it's no big thing." She took a deep breath. "Are you gay or aren't you?" She took another deep breath.

I smiled up at her and said nothing. I certainly couldn't say *I don't know*. Actually, I was at a loss as to what to say. I could not bring myself to deny what I had just this past summer decided to embrace; besides, to say no would be to admit being one of the squares. Yet, to say yes might commit me to proving it, like with the vodka. And Ginger was a woman of the world, not one of my high school girl friends with whom kissing and cuddling and fantasizing sufficed. And I had never made love to a woman before. Ginger, of course, had made up her mind that *I* was a woman of the world and knew "everything," having made love to all the women about whom I talked with such intensity.

I stood up, feeling the need to have our eyes on a level.

"C'mon, now, you can't just not say *anything*, girl. Are you or aren't you?" Ginger's voice was pleading as well as impatient.

She was right. I couldn't just not answer. I opened my mouth, not knowing what was going to come out.

"Yes," I said. Maybe it would all stop there.

Ginger's brown face broke into her wonderful full-cheeked half-smile, half-grin. Instinctively, I grinned back. And joining hands there on the top of the hill, with the sound of the car radio drifting upward through the open door below, we stood grinning at each other while the sun went down.

Ginger.
Snapping little dark eyes, skin the color of well-buttered caramel, and a body like the Venus of Willendorf. Ginger was gorgeously fat, with an open knowledge about her body's movement that was delicate and precise. Her breasts were high and ample. She had pads of firm fat upon her thighs, and round dimpled knees. Her swift, tapered hands and little feet were also deeply dimpled. Her high putchy cheeks and great mischievous smile was framed by wide bangs and a short pageboy that was sometimes straightened, sometimes left to wave tightly over her ears.

Whenever Ginger went to the beauty parlor she came back feather-bobbed and adorable, but much less real. Shortly after we met at the plant, she began to resist Cora's nagging, and stopped going to the hairdresser's altogether.

"What's the matter? Cat got your tongue?" Ginger turned back to me; our hands, still joined, fell apart.

"It's getting late," I answered. I was hungry.

Ginger's brow puckered and she sucked her teeth into the fading light. "Are you for real? What'd ya mean, it's getting late? Is that all you can think about?"

Oh. Obviously that was not the right thing to say. What am I supposed to do now?

Ginger's round face was a hand's span away from my own. She spoke softly, with her usual cockiness. Her close voice and the smell of her face powder made me at once both uneasy and excited.

"Why don't you kiss me? I don't bite."

Her words were bold, but beneath them I could feel fear belying their self-assurance.

Oh, hell, I thought. What am I doing here, anyway? I should have known it wasn't going to stop there—I knew it, I knew it and suppose she wants me to take her to. . . oh shit! What am I going to do now?

Afraid to lose some face I never had, obediently, I bent forward slightly. I started to kiss Ginger's cupid's-bow mouth, and her soft lips parted. My heart went snatch-grab. Down the hill, the car radio was just finishing the news. I felt Ginger's quick breath upon my face, expectant and slightly tinged with cough drops and cigarettes and coffee. It was warm and exciting in the chilly night air and I kissed her again thinking, this isn't a bad idea at all. . .

When Ginger and I got back to the house, Charlie had left for work with his Railroad Express supply truck. Cora and the boys had already eaten dinner, and the two younger ones were ready for bed. As we came in the front door, Cora was just coming downstairs with her husband's dinner tray. Ginger had explained to me that her father never left his room any more except to go to the bathroom.

Cora and CeCe had just come back from marketing, and Cora was tired. Her henna-red curly hair was caught behind each ear with a baby-blue ribbon, and untidy bangs almost covered her heavily made-up eyes.

"We ate Chinese tonight to give me a break. And we didn't leave any for you girls because I didn't know if you were going to come home. Ginger, don't forget to leave your house-money on the table."

There was only a hint of triumphant reproach in Cora's voice. Chinese food was a rare treat.

I usually spent the night at Ginger's house on the Thursdays we got paid. While Ginger put away the dishes her brothers had washed, and made the boys' lunches for school, I went upstairs to take a quick bath. The morning started early, at 5:00 A.M., when Cora rose to take care of her husband before she went to her job.

"And don't leave that water running in the tub the way you like to, neither!" Cora called out to me from the room she and Charlie shared as I passed by. "You're not in New York now and water costs money!"

Ginger's room was downstairs at the front of the house with its own entrance. It was rather secluded from the rest of the house, once everyone had retired.

By the time Ginger finished taking her shower, I was already in bed. I lay with my eyes closed, wondering if I could pretend to be asleep, and if not, what would be the sophisticated and dykely thing to do.

Ginger took much longer than usual preparing herself for bed. She sat at her little desk-table, creaming her legs with Jergen's lotion and braiding her hair, humming snatches of songs under her breath as she buffed her nails.

"If I came home tonight, would you still be my. . ."

"Come on a my house, my house a come on, come on. . ."

"I saw the harbor lights, they only told me we were. . ."

In between anxieties about my anticipated performance, I began to feel the rising excitement of the hill return. It challenged the knot of terror I felt at the thought of Ginger's unknown expectations, at the thought of sexual confrontation, at the thought of being tried and found wanting. I smelled the little breezes of Cashmere Bouquet powder and Camay soap as Ginger moved her arm back and forth, buffing away. What was taking her so long?

It didn't occur to me that Ginger, despite her show of coolness and bravado, was as nervous as I. After all, this wasn't just playing around with some hometown kid at the plant. This was actually going to bed with a real live New York City Greenwich Village Bulldagger.

"Aren't you coming to bed," I asked, finally, a little surprised at the urgency of my voice.

"Well, I thought you'd never ask." With a relieved chuckle, Ginger shed her robe, snapped off the dresser lamp, and bounced into bed beside me.

Until the very moment that our naked bodies touched in that old brass bed that creaked in the insulated sunporch on Walker Road, I had no idea what I was doing there, nor what I wanted to do there. I had no idea what making love to another woman meant. I only knew, dimly, it was something I wanted to happen, and something that was different from anything I had ever done before.

I reached out and put an arm around Ginger, and through the scents of powder and soap and hand cream I could smell the rising flush of her own spicy heat. I took her into my arms, and she became precious beyond compare. I kissed her on her mouth, this time with no thought at all. My mouth moved to the little hollow beneath her ear.

Ginger's breath warmed my neck and started to quicken. My hands moved down over her round body, silky and fragrant, waiting. Uncertainty and doubt rolled away from the mouth of my wanting like a great stone, and my unsureness dissolved in the directing heat of my own frank and finally open desire.

Our bodies found the movements we needed to fit each other. Ginger's flesh was sweet and moist and firm as a winter pear. I felt her and tasted her deeply, my hands and my mouth and my whole body moved against her. Her flesh opened to me like a peony and the unfolding depths of her pleasure brought me back to her body over and over again throughout the night. The tender nook between her legs, moist and veiled with thick crispy dark hair.

I dove beneath her wetness, her fragrance, the silky insistence of her body's rhythms illuminating my own hungers. We rode each other's need. Her body answered the quest of my fingers my tongue my desire to know a woman, again and again, until she arced like a rainbow, and shaken, I slid back through our heat, coming to rest upon her thighs. I surfaced dizzy and blessed with her rich myrrh-taste in my mouth, in my throat, smeared over my face, and the loosening grip of her hands in my hair and the wordless sounds of her satisfaction lulling me like a song.

Once, as she cradled my head between her breasts, Ginger whispered, "I could tell you knew how," and the pleasure and satisfaction in her voice started my tides flowing again and I moved down against her once more, my body upon hers, ringing like a bell.

I never questioned where my knowledge of her body and her need came from. Loving Ginger that night was like coming home to a joy I was meant for, and I only wondered, silently, how I had not always known that it would be so.

Ginger moved in love like she laughed, openly and easily, and I moved with her, against her, within her, an ocean of brown warmth. Her sounds of delight and the deep shudders of relief that rolled through her body in the wake of my stroking fingers filled me with delight and a hunger for more of her. The sweetness of her body meeting and filling my mouth, my hands, wherever I touched, felt right and completing, as if I had been born to make love to this woman, and was remembering her body rather than learning it deeply for the first time.

In wonder, but without surprise, I lay finally quiet with my arms around Ginger. So this was what I had been so afraid of not doing properly. How ridiculous and far away those fears seemed now, as if loving were some task outside of myself,

rather than simply reaching out and letting my own desire guide
me. It was all so simple. I felt so good I smiled into the darkness.
Ginger cuddled closer.

"We better get some sleep," she muttered. "Keystone tomorrow." And drifted off into slumber.

There was an hour or so before the alarm went off and I
lay awake, trying to fit everything together, trying to reassure
myself that I was in control and did not need to be afraid. And
what, I wondered, was my relationship now to this delicious
woman who lay asleep on my arm? Ginger by night now seemed
so different from the Ginger I knew in the day. Had some beautiful and mythic creature created by my own need suddenly
taken the place of my jovial and matter-of-fact buddy?

Once earlier, Ginger had reached out to touch the wet
warmth of my own body and I had turned her hand aside without thinking, without knowing why. Yet I knew that I was still
hungry for her cries of joy and the soaring wonder of her body
moving beneath mine, guided by a power that flowed through
me from that charged core pressed against her.

Ginger was my friend, the only friend I had made in this
strange town, and I loved her, but with caution. We had slept
together. Did that mean we were lovers?

*A few months after Gennie's death I walked down Broadway
late one Saturday afternoon. I had just had another argument
with my mother, and I was going to the A&P to get milk. I dawdled along the avenue looking into shop windows, not wanting
to return to the tensions and misunderstandings waiting for me
at home.*

*I paused in front of Stolz's Jewelers, admiring their new dis-
play. In particular, I marked a pair of hanging earrings of black
opals, set into worked silver. "Gennie will love those," I thought,
"I must remember to tell her. . ." and then it hit me again that
Gennie was dead, and that meant that she would never be there
ever again. It meant that I could not ever tell her anything
more. It meant that whether I loved her or was angry at her
or wanted her to see a new pair of earrings, none of that mattered or would ever matter to her again. I could share nothing at
all with her any more because she was gone.*

*And even after all the past weeks of secret mourning, Gennie's
death became real to me in a different way.*

*I turned away from the jewelry store window. And right then
and there in the middle of Broadway and 151st Street on a Sat-*

urday afternoon at the beginning of the summer of my sixteenth year, I decided that I would never love anybody else again for the rest of my life. Gennie had been the first person in my life I was conscious of loving. And she had died. Loving hurt too much. My mother had turned into a demon intent on destroying me. You loved people and you came to depend on their being there. But people died or changed or went away and it hurt too much. The only way to avoid that pain was not to love anyone, and not to let anyone get too close or too important. The secret to not being hurt like this again, I decided, was never depending on anyone, never needing, never loving.

It is the last dream of children, to be forever untouched.

I heard the oil-burner in the basement at Walker Road kick over at 4:30 A.M. and Ginger shifted and sighed softly in her sleep. I started to kiss her awake and stopped, as the smells of our loving and the moist top of her sleepy head engulfed me in a sudden wave of tenderness so strong that I pulled back.

"You better watch out," I said to myself soundlessly in the darkness. The alarm went off, and Ginger and I, galvanized by the hectic morning routine of the house, grabbed our robes and raced upstairs to the bathroom.

One more minute and we would have to stand in line with the boys. There was just time for a hurried hug and a kiss over the washbowl, as Ginger brushed out the tangles in her hair that had become unbraided during the night.

Charlie dropped us off on the other side of the railroad tracks, a block away from the plant. Ginger stopped in and bought buttered rolls and coffee for us in the luncheonette across the street from Keystone.

"We gonna need something to keep us awake today after last night," she grunted, then grinned, nudging me under the cover of pushing through the mob at the entrance to the plant building. We winked at each other as we waited in the crowd for the freight elevator to take us up into hell.

All day, I watched Ginger carefully for a lead as to how we were going to treat the extraordinary events of the night before. A piece of me was invested in her image of me as the gay young blade, the seasoned and accomplished lover from the big city.

(Later, Ginger told me that it was my questioning why she always had to make school lunch for the boys every morning before her work that made Cora conclude one day, "She's got to be a bulldagger!")

I enjoyed paying court to Ginger, and being treated, in private, like a swain. It gave me a sense of power and privilege that was heady, if illusory, since I knew on another level it was all play-acting. On one level it was play-acting for Ginger, too, because she would not allow herself to regard a relationship between two women as anything other than a lark. She could not consider it important, even as she sought it and cherished it.

At the same time, on a true and deeper level, Ginger and I met as two young Black women in need of each other's warmth and blood-assurance, able to share the passions within our bodies, and no amount of pretending that we were pretending could change that. Yet, we were both very much invested in the denial of our importance to each other. For different reasons, we both needed to pretend we didn't care.

Each of us was very busy being cool, ignoring and misnaming the passionate intensity with which we came together wherever possible, usually on that old brass bed in the insulated sunporch, that drafty haven on Walker Road which we turned tropical with the heat of our young bodies' wildness.

As long as I convinced myself that I wasn't really involved emotionally with Ginger, I could delight in this new experience. Her favorite expression was, "Be cool, girl," and I congratulated myself on how cool I *was*. It didn't bother me, I maintained, that Ginger went out on dates which Cora arranged.

With her typical aplomb, Cora welcomed my increased presence around the house with the rough familiarity and browbeating humor due another one of her daughters. If she recognized the sounds emanating from the sunporch on the nights I slept over, or our haggard eyes the next day, she ignored them. But she made it very clear that she expected Ginger to get married again.

"Friends are nice, but marriage is marriage," she said to me one night as she helped me make a skirt on her machine, and I wondered why Ginger had asked me over and then gone to the movies with a friend of Cora's from American Cyanimid. "And when she gets home don't be thumping that bed all night, neither, because it's late already and you girls have work tomorrow."

But I thought of little else at work now other than the night pleasures of Ginger's body, and how I could arrange to get her over to Mill River Road for an hour or so after work. It was a little more private than Walker Road, except that my old bed creaked so badly that we always had to put the mattress on the floor.

19 The week before Christmas I fell off my stool at work, hitting my head against the brick half-wall that separated us from the cutters, and getting a mild concussion. I was in the hospital when Ginger brought me a telegram from my sister saying that my father had had another severe stroke. It was Christmas Eve. I signed myself out of the hospital and caught a train for New York City.

I had not seen any member of my family for a year and a half.

The next few weeks were a haze of headache, and other people's emotions swirling around me. I went back to work after Christmas, commuting to and from New York City to visit my father in the hospital. Sometimes Ginger came with me after work.

The fog was heavy and chilling over the streets of Stamford the night my father died. No cars moved. I walked two miles to the station to catch the 9:30 train to New York. Ginger walked with me as far as Crispus Attucks. I was terrified I was going to trip on a curbstone, the fog was so thick. The streetlights glowed faintly like distant moons. The streets were empty and eerily quiet, as if the whole world had died, not only my father in that dim oxygenated room on the terminal ward of the Medical Center in New York.

During the week after my father's death, I stayed at my mother's house. Most of the time she was sedated against her frenzied and awful grief, and Helen and I handled the flow of people passing through the house. Phyllis was married and expecting her second child in two weeks, and could only attend the funeral. She lent me a dark grey coat to wear to the church.

During the week, I fought hard to remind myself that I was now a stranger in this house. But it did give me a new perspective on my mother. There had only been one human being whom she had ever entertained upon the earth as her equal; this was my father, and now he was dead. I saw the desolate loneliness that this exclusiveness had won her, and against which she only occasionally closed her hawk-grey eyes. But she looked through me and my sisters as if we were glass.

I saw my mother's pain, and her blindness, and her strength, and for the first time I began to see her as separate from me, and I began to feel free of her.

My sister Helen withdrew into her flippant shell for protection, and endlessly played a record which she had just gotten on the phonograph in the parlor. Day and night, over and over, for seven days:

I get the blues when we dance
I get the blues in advance
For I know you'll be gone
and I'll be here all alone
So I get the blues in advance.

Some get the blues from a song
Some when love has come and gone
You don't know how I cry
When you tell me goodbye. . .

Returning to Stamford after the funeral, I realized that I needed to be even further away from New York. I decided to make
as much money as I could and go to Mexico as soon as possible.

To that end and because Cora invited me, I gave up my room
on Mill River Road with its creaky bed, and moved my belongings into the sunporch on Walker Road. The ten dollars a week
room and board was less than what I was spending for both before. Cora said the extra cash was a help to her already strained
budget, and besides, I was eating her out of house and home
anyway.

Ginger told me that a new girl, Ada, had been hired to run
my machine at the plant. When I returned, since I was a member of the union, I was given another job. I was moved on to an
X-ray machine in the reading room, where the finished elec-
tronic crystals were fine-read according to strength of charge,
then racked for packing.

Although this job paid the same $1.10 an hour, all the jobs
in the RR were preferable and sought after. The room was in
the middle of the floor, enclosed by glass panels, and the fierce
sensory assaults of the rest of the plant were somewhat muted.

We sat at our machines in a circle, facing outward, our backs
to each other to discourage talking. There were six commercial
X-ray machines and a desk in the middle for Rose, our forewoman. We were never long away from her watchful eye.

But working in the RR meant there was a chance to make
piecework bonus.

Each reader obtained her crystals from the washing cage in
boxes of two hundred. Taking them back to our machines, we
inserted the tiny, ¾-inch squares of wafer-thin rock one by one
into the throat of the X-ray machine, twirled the dial until the
needle jumped to its highest point, powered by the tiny X-ray

beam flashed across the crystal, snatched it off the mount, racked it in the proper slot, and then shot another crystal into the machine. With concentration and dexterity, the average amount one could read in a day was one thousand crystals.

By not taking the time to flip down the protective shield that kept the X ray from hitting our fingers, we could increase that number to about eleven hundred. Any crystals over twelve hundred read in one day were paid for as piecework, at the rate of $2.50 a hundred. Some of the women who had been at Keystone for years had perfected the motions and moved so swiftly that they were able to make from five to ten dollars some weeks in bonus. For most of them, the tips of their fingers were permanently darkened from exposure to X ray. Before I finally left Keystone Electronics, there were dark marks on my fingers also, that only gradually faded.

After each crystal was read, it was flipped out of the machine and rapidly slipped into one of five slots in a rack that sat to the side of each of our machines. From these racks, periodically, a runner from the packing department would collect the crystals of whatever category was needed for the packers. Since it was not possible to keep track of the crystals after they were read, a tally was kept at the washing cage of how many boxes of crystals were taken daily by each reader. It was upon this count that our bonuses were based.

Throughout the day, Rose came by each machine regularly and spot-checked crystals from each of our racks, checking to make sure that no one racked unread crystals, or rushed through crystals with incorrect readings in order to raise our counts and make bonus.

The first two weeks I worked in the RR I talked to no one, raced my readings every day, never flipped the shield, and made three dollars in bonus. I decided I would have to reassess the situation. Ginger and I talked about it one night.

"You'd better slow down a little at work. The word's going out you're an eager beaver, brown-nosing Rose."

I was offended. "I'm not ass-kissing, I'm trying to make some money. There's nothing wrong with that, is there?"

"Don't you know those rates are set high like that so nobody can beat them? If you break your ass to read so many, you're going to show up the other girls, and before you know it they're going to raise the day rate again, figuring if you can do it so can everybody. And that just makes everybody look bad. They're

never going to let you make any money in that place. All the
books you read and you don't know that yet?" Ginger rolled
over and tapped the book I was reading on my pillow.

But I was determined. I knew I could not take Keystone
Electronics for much longer, and I knew I needed some money
put aside before I left. Where would I go when I got back to
New York? Where would I live until I got a job? And how long
would I have to look for work? And on the horizon like a dim
star, was my hope of going to Mexico. I had to make some
money.

Ginger and Ada, her new workmate, went to the movies more
and more often now that I was living at the Thurmans', and I
was determined not to care. But my sixth sense told me I had to
get away, and soon.

My daily rate of crystals began to increase steadily. Rose
came by more and more often to my machine, but could find
nothing wrong with my crystals, nor their slotting. She even
went so far as to ask me to turn out my jeans pockets one evening. I was outraged, but complied. By the next payday, I had
made an additional thirty dollars in bonus money for two weeks.
That was almost as much as my weekly wages. It became the
talk of the RR women.

"How does she manage to do all those?"

"Just wait and see. She's going to burn her fingers off before
she's through." The women lowered their voices as I came back
from the cage with a fresh box of crystals. But Ada, who had
stopped by for a brief chat, did not care whether or not I heard
her parting words.

"I don't know what she's doing with them crystals, but I bet
she's not reading them!"

She was right. I could not even tell Ginger how I was managing to pull down such high bonuses, although she often asked.
The truth was, I would slip crystals into my socks every time I
went to the bathroom. Once inside the toilet stall, I chewed
them up with my strong teeth and flushed the little shards of
rock down the commode. I could take care of between fifty and
a hundred crystals a day in that manner, taking a handful from
each box I signed out.

I knew Ginger was hurt by my silence, and by what she saw
as my disloyalty to the other RR women. I was angered by the
feeling of persistent guilt that her words aroused in me, but I
could say nothing. I could also say nothing about the increasing
time she and Ada spent together.

I longed for a chance to be alone, to enjoy the privacy that was not possible once I started to share the sunporch on Walker Road. I hated the amount of time I spent thinking about Ginger and Ada. I began to feel more and more desperate to get out of Stamford, and my bonuses went up.

One day in the beginning of March, I saw Rose talking to Bernie, the plant's efficiency expert, and looking after me speculatively as I came out of the john. I knew my days at Keystone were numbered. That week I made forty dollars in bonuses.

On Friday, Rose told me that the plant was cutting back readers and they were going to have to let me go. Since I was a member of the union, they gave me two weeks severance pay, so I would leave immediately and not make a fuss. Even though it was what I wanted to happen, I still cried a little on the way home. "Nobody likes to be fired," Ginger said and held my hand.

Cora was sorry to lose the extra income. Ginger said she'd miss me, but I could tell she was also secretly relieved, as she confided to me months later. I made plans to return to New York City.

20

I don't know why I was seized with such a desire to go to Mexico. Ever since I could remember Mexico had been the accessible land of color and fantasy and delight, full of sun, music and song. And from civics and geography in grade school, I knew it was attached to where I lived, and that intrigued me. That meant, if need be, I could always walk there.

I was happy to learn that Jean's boyfriend, Alf, who was in Mexico painting, would soon be coming home.

When I returned to New York after my father's death, going to Mexico became my chief goal. I saw very little of my mother. Where I would have expected grief for my father, there was only numbness. I stayed with Jean and her friends in a West Side apartment while I hunted for work. I eventually went to work as a clinic clerk in a Health Center, and moved in to share an apartment with Rhea Held, a progressive white woman who was a friend of Jean and Alf's.

No matter what emotional scrapes I got into that summer, the idea of Mexico shone like a beacon that I could count on, keeping me steady. The money I was saving from work, together with the small amount I had received from my father's insurance, would make it possible. I was determined to go, and that determination was fed by the deepening political gloom and red-baiting hysteria.

I became deeply involved in working with the Committee to Free the Rosenbergs; even so, the months in New York between my return from Stamford and my going to Mexico were very much a sojourn to me.

Rhea Held and I lived quite well together in the bright, sunny seventh-floor walk-up apartment on Seventh Street on the Lower East Side, now becoming known as the East Village. It was at times difficult and new—learning to live with Rhea, learning to share space with anyone, and a white woman, too, especially since I had no deep emotional bonds with her, only warm and casual pleasantries.

The work at the health center was interestingly medical and the hours, not tedious. I felt set apart from the other women with whom I worked, by virtue of their lunch-talk about weekend dates (while my noontime fantasies were still filled with the remembered joys of Ginger's bed).

Spring moved to summer. We demonstrated, picketed, stuffed envelopes, rang doorbells, and went to Washington for the Rosenbergs.

The second time I came to Washington, I traveled by bus. The trip took six hours and we boarded the buses at Union Square at 6:00 A.M. on a Sunday morning. It was not a pleasure trip, this time. We were seeking life for the parents of two little boys who traveled on the same bus in which I was riding. The Rosenbergs were about to be sacrificed, and this was a last-ditch visit to the white house to beg for a stay of execution.

Sunday morning, drizzly and cold for early June. I marched up and down with Jean and Rhea and the other women I had come with, hoping it would make a difference, still not really believing that any country I was associated with could murder these children's parents and call it legal. And they were white, too, which made it even harder for me to believe.

This time, whether or not I could eat vanilla ice cream at a soda fountain never came up. I had neither the money nor the time to find out. We picketed the white house, sang our brave

*little songs, handed in our petitions of mercy, and then climbed
back into the buses for the long wet ride home.*

*One week later, President Eisenhower signed into law an executive decree that said I could eat anything I wanted to anywhere in Washington, D.C., including vanilla ice cream. It
didn't mean too much to me by then.*

In the evenings after work, I saw Jean and Alf, who were
now married, or went to meetings with Rhea. Meetings where
frightened people tried to keep some speck of hope alive,
despite political disagreement, while all around us was the
possible threat of dying like the Rosenbergs, or at least the
threat of losing jobs or being fingered for life. Downtown at
political meetings and uptown at the Harlem Writers Guild,
friends, acquaintances, and simple people were terrorized at the
thought of having to answer, "Are you or have you ever been a
member of the Communist Party?"

The Rosenbergs' struggle became synonymous for me with
being able to live in this country at all, with being able to survive in hostile surroundings. But my feelings of connection with
most of the people I met in progressive circles, were as tenuous
as those I had with my co-workers at the Health Center. I could
imagine these comrades, Black and white, among whom color
and racial differences could be openly examined and talked
about, nonetheless one day asking me accusingly, "Are you or
have you ever been a member of a homosexual relationship?"
For them, being gay was "bourgeois and reactionary," a reason
for suspicion and shunning. Besides, it made you "more susceptible to the FBI."

The Rosenbergs were electrocuted on June 19, 1953—two
weeks after we had picketed the white house. I walked away
from the memorial rally in Union Square Park into the warm
Village night, tears streaming down my face for them, for their
sons, for all our wasted efforts, for myself—wondering whether
there was any place in the world that was different from here,
anywhere that could be safe and free, not really even sure of
what being safe and free could mean. But it did not mean being
lonely, disillusioned, betrayed. I felt like I was thirty years old.

I ran into Bea coming out of a music store next to Rienzi's
Coffee Shop. I was grateful for her face, familiar yet different
from the ones with which I had shared the grief and intensity
of the last few weeks. I invited her home to Seventh Street for
more coffee. Rhea had left for the weekend, seeking her own
solace for the failure and grief we both shared.

Bea and I had met at Bennington College the year before in spring when I was visiting Jill. Bea was also there visiting a friend. Our eyes had met several times during that crazy drunken weekend, and once at 2:00 A.M. in the cafeteria, Bea and I had talked while the others slept, deciding that she and I felt separated from the other girls because we were both a few months older, and we lived alone; that is, we were responsible for ourselves. There was some brief, guarded intellectual conversation about a shared appreciation of so many beautiful girls in one dormitory. Since then, Bea had broken up with a lover and was living in Philadelphia with a group of other women who had rented a house together. In the meantime, I had been to Stamford and met Ginger.

We walked east across town holding hands, my tears and her sympathetic silence both mute memorials for Ethel and Julius Rosenberg. I began to feel eased. It was obvious to both of us that in the past year we had each moved beyond investigative discussions about loving women. I felt this—something in the frankness with which we held each other as we walked.

That night, I invited Bea to stay over. The rest was surprisingly easy. I made love to a woman for the first time in my very own bed. This was home, feeling the physical tensions of the last months of hope and despair loosen inside of me, as if a long fast had broken. The sense of relief was only lessened by Bea's unresponsiveness. The quiet stillness of her sculptured body was disappointing beside the remembered passion of Ginger.

For the next few months, outside of work, I concentrated my energies on preparations to go to Mexico and being long-distance lovers with Bea. We saw each other every other weekend, on the average, alternating between the YWCA in Philadelphia and New York. Bea had roommates and I had Rhea, who determinedly knew nothing of my sexual life. More often than not, I went to Philadelphia since the Y there was cheaper and had better beds.

Meeting other lesbians was very difficult, except for the bars which I did not go to because I did not drink. One read *The Ladder* and the Daughters of Bilitis newsletter and wondered where all the other gay-girls were. Often, just finding out another woman was gay was enough of a reason to attempt a relationship, to attempt some connection in the name of love without first regard to how ill-matched the two of you might really be. Such were the results of loneliness, and this was certainly the case between Bea and me. For starters, our backgrounds and outlooks on important issues could not have been more different. Her family was old, mainline, white, and monied. Psychologically, she had left very little of them behind. Most importantly, our attitudes toward sex were totally different.

Sexual expression with Bea was a largely theoretical satisfaction, a very pleasant pastime, and one to which she had great intellectual commitment but apparently little visceral response. It was hard to believe her protestations and assurances that this had nothing to do with me. Whatever fears of reprisal from her upper-class family had turned her off, they had been quite successful. Despite our hours of love-making, our most impassioned shared connections were our love of guitars and old music.

I would take the night train to Philly and then a bus to the Arch Street YWCA, where Bea would have rented a room for us for the weekend. The rooms were small and plain and all alike, with single beds.

Bea's face was square and rosy-cheeked, with a rosebud mouth whose corners always pointed down. She had wide, light blue eyes and strong beautiful teeth. Her blonde body was smooth and without fault—small-breasted, long-waisted, with sturdy hips and long smooth legs. It was a body not unlike the ivory statues I used to buy in Oriental import stores when I was in high school, with the money that I stole from my father's pants pockets.

At first, I looked forward to our weekends with wild anticipation. The hope that this time it was going to be different. Bea's acknowledged gayness was some connection, some living reality within the emotional desert around which I existed. And she was always quite honest about what she didn't feel.

So weekend after weekend, in YWCA bed after YWCA bed, I ran my hot searching mouth over her as against a carved mound of smooth stone, until lip-bruised and panting with frustration, I fell back for a brief rest.

"That was really nice," she would say. "I think I almost felt something."

The scenario was always depressingly the same. We were both strong, physically healthy young women with lots of energies. Starting Friday night, I would make almost non-stop love to Bea for two days on our single bed while she sighed sadly. By Sunday noon, distraught and ravenous, I would come up for air, raving like a maniac, a sex fiend, a debaucher of virgins. We would dress to music—Bea had perfect pitch—and then essay forth, blinking, into daylight. Companionable in our spent frustrations, hand in hand, we would go to the Rodin Museum and then get something to eat in a diner before I caught my train back to New York. I grew fond of her forthrightness and her wit. And in a way, we even grew to love each other.

Sometimes to this day, whenever I think of Philadelphia, which is as infrequently as possible, I think of it as a boring grey-stone backdrop to a well-worn triangle, circumscribing the Arch Street YWCA, the Rodin Museum, and the 30th Street Station.

Across the table from me, Bea chewed each mouthful thirty-two times and told me how much she looked forward to our being together again I was beside myself. Every Sunday night, I got onto the train vowing to myself that I would never see her again. That's the way it would be for about a week. Then she would call me or I would call her, and one of us would be on the next Friday train to or from Philly. The prospect of breaching that insurmountable calm endlessly sparked my desire.

By Thanksgiving, we were planning to go to Mexico together. I knew this was a mistake, but I did not have the strength to say no. Finally, two weeks before we were planning to leave, on the way to the station one Sunday evening, I told Bea we had to stop seeing each other. That I was going to Mexico alone. No explanations, no preliminaries. It was self-preservation on my part, and I was horrified at my own cruelty. But I did not know any other way to do it. Bea stood in the gateway of the 30th Street station and wept as I ran for my train.

When I got home I sent her a telegram. It said, "I'M SORRY."

I had believed that if I could bring myself to say it, harsh as it was, that would be the end of it, and I could go off and be guilty in private, as I made last-minute arrangements for my trip. But I had reckoned without Bea's thoroughness and determination.

The whole disastrous affair terminated with Bea coming to New York the following day and camping on the steps of our seventh-floor landing outside the apartment, trying to catch hold of me. I was hiding out at Jean and Alf's place, having been warned by an incredulous Rhea that a weeping girl was trying to find me. Rhea ran interference, making excuses to Bea as she went in and out of the apartment to work. Luckily, I had already quit my job at the Health Center, for Bea had gone there first.

Bea sat on the landing for two days, with quick forays downstairs to the corner foodshop for Cokes and trips to the john. She finally gave up and went back to Philadelphia.

She left me a note saying that what she really wanted to know was why, this way. I couldn't tell her; I didn't know why myself. But I felt like a monster. I had made a desperate bid for self-preservation—or what felt like self-preservation—in the only way I knew how. I hadn't wanted to hurt anyone. But I had. I promised myself never to get involved like that again.

Guilt can be very useful.

For the three days this went on in the hallway, Rhea was her usual quizzical and accepting self. I had to tell her about the affair, couched in the fact that it was now over. What she thought about Bea I never stopped long enough to ask, but what she said made good sense to me.

"Just because you're strong doesn't mean you can let other people depend on you too much. It's not fair to them, because when you can't be what they want they're disappointed, and you feel bad." Rhea was sometimes very wise, just not for herself.

I never forgot that conversation, and we never discussed Bea again. I left for Mexico a week later.

It was eleven months after I had come back from Stamford, and two weeks before my nineteenth birthday.

I leaned back in my airplane seat, in the first skirt I'd bought in two years. The Air France night flight to Mexico City was half-empty. Rhea had made a surprise going-away party for me the night before, but even so I had been hounded by nightmares of arriving at the airport with no clothes on, or having forgotten my suitcases, or my passport, or neglected to buy a ticket. Not until I looked down and saw the lights of the city spread like electric lace across the night, did I actually believe I had gotten out of New York in one piece and under my own steam. Alive.

In the back of my head, I could hear Bea sobbing disconsolately in the stairwell. I felt like I was fleeing New York with the hounds of hell at my heels.

The stewardess was very solicitous of me. She said it was because this was my first flight, and I was so young to be traveling so far alone.

21

From the Palace of Fine Arts to El Angel de la Reforma, along the broad Avenida Insurgentes, lay the central hub of the Districto Federal, Mexico City. It was a sea of strange sounds and smells and experiences that I swam into with delight daily. It took me two days to adjust to the high altitude of the city, and to the realization that I was in a foreign country, alone, with only rudimentary language skills.

The first day I explored tentatively. By the second day, alight with the bustle and easy warmth of the streets, I felt filled with the excitement of curiosity and more and more at home. I walked miles and miles through the city, past modern stores and old museums, and families eating beans and tortillas over a brazier between two buildings.

Moving through street after street filled with people with brown faces had a profound and exhilarating effect upon me, unlike any other experience I had ever known.

Friendly strangers, passing smiles, admiring and questioning glances, the sense of being somewhere I wanted to be and had chosen. Being noticed, and accepted without being known, gave me a social contour and surety as I moved through the city sightseeing, and I felt bold and adventurous and special. I reveled in the attention of the shopkeepers around the hotel, from whom I bought my modest provisions.

"¡Ah, la Señorita Moreña! [*moreña* means dark] buenas dias!" The woman from whom I bought my newspaper on the corner of Reforma reached up and patted my short natural hair. "¡Ay, que bonita! ¿Está la Cubana?"

I smiled in return. Because of my coloring and my haircut, I was frequently asked if I was Cuban. "Gracias, senora," I replied, settling the bright *rebozo* I had bought the day before around my shoulders. "No, yo estoy de Nueva York."

Her bright dark eyes widened in amazement and she patted the back of my hand with her dry wrinkled fingers, still holding the coin I had just given her. "Ay, con Dios, niña," she called after me, as I moved on up the street.

By noon, it amazed me that the streets of a city could be so busy and so friendly at the same time. Even with all the new building going on there was a feeling of color and light, made more festive by the colorful murals decorating the sides of high buildings, public and private. Even the university buildings were covered with mosaic murals in dazzling colors.

Lottery-sellers at every corner, and strolling through Chapultepec Park, with strings of gaily colored tickets pinned to their shirts. Children in uniforms coming home from school in groups, and other children, equally bright-eyed, too poor to go to school, sitting crosslegged with their parents on a blanket in the shadow of a building, cutting out soles for cheap sandals from the worn-out treads of discarded tires.

The National Pawn Shop across from the Seguro Social on Friday at noon, long lines of young government workers redeeming guitars and dancing shoes for the weekend ahead. Wide-eyed toddlers who took my hand and led me over to their mothers' wares, set out upon tables shielded by blankets from the sun. People in the street who smiled without knowing me, just because that was what you did with strangers.

There was a beautiful park called the Alameda which ran for blocks through the middle of the district, from Netzahuacoytl down behind the Palacio de Bellas Artes. Some mornings, I left my hotel as soon as it was light, taking a bus to the center of the city to walk in the Alameda. I would have loved to walk there in the astonishing moonlight, but I had heard that single women did not go out alone after dark in Mexico City, so I spent my evenings those early days in Mexico reading *War and Peace*, which I had never been able to get into before.

I got down from the bus in front of the Fine Arts Museum, breathing in the clean smells of wet bushes and morning blossoms and the beautiful delicate trees. Before I entered the park, I bought a *pan dulce* from a delivery boy pedaling past, his huge sombrero with the upturned brim carefully balanced upon his head and piled high with the tasty little buns, still warm from his mother's ovens.

Marble statues dotted the paths throughout the park, where later on in the day workers from the buildings across the street would take their lunchtime *paseo*. My favorite statue was one of a young naked girl in beige stone, kneeling, closely folded in upon herself, head bent, greeting the dawn. As I walked through the fragrant morning quiet in the Alameda, the nearby sounds of traffic increasing yet dimming, I felt myself unfolding like some large flower, as if the statue of the kneeling girl had come alive, raising her head to look full-faced into the sun. As I stepped out into the early morning flow of the *avenida* I felt the light and beauty of the park shining out of me, and the woman lighting her coals in a brazier on the corner smiled back at it in my face.

It was in Mexico City those first few weeks that I started to
break my life-long habit of looking down at my feet as I walked
along the street. There was always so much to see, and so many
interesting and open faces to read, that I practiced holding my
head up as I walked, and the sun felt hot and good on my face.
Wherever I went, there were brown faces of every hue meeting
mine, and seeing my own color reflected upon the streets in
such great numbers was an affirmation for me that was brand-
new and very exciting. I had never felt visible before, nor even
known I lacked it.

I had not made any friends in Mexico City, although I existed
quite happily on part-English, part-Spanish conversations with
the chambermaid about the weather, my clothes, and the bidet;
with the señora from whom I bought my daily evening meal of
two hot tamales wrapped in cornhusks and a bottle of blue-
labeled milk; and with the day clerk of the small second-class
hotel where I had my tiny room.

At the end of my first week, I went out to the new bemuraled
University City and registered for two courses in the history and
ethnology of Mexico, and in folklore. I began to think of looking around for cheaper and more permanent living accommodations. Even with eating inexpensive foods bought from street
vendors, not being able to cook was cutting into my small store
of money. It also restricted my diet greatly, since I ate only
those foods I could be sure would not give me the diarrhea
which was the visitors' downfall in Mexico City.

One day, after two weeks in and around the District, I traveled south to Cuernavaca by bus to see Frieda Mathews and her
young daughter Tammy. Frieda's name had been given to me by
a friend of Rhea's who had been a nurse with Frieda in the
Lincoln Brigade during the Spanish Civil War. I had been visiting
museums and pyramids, wandering the streets of the city, and
generally satisfying my hunger and curiosity for the feel of this
new place. Although I was feeling more and more at home, I began to feel the need for someone to talk to in English. Classes at
Ciudad Universitaria began the following week.

Cuernavaca was a garden spot south of the District and closer
to sea level, in the Morelos Valley about forty-five miles from
Mexico City.

When I telephoned, Frieda greeted me warmly and immediately invited me down to Cuernavaca to spend the day. She and
Tammy met me at the bus. The weather was warmer and sunnier
than in the District, and there was a much more relaxed air
about the town square.

As soon as the bus pulled into the square, I recognized the tall blond american woman and the tanned smiling young girl beside her. Frieda looked like she sounded over the phone, a calm, intelligent, and forthright woman in her early forties. Frieda and Tammy had lived in Cuernavaca for nine years, and Frieda was always hungry for news from New York, her original home. "Is the Essex Street Market still open, and what are the writers doing?"

We spent the morning talking about mutual acquaintances and then wandered through the markets on Guerrero buying foodstuffs for dinner, which Tammy brought back to their housekeeper to cook. Later, we sat drinking foamy *café con leche* at a table in the open-air cafe that occupied one whole corner of the town square. Strolling musicians were tuning their guitars in the afternoon sun, and the *chamaquitos*, street urchins, descended upon us begging for pennies, then ran away laughing as Tammy engaged them in rapid spanish. In short order, other americans, all of them white and most of them women, strolled over to our table to see who was this new face in town. Frieda introduced me to a host of cordial welcomes.

After the day spent in the easy beauty of Cuernavaca and easy-going company of Frieda and her friends, it took little urging on Frieda's part to persuade me to consider moving down to Cuernavaca. I was still anxious to find cheaper lodgings than the Hotel Fortin. I could commute to the District for classes, she assured me. Many people in Cuernavaca worked in Mexico City, and transportation by bus or group *taximetro* was very inexpensive.

"I think you'll be happier living here than in Mexico City," Frieda offered. "It's a lot quieter. You can probably get one of the small houses in the compound over at Humboldt Number Twenty-four, which is a pretty place to live."

Tammy, who was twelve, was delighted to have somebody come to town who was closer to her age than Frieda and her friends.

"And Jesús can help you with your things from the District," Frieda added. With her divorce settlement, Frieda had bought a small farm in Tepotzlán, a tiny village further up the mountain. Jesús managed the farm, she explained. They had once been lovers. "But that's all quite different now," Frieda said brusquely, as Tammy called to us from the patio to come see her *patoganso*, a duck so big it could have been a goose.

I went to see about the little house in the compound that same afternoon.

I was open to anything. Cuernavaca felt like a gift. The house consisted of one large room, with huge windows facing the mountains, and a bathroom, kitchen, and tiny dining alcove; my own little house with trees and flowers and bushes around a path that led to my own front door, where no one else would enter except by my invitation. The one-and-a-half hour trip over the mountains to make my 8:00 A.M. class in the mornings seemed a minor inconvenience. On the bus back to Mexico City, I made up my mind to move.

Jesús came to pick me up with my bags and my typewriter one afternoon after school. It was late afternoon as we drove around and around the mountain on the new *autopiso* from the Federal District to Cuernavaca. The top of his old Chrysler convertible was down. Mariachi music twanged out of the turned-up radio as we careened around curve after curve, each one revealing a brand-new vista, a new landscape. (And I had once thought of Stamford, Conn., as "the country!") The thunderheads on the horizon as we came around the crest of Morelos mountain shone purple-edged and brilliant in the lowering sun, and I was happier than I'd been in what seemed like a very long time. What was even better, I was wholly conscious that I was.

I settled back against the worn upholstery of the capacious seat. As we rode down into the valley toward Cuernavaca that March evening, with a *mañanitas* blaring from the radio, the back seat full of my bags and typewriter, the screech of Jesús's tires around the curves and his ready reassuring guffaw, I knew I was quite glad to be exactly where I was.

> . . . la luna se oculto,
> Levantate, Amiga mía,
> mira que le amanaceo.

La Señora. La Periodista. La Morenita. La Alta Rubia. La Chica. The people who worked in the compound at Humboldt No. 24 had names for most of the *norteamericanas* who lived and visited there. A bit nickname, a bit designation, a bit endearment. Nobody who was disliked had one. They were never used in anger or displeasure. The Lady. The Newspaperwoman. The Dark One. The Tall Blond. The Little One.

By 1954, Cuernavaca had earned a name as a haven for political and spiritual refugees from the north, a place where american middle-class non-conformists could live more simply, cheaply, and quietly than in Acapulco or Taxco, where all the movie stars went. A small beautiful town, largely supported by the expatriates from many different countries who lived there.

Along Cuernavaca's sleepy streets were iron gates and high adobe walls bright with sun, and with brilliant jacaranda trees dripping their flowers over the walls from inside.

Beside the walls, little boys sat napping with their burros, taking a rest halfway up the hilly packed-mud streets. Behind the iron gates, american Cuernavaca led a complex and sophisticated life.

A high percentage of single women of moderate means, mostly from California and New York, owned shares in the little tourist shops that lined the Plaza; others supplemented whatever income they had by working in those shops, or teaching and nursing a few days a week in Mexico City. Some of these women were divorced and living on alimony; others were nurses like Frieda who had served in the Lincoln Brigade and run into trouble with the american government because of it. Members of the brigade had been granted citizenship by Mexico. There were members of the red-baited Hollywood Ten and their families, whitelisted out of work in the movie industry, and eking out a living in less-expensive Mexico by editing and ghostwriting. There were victims of other McCarthyist purges, still going on in full swing. We had in common many of Rhea's friends, and many of the people I had met while working on the Rosenberg committee in the years before.

For the american colony in Cuernavaca, the political atmosphere was one of guarded alertness. There was not the stench of terror and political repression so present in New York; we were 3,500 miles away. But any idea that immunity from McCarthyism might be conferred by borders had been shattered two years before in the minds of anyone who had ever been the least bit politically active. FBI agents had descended upon Mexico and hustled Morton Sobell, alleged co-conspirator of Ethel and Julius Rosenberg, out of Mexico and right back across the border to stand trial for treason.

Caution and fear of newcomers was everywhere, mixed up with a welcoming excitement at any new face. Expectation of some new political disaster from the north, as yet unspecified, was also everywhere. So were the ripe luscious bougainvillea with their flame-red voluptuous flowers, and the delicate and persistent showers of jacaranda blossoms, with their small white and pink and purple petals, behind which all of these anxieties flourished.

It was here in the breathtaking dawns and quick hill-twilights of Cuernavaca that I learned it really is easier to be quiet in the woods. One morning I came down the hill toward the square at dawn to catch my ride to the District. The birds suddenly cut loose all around me in the unbelievable sweet warm air. I had never heard anything so beautiful and unexpected before. I felt shaken by the waves of song. For the first time in my life, I had an insight into what poetry could be. I could use words to recreate that feeling, rather than to create a dream, which was what so much of my writing had been before.

The little blind bird-boy, Jeroméo, slept on a stone bench next to the bandstand in the center of the square, near his cages of brightly-colored birds for sale. In the pre-dawn darkness, the birds high in the trees sensed the coming of the sun, and as the moist fragrant air filled with an orchestra of song from the birds in the trees surrounding the Plaza, the caged birds filled the square with their singing answer.
Jeroméo went on sleeping.

In the afternoons when I came home from the District I went sightseeing in the Morelos Valley, or sat with Frieda and her friends in the square over coffee. Sometimes I went swimming with them in Ellen Perl's pool.

The women I met through Frieda were older and far more experienced than I. I learned later that they speculated at length in private as to whether or not I was gay, and whether or not I knew it. It never occurred to me that they were gay, or at least bisexual, themselves. I never suspected because a large part of their existence was devoted toward concealing that fact. These women pretended to be straight in a way they never would have pretended to be conservative. Their political courage was far greater than their sexual openness. To my provincially New York and naïve eyes, "gay-girls" were just that—young, obvious, and definitely bohemian. Certainly not progressive, comfortable, matronly, and over forty, with swimming pools, dyed hair, and young second husbands. As far as I knew all the american women in the Plaza were straight, just emancipated.

Weeks later, I mentioned as much to Eudora on our way to the pyramids at Teotíhuacan, and she almost laughed us off the road into a ditch.

22

Eudora. Mexico. Color and light and Cuerna-vaca and Eudora.

At the compound, Easter Saturday, she was just coming out of a week's drinking binge which started with the firing of Robert Oppenheimer, the atomic scientist, in the states. I was full of the Good Friday festivities in Mexico City, which I had attended with Frieda and Tammy the day before. They had gone to Tepotzlán. I was sunning myself on my front lawn.

"Hello, down there! Aren't you overdoing it?" I looked up at the woman whom I had noticed observing me from an upper window in the two-story dwelling at the edge of the compound. She was the only woman I'd seen wearing pants in Mexico except at the pool.

I was pleased that she had spoken. The two women who lived separately in the double house at that end of the compound never appeared at tables in the Plaza. They never spoke as they passed my house on their way to the cars or the pool. I knew one of them had a shop in town called La Señora, which had the most interesting clothes on the Square.

"Haven't you heard, only mad dogs and englishmen go out in the noonday sun?" I shaded my eyes so I could see her better. I was more curious than I had realized.

"I don't burn that easily," I called back. She was framed in the large casement window, a crooked smile on her half-shaded face. Her voice was strong and pleasant, but with a crack in it that sounded like a cold, or too many cigarettes.

"I'm just going to have some coffee. Would you like some?"

I stood, picked up the blanket upon which I'd been lying, and accepted her invitation.

She was waiting in her doorway. I recognized her as the tall grey-haired woman called La Periodista.

"My name's Eudora," she said, extending her hand and holding mine firmly for a moment. "And they call you La Chica, you're here from New York, and you go to the new university."

"Where did you find all that out?" I asked, taken aback. We stepped inside.

"It's my business to find out what goes on," she laughed easily. "That's what reporters do. Legitimate gossip."

Eudora's bright spacious room was comfortable and disheveled. A large easy chair faced the bed upon which she now perched crosslegged, in shorts and polo shirt, smoking, and surrounded by books and newspapers.

Maybe it was her direct manner. Maybe it was the openness with which she appraised me as she motioned me towards the chair. Maybe it was the pants, or the informed freedom and authority with which she moved. But from the moment I walked into her house, I knew Eudora was gay, and that was an unexpected and welcome surprise. It made me feel much more at home and relaxed, even though I was still feeling sore and guilty from my fiasco with Bea, but it was refreshing to know I wasn't alone.

"I've been drinking for a week," she said, "and I'm still a little hung-over, so you'll have to excuse the mess."

I didn't know what to say.

Eudora wanted to know what I was doing in Mexico, young, Black, and with an eye for the ladies, as she put it. That was the second surprise. We shared a good laugh over the elusive cues for mutual recognition among lesbians. Eudora was the first woman I'd met who spoke about herself as a lesbian rather than as "gay," which was a word she hated. Eudora said it was a north american east-coast term that didn't mean anything to her, and what's more most of the lesbians she had known were anything but gay.

When I went to the market that afternoon, I brought back milk and eggs and fruit for her. I invited her to dinner, but she wasn't feeling much like eating, she said, so I fixed my dinner and brought it over and ate with her. Eudora was an insomniac, and we sat talking late late into the night.

She was the most fascinating woman I had ever met.

Born in Texas forty-eight years before, Eudora was the youngest child in an oil-worker's family. She had seven older brothers. Polio as a child had kept her in bed for three years, "so I had a lot of catchin' up to do, and I never knew when to stop."

In 1925, she became the first woman to attend the University of Texas, integrating it by camping out on the university grounds for four years in a tent with her rifle and a dog. Her brothers had studied there, and she was determined to also. "They said they didn't have living accommodations for women," Eudora said, "and I couldn't afford a place in town."

She'd worked in news all her life, both print and radio, and had followed her lover, Franz, to Chicago, where they both worked for the same paper. "She and I were quite a team, all right. Had a lot of high times together, did a lot of foolishness, believed a lot of things.

"Then Franz married a foreign correspondent in Istanbul," Eudora continued, drily, "and I lost my job over a byline on the Scottsboro case." She worked for a while in Texas for a Mexican paper, then moved into Mexico City for them.

When she and Karen, who owned La Señora, were lovers, they had started a bookstore together in Cuernavaca in the more liberal forties. For a while it was a rallying place for disaffected americans. This was how she knew Frieda.

"It was where people came to find out what was really going on in the states. Everybody passed through." She paused. "But it got to be a little too radical for Karen's tastes," Eudora said carefully. "The dress shop suits her better. But that's a whole other mess, and she still owes me money."

"What happened to the bookstore?" I asked, not wanting to pry, but fascinated by her story.

"Oh, lots of things, in very short order. I've always been a hard drinker, and she never liked that. Then when I had to speak my mind in the column about the whole Sobell business, and the newspaper started getting itchy, Karen thought I was going to lose that job. I didn't, but my immigration status was changed, which meant I could still work in Mexico, but after all these years I could no longer own property. That's the one way of getting uppity americans to keep their mouths shut. Don't rock big brother's boat, and we'll let you stay. That was right up Karen's alley. She bought me out and opened the dress shop."

"Is that why you broke up?"

Eudora laughed. "That sounds like New York talk." She was silent for a minute, busying herself with the overflowing ashtray.

"Actually, no," she said finally. "I had an operation, and it was pretty rough for both of us. Radical surgery, for cancer. I lost a breast." Eudora's head was bent over the ashtray, hair falling forward, and I could not see her face. I reached out and touched her hand.

"I'm so sorry," I said.

"Yeah, so am I," she said, matter-of-factly, placing the polished ashtray carefully back on the table beside her bed. She looked up, smiled, and pushed the hair back from her face with the heels of her hands. "There's never enough time to begin with, and still so damn much I want to do."

"How are you feeling now, Eudora?" I remembered my nights on the female surgery floor at Beth David. "Did you have radiation?"

"Yes I did. It's almost two years since the last one, and I'm fine now. The scars are hard to take, though. Not dashing or romantic. I don't much like to look at them myself." She got up, took down her guitar from the wall, and started to tune it. "What folksongs are they teaching you in that fine new university up the mountain?"

Eudora had translated a number of texts on the history and ethnology of Mexico, one of which was a textbook assigned for my history class. She was witty and funny and sharp and insightful, and knew a lot about an enormous number of things. She had written poetry when she was younger, and Walt Whitman was her favorite poet. She showed me some clippings of articles she had written for a memorial-documentary of Whitman. One sentence in particular caught my eye.

I met a man who'd spent his life in thinking, and could understand me no matter what I said. And I followed him to Harleigh in the snow.

The next week was Easter holidays, and I spent part of each afternoon or evening at Eudora's house, reading poetry, learning to play the guitar, talking. I told her about Ginger, and about Bea, and she talked about her and Franz's life together. We even had a game of dirty-word Scrabble, and although I warned her I was a declared champion, Eudora won, thereby increasing my vocabulary no end. She showed me the column she was finishing about the Olmec stone heads, and we talked about the research she was planning to do on African and Asian influences in Mexican art. Her eyes twinkled and her long graceful hands flashed as she talked, and by midweek, when we were not together, I could feel the curves of her cheekbone under my lips as I gave her a quick goodbye kiss. I thought about making love to her, and ruined a whole pot of curry in my confusion. This was not what I had come to Mexico to do.

There was an air about Eudora when she moved that was both delicate and sturdy, fragile and tough, like the snapdragon she resembled when she stood up, flung back her head, and brushed her hair back with the palms of her hands. I was besotted.

Eudora often made fun of what she called my prudishness, and there was nothing she wouldn't talk about. But there was a reserve about her own person, a force-field around her that I did

not know how to pass, a sadness surrounding her that I could
not breach. And besides, a woman of her years and experience—
how presumptuous of me!

We sat talking in her house later and later, over endless cups
of coffee, half my mind on our conversation and half of it
hunting for some opening, some graceful, safe way of getting
closer to this woman whose smell made my earlobes burn. Who,
despite her openness about everything else, turned away from
me when she changed her shirt.

On Thursday night we rehung some of her bark paintings
from Tehuantepec. The overhead fan hummed faintly; there
was a little pool of sweat sitting in one wing of her collarbone. I
almost reached over to kiss it.

"Goddammit!" Eudora had narrowly missed her finger with
the hammer.

"You're very beautiful," I said suddenly, embarrassed at
my own daring. There was a moment of silence as Eudora put
down her hammer.

"So are you, Chica," she said, quietly, "more beautiful than
you know." Her eyes held mine for a minute so I could not turn
away.

No one had ever said that to me before.

It was after 2:00 A.M. when I left Eudora's house, walking
across the grass to my place in the clear moonlight. Once inside
I could not sleep. I tried to read. Visions of Eudora's dear one-
sided grin kept coming between me and the page. I wanted to
be with her, to be close to her, laughing.

I sat on the edge of my bed, wanting to put my arms around
Eudora, to let the tenderness and love I felt burn away the sad
casing around her and speak to her need through the touch of
my hands and my mouth and my body that defined my own.

"It's getting late," she had said. "You look tired. Do you
want to stretch out?" She gestured to the bed beside her. I
came out of my chair like a shot.

"Oh, no, that's all right," I stammered. All I could think of
was that I had not had a bath since morning. "I—I need to take
a shower, anyway."

Eudora had already picked up a book. "Goodnight, Chica,"
she said without looking up.

I jumped up from the edge of my bed and put a light under the water-heater. I was going back.

"What is it, Chica? I thought you were going to bed." Eudora was reclining exactly as I had left her an hour before, propped up on a pillow against the wall, the half-filled ashtray next to her hand and books littering the rest of the three-quarter studio bed. A bright towel hung around her neck against the loose, short-sleeved beige nightshirt.

My hair was still damp from the shower, and my bare feet itched from the dew-wet grass between our houses. I was suddenly aware that it was 3:30 in the morning.

"Would you like some more coffee?" I offered.

She regarded me at length, unsmiling, almost wearily.

"Is that what you came back for, more coffee?"

All through waiting for the *calendador* to heat, all through showering and washing my hair and brushing my teeth, until that very moment, I had thought of nothing but wanting to hold Eudora in my arms, so much that I didn't care that I was also terrified. Somehow, if I could manage to get myself back up those steps in the moonlight, and if Eudora was not already asleep, then I would have done my utmost. That would be my piece of the bargain, and then what I wanted would somehow magically fall into my lap.

Eudora's grey head moved against the bright serape-covered wall behind her, still regarding me as I stood over her. Her eyes wrinkled and she slowly smiled her lopsided smile, and I could feel the warm night air between us collapse as if to draw us together.

I knew then that she had been hoping I would return. Out of wisdom or fear, Eudora waited for me to speak.

Night after night we had talked until dawn in this room about language and poetry and love and the good conduct of living. Yet we were strangers. As I stood there looking at Eudora, the impossible became easier, almost simple. Desire gave me courage, where it had once made me speechless. With almost no thought I heard myself saying,

"I want to sleep with you."

Eudora straightened slowly, pushed the books from her bed with a sweep of her arm, and held out her hand to me.

"Come."

I sat down on the edge of the bed, facing her, our thighs touching. Our eyes were on a level now, looking deeply into each other. I could feel my heart pounding in my ears, and the high steady sound of the crickets.

"Do you know what you're saying?" Eudora asked softly, searching my face. I could smell her like the sharp breath of wildflowers.

"I know," I said, not understanding her question. Did she think I was a child?

"I don't know if I can," she said, still softly, touching the sunken place on her nightshirt where her left breast should have been. "And you don't mind this?"

I had wondered so often how it would feel under my hands, my lips, this different part of her. Mind? I felt my love spread like a shower of light surrounding me and this woman before me. I reached over and touched Eudora's face with my hands.

"Are you sure?" Her eyes were still on my face.

"Yes, Eudora." My breath caught in my throat as if I'd been running. "I'm very sure." If I did not put my mouth upon hers and inhale the spicy smell of her breath my lungs would burst.

As I spoke the words, I felt them touch and give life to a new reality within me, some half-known self come of age, moving out to meet her.

I stood, and in two quick movements slid out of my dress and underclothes. I held my hand down to Eudora. Delight. Anticipation. A slow smile mirroring my own softened her face. Eudora reached over and passed the back of her hand along my thigh. Goose-flesh followed in the path of her fingers.

"How beautiful and brown you are."

She rose slowly. I unbuttoned her shirt and she shrugged it off her shoulders till it lay heaped at our feet. In the circle of lamplight I looked from her round firm breast with its rosy nipple erect to her scarred chest. The pale keloids of radiation burn lay in the hollow under her shoulder and arm down across her ribs. I raised my eyes and found hers again, speaking a tenderness my mouth had no words yet for. She took my hand and placed it there, squarely, lightly, upon her chest. Our hands fell. I bent and kissed her softly upon the scar where our hands had rested. I felt her heart strong and fast against my lips. We fell back together upon her bed. My lungs expanded and my breath deepened with the touch of her warm dry skin. My mouth finally against hers, quick-breathed, fragrant, searching, her hand entwined in my hair. My body took charge from her flesh. Shifting slightly, Eudora reached past my head toward the lamp above us. I caught her wrist. Her bones felt like velvet and quicksilver between my tingling fingers.

"No," I whispered against the hollow of her ear. "In the light."

Sun poured through the jacarandas outside Eudora's window. I heard the faint and rhythmical whirr-whoosh of Tomas's scythe as he cut back the wild banana bushes from the walk down by the pool.

I came fully awake with a start, seeing the impossible. The junebug I had squashed with a newspaper at twilight, so long before, seemed to be moving slowly up the white-painted wall. It would move a few feet up from the floor, fall back, and then start up again. I grabbed for my glasses from the floor where I had dropped them the night before. With my glasses on, I could see that there was a feather-thin line of ants descending from the adobe ceiling down the wall to the floor where the junebug was lying. The ants, in concert, were trying to hoist the carcass straight up the vertical wall on their backs, up to their hole on the ceiling. I watched in fascination as the tiny ants lifted their huge load, moved, lost it, then lifted again.

I half-turned and reached over to touch Eudora lying against my back, one arm curved over our shared pillow. The pleasure of our night flushed over me like sun on the walls of the light-washed colorful room. Her light brown eyes opened, studying me as she came slowly out of sleep, her sculptured lips smiling, a little bit open, revealing the gap beside her front teeth. I traced her mouth with my finger. For a moment I felt exposed, unsure, suddenly wanting reassurance that I had not been found wanting. The morning air was still dew-damp, and the smell of our loving lay upon us.

As if reading my thoughts, Eudora's arm came down around my shoulders, drawing me around and to her, tightly, and we lay holding each other in the Mexican morning sunlight that flooded through her uncovered casement windows. Tomas, the caretaker, sang in soft Spanish, keeping time with his scythe, and the sounds drifted in to us from the compound below.

"What an ungodly hour," Eudora laughed, kissing the top of my head and jumping over me with a long stride. "Aren't you hungry?" With her towel around her neck, Eudora made *huevos*, scrambled eggs Mexican-style, and real *café con leche* for our breakfast. We ate at the gaily painted orange table between the tiny kitchen and her bedroom, smiling and talking and feeding each other from our common plate.

There was room for only one of us at the square shallow sink in the kitchen. As I washed dishes to insure an ant-free afternoon, Eudora leaned on the doorpost, smoking lazily. Her hipbones flared like wings over her long legs. I could feel her quick breath on the side of my neck as she watched me. She dried the dishes, and hung the towel over a tin mask on the kitchen cabinet.

"Now let's go back to bed," she muttered, reaching for me through the Mexican shirt I had borrowed to throw over myself. "There's more."

By this time the sun was passing overhead. The room was full of reflected light and the heat from the flat adobe over us, but the wide windows and the lazy ceiling fan above kept the sweet air moving. We sat in bed sipping iced coffee from a pewter mug.

When I told Eudora I didn't like to be made love to, she raised her eyebrows. "How do you know?" she said, and smiled as she reached out and put down our coffee cup. "That's probably because no one has ever really made love to you before," she said softly, her eyes wrinkling at the corners, intense, desiring.

Eudora knew many things about loving women that I had not yet learned. Day into dusk. A brief shower. Freshness. The comfort and delight of her body against mine. The ways my body came to life in the curve of her arms, her tender mouth, her sure body—gentle, persistent, complete.

We run up the steep outside steps to her roof, and the almost full moon flickers in the dark center wells of her eyes. Kneeling, I pass my hands over her body, along the now-familiar place below her left shoulder, down along her ribs. A part of her. The mark of the Amazon. For a woman who seems spare, almost lean, in her clothing, her body is ripe and smooth to the touch. Beloved. Warm to my coolness, cool to my heat. I bend, moving my lips over her flat gentle stomach to the firm rising mound beneath.

On Monday, I went back to school. In the next month, Eudora and I spent many afternoons together, but her life held complications about which she would say little.

Eudora had been all over Mexico. She regaled me with tales of her adventures. She seemed always to have lived her life as if it were a story, a little grander than ordinary. Her love of Mexico, her adopted land, was deep and compelling, like an answer to my grade-school fantasies. She knew a great deal about the folkways and beliefs of the different peoples who had swept across the country in waves long ago, leaving their languages and a small group of descendants to carry on the old ways.

We went for long rides through the mountains in her Hudson convertible. We went to the Brincas, the traditional Moorish dances in Tepotzlán. She told me about the Olmec stone heads of African people that were being found in Tabasco, and the ancient contacts between Mexico and Africa and Asia that were just now coming to light. We talked about the legend of the China Poblana, the Asian-looking patron saint of Puebla. Eudora could savor what was Zapotec, Toltec, Mixtec, Aztec in the culture, and how much had been so terribly destroyed by Europeans.

"That genocide rivals the Holocaust of World War II," she asserted.

She talked about the nomadic Lacondonian Indians, who were slowly disappearing from the land near Comitán in Chiapas, because the forests were going. She told me how the women in San Cristobál de las Casas give the names of catholic saints to their goddesses, so that they and their daughters can pray and make offerings in peace at the forest shrines without offending the catholic church.

She helped me plan a trip south, to Oaxaca and beyond, through San Cristobál to Guatemala, and gave me the names of people with whom I could stay right through to the border. I planned to leave when school was over, and secretly, more and more, hoped she could come with me.

Despite all the sightseeing I had done, and all the museums and ruins I had visited, and the books I had read, it was Eudora who opened those doors for me leading to the heart of this country and its people. It was Eudora who showed me the way to the Mexico I had come looking for, that nourishing land of light and color where I was somehow at home.

"I'd like to come back here and work for a while," I said, as Eudora and I watched women dying wool in great vats around the market. "If I can get papers."

"Chica, you can't run away to this country or it will never let you go. It's too beautiful. That's what the *café con leche* crowd can never admit to themselves. I thought it'd be easier here, myself, to live like I wanted to, say what I wanted to say, but it isn't. It's just easier not to, that's all. Sometimes I think I should have stayed and fought it out in Chicago. But the winters were too damned cold. And gin was too damned expensive." She laughed and pushed back her hair.

As we got back into the car to drive home, Eudora was unusually quiet. Finally, as we came over the tip of Morelos, she said, as if we'd continued our earlier conversation, "But it would be good if you came back here to work. Just don't plan on staying too long."

Eudora and I only went to the Plaza once together. Although she knew the people who hung out there, she disliked most of them. She said it was because they had sided with Karen. "Frieda's all right," she said, "but the rest of them don't deserve a pit to hiss in."

We sat at a small table for two, and Jeroméo ambled over with his bird cages to show his wares to the newcomers. The ever-present *chamaquitos* came to beg *centavos* and errands. Even the strolling mariachi players passed by to see if we were a likely prospect for serenading. But only Tammy, irrepressible and pre-adolescent, bounded over to our table and leaned possessively against it, eager for conversation.

"Are you coming shopping with me tomorrow?" she inquired. We were going to buy a turtle to keep her duck company.

I told her yes, hugged her, and then patted her fanny. "See you tomorrow," I said.

"Now the tongues can wag again," Eudora said, bitterly. I looked at her questioningly.

"Nobody knows anything about us," I said, lightly. "And besides, everybody minds their own business around here."

Eudora looked at me for a moment as if she was wondering who I was.

The sun went down and Jeroméo covered his birds. The lights on the bandstand came on, and Maria went around, lighting candles on the tables. Eudora and I paid our bill and left, walking around the closed market and down Guerrero hill toward Humboldt No. 24. The air was heavy with the smell of flowers and woodfire, and the crackle of frying grasshoppers from the vendors' carts lining Guerrero hill.

The next afternoon when Tammy and I came from the market, we joined Frieda and her friends at their table. Ellen was there, with her cat, and Agnes with her young husband Sam, who was always having to go to the border for something or other.

"Did we interrupt something?" I asked, since they had stopped talking.

"No, dear, just old gossip," Frieda said, drily.

"I see you're getting to know everybody in town," Agnes said brightly, sitting forward with a preliminary smile. I looked up to see Frieda frowning at her.

"We were just saying how much better Eudora looks these days," Frieda said, with finality, and changed the subject. "Do you kids want *café* or *helada*?"

It bothered me that Frieda sometimes treated me like her peer and confidante, and at other times like Tammy's contemporary.

Later, I walked Frieda and Tammy home, and just before I turned off, Frieda said off-handedly, "Don't let them razz you about Eudora, she's a good woman. But she can be trouble."

I pondered her words all the way up to the compound.

That spring, McCarthy was censured. The Supreme Court decision on the desegregation of schools was announced in the english newspaper, and for a while all of us seemed to go crazy with hope for another kind of america. Some of the *café con leche* crowd even talked about going home.

SUPREME COURT OF U. S. DECIDES AGAINST SEPARATE EDUCATION FOR NEGROES. I clutched the Saturday paper and read again. It wasn't even a headline. Just a box on the lower front page.

I hurried down the hill towards the compound. It all felt monumental and confusing. The Rosenbergs were dead. But this case which I had only been dimly aware of through the NAACP's *Crisis*, could alter the whole racial climate in the states. The supreme court had spoken. For me. It had spoken in the last century, and I had learned its "separate but equal" decision in school. Now something had actually changed, might actually change. Eating ice cream in Washington, D. C. was not the point; kids in the south being able to go to school was.

Could there possibly, after all, be some real and fruitful relationship between me and that malevolent force to the north of this place?

The court decision in the paper in my hand felt like a private promise, some message of vindication particular to me. Yet everybody in the Plaza this morning had also been talking about it, and the change this could make in american life.

For me, walking hurriedly back to my own little house in this land of color and dark people who said *negro* and meant something beautiful, who noticed me as I moved among them—this decision felt like a promise of some kind that I half-believed in, in spite of myself, a possible validation.

Hope. It was not that I expected it to alter radically the nature of my living, but rather that it put me actively into a context that felt like progress, and seemed part and parcel of the wakening that I called *Mexico*.

It was in Mexico that I stopped feeling invisible. In the streets, in the buses, in the markets, in the Plaza, in the particular attention within Eudora's eyes. Sometimes, half-smiling, she would scan my face without speaking. It made me feel like she was the first person who had ever looked at me, ever seen who I was. And not only did she see me, she loved me, thought me beautiful. This was no accidental collision.

I never saw Eudora actually drinking, and it was easy for me to forget that she was an alcoholic. The word itself meant very little to me besides derelicts on the Bowery. I had never known anyone with a drinking problem before. We never discussed it, and for weeks she would be fine while we went exploring together.

Then something, I never knew what, would set her off. Sometimes she'd disappear for a few days, and the carport would be empty when I came from school.

I hung around the compound in those afternoons, waiting to see her car drive in the back gate. Once I asked her afterwards where she'd been.

"In every *cantina* in Tepotzlán," she said matter-of-factly. "They know me." Her eyes narrowed as she waited for me to speak.

I did not dare to question her further.

She would be sad and quiet for a few days. And then we would make love.

Wildly. Beautifully. But it only happened three times.

Classes at the university ended. I made my plans to go south—Guatemala. I soon realized that Eudora was not coming with me. She had developed bursitis, and was often in a lot of pain. Sometimes in the early morning I heard furious voices coming through Eudora's open windows. Hers and La Señora's.

I gave up my little house with its simple, cheerful long-windowed room, and stored my typewriter and extra suitcase

at Frieda's house. I was going to spend my last evening with
Eudora, then take the second-class bus at dawn south to Oaxaca.
It was a fifteen-hour trip.

Tomás's burro at the gate. Loud voices beneath the birdsong
in the compound. La Señora almost knocking me over as she
swept past me down Eudora's steps. Tomás standing in Eudora's
entryway. On the orange table an unopened bottle of pale
liquor with no label.

"Eudora! What happened?" I cried. She ignored me, speaking
to Tomás in spanish, "And don't give La Señora anything of
mine again, understand? Here!" She handed him two pesos
from the wallet on the table.

"Con su permiso," he said with relief, and left quickly.

"Eudora, what's wrong?" I moved toward her, and she
caught me at arm's length.

"Go home, Chica. Don't get involved in this."

"Involved in what? What's going on?" I shrugged off her
hands.

"She thinks she can steal my bookstore, ruin my life, and still
have me around whenever she wants me. But she's not going to
get away with it any more. I'm going to get my money!" Eudora hugged me tightly for a moment, then pushed me away.
There was a strange acrid smell upon her.

"Goodbye, Chica. Go on back to Frieda's house. This doesn't
concern you. And have a good trip. When you come back next
time we'll go to Jalisco, to Guadalajara, or maybe up to Yuca-
tan. They're starting a new dig there I'm going to cover. . ."

"Eudora, I can't leave you like this. Please. Let me stay!" If
only I could hold her. I reached out to touch her again, and Eudora whirled away, almost tripping over the table.

"No, I said." Her voice was nasty, harsh, like gravel. "Get
out! What makes you think you can come into someone's life
on a visa and expect. . ."

I flinched in horror at her tone. Then I recognized the smell
as tequila, and I realized she had been drinking already. Maybe
it was the look on my face that stopped her. Eudora's voice
changed. Slowly, carefully—almost gently—she said, "You can't
handle this, Chica. I'll be all right. But I want you to leave, right
now, because it's going to get worse, and I do not want you
around to see it. Please. Go."

It was as clear and as direct as anything Eudora had ever said
to me. There was anger and sadness beneath the surface of her
words that I still did not understand. She picked up the bottle

from the table and flopped into the armchair heavily, her back to me. I had been dismissed.

I wanted to burst into tears. Instead, I picked up my suitcase. I stood there, feeling like I'd been kicked in the stomach, feeling afraid, feeling useless.

Almost as if I'd spoken, Eudora's voice came muffled through the back of the armchair.

"I said I'll be all right. Now go."

I moved forward and kissed the top of her tousled head, her spice-flower smells now mixed with the acrid smell of tequila.

"All right, Eudora, I'm going. Goodbye. But I'm coming back. In three weeks, I'll be back."

It was not only a cry of pain, but a new determination to finish something I had begun, to stick with—what? A commitment my body had made? or with the tenderness which flooded through me at the curve of her head over the back of the chair?

To stick with something that had passed between us, and not lose myself. And not lose myself.

Eudora had not ignored me. Eudora had not made me invisible. Eudora had acted directly towards me.

She had sent me away.

I was hurt, but not lost. And in that moment, as in the first night when I held her, I felt myself pass beyond childhood, a woman connecting with other women in an intricate, complex, and ever-widening network of exchanging strengths.

"Goodbye, Eudora."

When I arrived back in Cuernavaca just before the rains—tired, dirty, and exhilarated—I headed for Frieda's house and my clean clothes. She and Tammy had just come in from the farm in Tepotzlán.

"How's Eudora?" I asked Frieda, as Tammy fetched us cool drinks from the kitchen.

"She's left town, moved up to the District, finally. I hear she's reporting for a new daily up there."

Gone. "Where's she living?" I asked dully.

"Nobody has her address," Frieda said, quickly. "I understand there was one hell of a brawl up at the compound between her and La Señora. But evidently they must have gotten their business settled, because Eudora left soon afterwards. It all happened right after you left." Frieda sipped her *fresca* slowly. Glancing at me, she took some change from her pocket and sent Tammy to the market for bread.

I carefully kept what I hoped was an impassive expression on
my face as I toyed with my fruit drink, screaming inside. But
Frieda put her drink down, leaned forward, and patted me on
the arm reassuringly.

"Now don't worry about her," she said kindly. "That was the
best thing in the world Eudora could have done for herself, getting out of this fishbowl. If I wasn't afraid of losing Tammy to
her father in the states, I think I'd leave tomorrow." She settled
back in her chair, and fixed me with her level, open gaze.

"Anyway, you're going back home next week, aren't you?"

"Yes," I said, knowing what she was saying and that she was
quite right.

"But I hope to come back some day." I thought of the ruins
at Chichen-Itzá, of the Olmec heads in Tabasco, and Eudora's
excited running commentaries.

"I'm sure you will, then," Frieda said, encouragingly.

I returned to New York on the night of July 4th. The humid
heat was oppressive after the dry hot climate of Mexico. As I
got out of the taxi on Seventh Street, the sound of firecrackers
was everywhere. They sounded thinner and higher than the fire-
works in Mexico.

23 I remember how being young and Black and
gay and lonely felt. A lot of it was fine, feeling
I had the truth and the light and the key, but a
lot of it was purely hell.

There were no mothers, no sisters, no heroes. We had to do it
alone, like our sister Amazons, the riders on the loneliest out-
posts of the kingdom of Dahomey. We, young and Black and
fine and gay, sweated out our first heartbreaks with no school
nor office chums to share that confidence over lunch hour. Just
as there were no rings to make tangible the reason for our happy secret smiles, there were no names nor reason given or shared
for the tears that messed up the lab reports or the library bills.

We were good listeners, and never asked for double dates, *but
didn't we know the rules*? Why did we always seems to think
friendships between women were important enough to *care*
about? Always we moved in a necessary remoteness that made
"What did you do this weekend?" seem like an impertinent

question. We discovered and explored our attention to women alone, sometimes in secret, sometimes in defiance, sometimes in little pockets that almost touched ("Why are those little Black girls always either whispering together or fighting?") but always alone, against a greater aloneness. We did it cold turkey, and although it resulted in some pretty imaginative tough women when we survived, too many of us did not survive at all.

I remember Muff, who sat on the same seat in the same dark corner of the Pony Stable Bar drinking the same gin year after year. One day she slipped off onto the floor and died of a stroke right there between the stools. We found out later her real name was Josephine.

During the fifties in the Village, I didn't know the few other Black women who were visibly gay at all well. Too often we found ourselves sleeping with the same white women. We recognized ourselves as exotic sister-outsiders who might gain little from banding together. Perhaps our strength might lay in our fewness, our rarity. That was the way it was Downtown. And Uptown, meaning the land of Black people, seemed very far away and hostile territory.

Diane was fat, and Black, and beautiful, and knew it long before it became fashionable to think so. Her cruel tongue was used to great advantage, spilling out her devastatingly uninhibited wit to demolish anyone who came too close to her; that is, when she wasn't busy deflowering the neighborhood's resident virgins. One day I noticed her enormous bosom which matched my own and it felt quite comforting rather than competitive. It was clothed in a CCNY sweatshirt, and I realized in profound shock that someone else besides me in the Village gay-girl scene was a closet student at one of the Uptown (meaning past 14th Street) colleges. We would rather have died than mention classes, or tests, or any books other than those everyone else was discussing. This was the fifties and the gulf between the Village gay scene and the college crowd was sharper and far more acrimonious than any town-gown war.

There were not enough of us. But we surely tried. I remember thinking for a while that I was the only Black lesbian living in the Village, until I met Felicia. Felicia, with the face of a spoiled nun, skinny and sharp-brown, sat on my sofa on Seventh Street, with her enormous eyelashes that curled back upon themselves twice. She was bringing me a pair of Siamese cats that had terrorized her junkie friends who were straight and

lived on a houseboat with the two cats until they brought their
new baby home from the hospital and both cats went bananas
back and forth all over the boat, jumping over everything including the box that the baby screamed in, because Siamese
cats are very jealous. So, instead of drowning the cats, they
gave them to Felicia whom I ran into having a beer at the Bagatelle that night and when Muriel mentioned I liked cats, Flee
insisted on bringing them over to my house right then and
there. She sat on my sofa with her box of cats and her curly
eyelashes and I thought to myself, "if she must wear false eyelashes you'd think she'd make them less obviously false."

We soon decided that we were really sisters, which was much
more than friends or buddies, particularly when we discovered
while reminiscing about the bad days that we had gone to the
same catholic school for six months in the first grade.

I remembered her as the tough little kid in 1939 who came
into class in the middle of winter, disturbing our neat tight
boredom and fear, bringing her own. Sister Mary of Perpetual
Help seated her beside me because I had a seat to myself in the
front row, being both bad-behaved and nearsighted. I remembered this skinny little kid who made my life hell. She pinched
me all day long, all the time, until she vanished sometime around
St. Swithin's Day, a godsent reward I thought, for what, I
couldn't imagine, but it almost turned me back to god and
prayer again.

Felicia and I came to love each other very much, even though
our physical relationship was confined to cuddling. We were
both part of the "freaky" bunch of lesbians who weren't into
role-playing, and who the butches and femmes, Black and white,
disparaged with the term Ky-Ky, or AC/DC. Ky-Ky was the
same name that was used for gay-girls who slept with johns for
money. Prostitutes.

Flee loved to snuggle in bed, but sometimes she hurt my
feelings by saying I had shaggy breasts. And too, besides, Flee
and I were always finding ourselves in bed together with other
people, usually white women.

Then I thought we were the only gay Black women in the
world, or at least in the Village, which at the time was a state of
mind extending all the way from river to river below 14th
Street, and in pockets throughout the area still known as the
Lower East Side.

I had heard tales from Flee and others about the proper
Black ladies who came downtown on Friday night after the last
show at Small's Paradise to find a gay-girl to go muff-diving

with, and bring her back up to Convent Avenue to sleep over while their husbands went hunting, fishing, golfing, or to an Alpha's weekend. But I only met one once, and her pressed hair and all too eagerly interested husband who had accompanied her this particular night to the Bagatelle, where I met her over a daiquiri and a pressed knee, turned me off completely. And this was pretty hard to do in those days because it seemed an eternity between warm beds in the cold mornings seven flights up on Seventh Street. So I told her that I never traveled above 23rd Street. I could have said 14th Street, but she had already found out that I went to college; therefore I thought 23rd was safe enough because CCNY Downtown was there. That was the last bastion of working-class academia allowed.

Downtown in the gay bars I was a closet student and an invisible Black. Uptown at Hunter I was a closet dyke and a general intruder. Maybe four people altogether knew I wrote poetry, and I usually made it pretty easy for them to forget.

It was not that I didn't have friends, and good ones. There was a loose group of young lesbians, white except for Flee and I, who hung out together, apart from whatever piece of the straight world we each had a separate place in. We not only believed in the reality of sisterhood, that word which was to be so abused two decades later, but we also tried to put it into practice, with varying results. We all cared for and about each other, sometimes with more or less understanding, regardless of who was entangled with whom at any given time, and there was always a place to sleep and something to eat and a listening ear for anyone who wandered into the crew. And there was always somebody calling you on the telephone, to interrupt the fantasies of suicide. That is as good a working definition of friend as most.

However imperfectly, we tried to build a community of sorts where we could, at the very least, survive within a world we correctly perceived to be hostile to us; we talked endlessly about how best to create that mutual support which twenty years later was being discussed in the women's movement as a brand-new concept. Lesbians were probably the only Black and white women in New York City in the fifties who were making any real attempt to communicate with each other; we learned lessons from each other, the values of which were not lessened by what we did not learn.

For both Flee and me, it seemed that loving women was something that other Black women just didn't do. And if they did, then it was in some fashion and in some place that was totally inaccessible to us, because we could never find them. Except for Saturday nights in the Bagatelle, where neither Flee nor I was stylish enough to be noticed.

(My straight Black girlfriends, like Jean and Crystal, either ignored my love for women, considered it interestingly avant-garde, or tolerated it as just another example of my craziness. It was allowable as long as it wasn't too obvious and didn't reflect upon them in any way. At least my being gay kept me from being a competitor for whatever men happened to be upon their horizons. It also made me much more reliable as a confidante. I never asked for anything more.)

But only on the full moon or every other Wednesday was I ever convinced that I really wanted it different. A bunch of us—maybe Nicky and Joan and I—would all be standing around having a beer at the Bagatelle, trying to decide whether to inch onto the postage-stamp dance floor for a slow intimate fish, garrison belt to pubis and rump to rump (but did we really want to get that excited after a long weekend with work tomorrow?), when I'd say sorry but I was tired and would have to leave now, which in reality meant I had an already late paper for english due the next day and needed to work on it all that night.

That didn't happen too often because I didn't go to the Bag very much. It was the most popular gay-girl's bar in the Village, but I hated beer, and besides the bouncer was always asking me for my ID to prove I was twenty-one, even though I was older than the other women with me. Of course "you can never tell with Colored people." And we would all rather die than have to discuss the fact that it was because I was Black, since, of course, gay people weren't racists. After all, didn't they know what it was like to be oppressed?

Sometimes we'd pass Black women on Eighth Street—*the invisible but visible sisters*—or in the Bag or at Laurel's, and our glances might cross, but we never looked into each other's eyes. We acknowledged our kinship by passing in silence, looking the other way. Still, we were always on the lookout, Flee and I, for that telltale flick of the eye, that certain otherwise prohibited openness of expression, that definiteness of voice which would suggest, I think she's gay. *After all, doesn't it take one to know one?*

I was gay and Black. The latter fact was irrevocable: armor, mantle, and wall. Often, when I had the bad taste to bring that fact up in a conversation with other gay-girls who were not Black, I would get the feeling that I had in some way breached some sacred bond of gayness, a bond which I always knew was not sufficient for me.

This was not to deny the closeness of our group, nor the mutual aid of those insane, glorious, and contradictory years. It is only to say that I was acutely conscious—from the ID "problem" at the Bag on Friday nights to the summer days at Gay Head Beach where I was the only one who wouldn't worry about burning—that my relationship as a Black woman to our shared lives was different from theirs, and would be, gay or straight. The question of acceptance had a different weight for me.

In a paradoxical sense, once I accepted my position as different from the larger society as well as from any single sub-society— Black or gay—I felt I didn't have to try so hard. To be accepted. To look femme. To be straight. To look straight. To be proper. To look "nice." To be liked. To be loved. To be approved. What I didn't realize was how much harder I had to try merely to stay alive, or rather, to stay human. How much stronger a person I became in that trying.

But in this plastic, anti-human society in which we live, there have never been too many people buying fat Black girls born almost blind and ambidextrous, gay or straight. Unattractive, too, or so the ads in *Ebony* and *Jet* seemed to tell me. Yet I read them anyway, in the bathroom, on the newsstand, at my sister's house, whenever I got a chance. It was a furtive reading, but it was an affirmation of some part of me, however frustrating.

If nobody's going to dig you too tough anyway, it really doesn't matter so much what you dare to explore. I had already begun to learn that when I left my parents' house.

Like when your Black sisters on the job think you're crazy and collect money between themselves to buy you a hot comb and straightening iron on their lunch hour and stick it anonymously into your locker in the staff room, so that later when you come down for a coffee break and open your locker the damn things fall out on the floor with a clatter and all ninety-five percent of your library co-workers who are very very white want to know what it's all about.

Like when your Black brother calls you a ball-buster and tricks you up into his apartment and tries to do it to you against the kitchen cabinets just, as he says, to take you down a peg or two, when all the time you'd only gone up there to begin with fully intending to get a little in the first place (because all the girls I knew who were possibilities were too damn complicating, and I was plain and simply horny as hell). I finally got out of being raped although not mauled by leaving behind a ring and a batch of lies and it was the first time in my life since I'd left my parents' house that I was in a physical situation which I couldn't handle physically—in other words, the bastard was stronger than I was. It was an instantaneous consciousness-raiser.

As I say, when the sisters think you're crazy and embarrassing; and the brothers want to break you open to see what makes you work inside; and the white girls look at you like some exotic morsel that has just crawled out of the walls onto their plate (but don't they love to rub their straight skirts up against the edge of your desk in the college literary magazine office after class); and the white boys all talk either money or revolution but can never quite get it up—then it doesn't really matter too much if you have an Afro long before the word even existed.

Pearl Primus, the African-American dancer, had come to my high school one day and talked about African women after class, and how beautiful and natural their hair looked curling out into the sun, and as I sat there listening (one of fourteen Black girls in Hunter High School) I thought, that's the way god's mother must have looked and I want to look like that too so help me god. In those days I called it a natural, and kept calling it natural when everybody else called it crazy. It was a strictly homemade job done by a Sufi Muslim on 125th Street, trimmed with the office scissors and looking pretty raggedy. When I came home from school that day my mother beat my behind and cried for a week.

Even for years afterward white people would stop me on the street or particularly in Central Park and ask if I was Odetta, a Black folksinger whom I did not resemble at all except that we were both big Black beautiful women with natural heads.

Besides my father, I am the darkest one in my family and I've worn my hair natural since I finished high school.

Once I moved to East Seventh Street, every morning that I had the fifteen cents I would stop into the Second Avenue Griddle on the corner of St. Mark's Place on my way to the subway and school and buy an english muffin and coffee. When I didn't have the money, I would just have coffee. It was a tiny little counter place run by an old Jewish man named Sol who'd been a seaman (among other things) and Jimmy, who was Puerto Rican and washed dishes and who used to remind Sol to save me the hard englishes on Monday; I could have them for a dime.

Toasted and dripping butter, those english muffins and coffee
were frequently the high point of my day, and certainly enough
to get me out of bed many mornings and into the street on that
long walk to the Astor Place subway. Some days it was the only
reason to get up, and lots of times I didn't have money for anything else. For over eight years, we shot a lot of bull over that
counter, and exchanged a lot of ideas and daily news, and most
of my friends knew who I meant when I talked about Jimmy
and Sol. Both guys saw my friends come and go and never said
a word about my people, except once in a while to say, "your
girlfriend was in here; she owes me a dime and tell her don't
forget we close exactly at seven."

So on the last day before I finally moved away from the Lower East Side after I got my master's from library school, I went
in for my last english muffin and coffee and to say goodbye to
Sol and Jimmy in some unemotional and acceptable-to-me way.
I told them both I'd miss them and the old neighborhood, and
they said they were sorry and why did I have to go? I told them
I had to work out of the city, because I had a fellowship for
Negro students. Sol raised his eyebrows in utter amazement,
and said, "Oh? I didn't know you was cullud!"

I went around telling that story for a while, although a lot of
my friends couldn't see why I thought it was funny. But this is
all about how very difficult it is at times for people to see who
or what they are looking at, particularly when they don't want
to.

Or maybe it does take one to know one.

24   It seemed preordained that Muriel and I should
meet.

When Ginger and I had been getting to know
each other over the cutting-room X-ray machines in the heat
and stink and noise of Keystone Electronics, she was constantly
telling me about this crazy kid called Mo who had worked at
my machine a year or so before. (It was her way of letting me
know that she knew I was gay and it was all right with her.)

"Yeah, she sure was a lot like you."

"How do you mean; did she look like me?"

"Very funny." Ginger cut her doll-baby-round eyes at me.
"She's white. Italian. But both you-all have that easy way about

you, and that soft way of talking. 'Cept you're this slick kitty from the city and she's a strictly local product. Used to say her father never let her smell the night air 'til she was eighteen.

"She wrote poetry, too. All-a-time, even on lunch hour."

"Oh." Somehow I knew there was more. What Ginger couldn't bring herself to tell me was that Muriel liked girls.

I saw Ginger one last time before I left for Mexico. She told me that her friend Mo had come back to live in Stamford because she had had a nervous breakdown in New York.

During the time I was in Mexico, Muriel was slowly crawling out from under the basket of shock treatments she had been thrust into. When she began seeing her friends again in Stamford, Ginger made sure she told her about "this crazy kid from New York City who worked your old machine a year before and who wrote poetry, too."

When I returned to New York from Mexico, I returned full of sun and great determination to re-order my life and someday get back to Mexico and, of course, Eudora. I moved back into my old Seventh Street walk-up and started the discouraging work of job-hunting.

One Sunday evening, the telephone rang, and Rhea answered.

"One of your cool-voiced young women," she said, handing me the phone with a smile. It was Ginger, whose smoky tones sounded anything but cool to me.

"H'ya doin', kiddo?" she began. "I have somebody here who wants to meet you." There was a short pause and then a little chuckle, and then a high, nervous voice saying, "Hello? Audre?"

We made a date.

As I opened the door into the malty dusk of the Page Three, it was still early, and Muriel was the only person standing at the bar. She looked like no one I had ever seen living in Stamford while I was there. Her mid-brown eyes were large and almond-shaped, with thick lashes that outlined each eye with darkness. They peered from a high and flat-cheeked face whose paleness was intensified by the almost straight dark hair that framed her head like a monk's cut, or an inverted bowl. Thick black eyebrows drew together like a scowl.

As usual, I was a little bit late, and she was waiting. Muriel always seemed shorter to me because of the way she stood, shoulders hunched and all folded in upon herself. She held a bottle of beer and a cigarette in her left hand, the pinky of which sported a wide silver band, and was perched archly upon its neighbor. I came to think of this typical stance of hers as Muriel's fetal-finger pose.

Her black turtleneck sweater fell low over her slightly rounded tummy, clad in a pair of well-creased woolen slacks, black with a fine white pinstripe. A soft black beret was pulled slightly to one side of her head, and just beneath her straight thick hair, tiny gold dots sparkled from the lobes of her barely visible ears.

On the bar beside her lay a worn suede jacket, and on top of that a pair of black leather fur-lined gloves. There was something romantically archaic about her sharp contrasts, and the neat polish on her black-laced oxford shoes made her seem vulnerable and schoolgirlish.

I thought she looked quite odd. Then, recalling the days that Gennie and I had wandered the streets together in our adventurous scenarios, I suddenly realized that Muriel had dressed for being a gambler.

What looked like a malocclusion was only a gap between her front teeth. It became visible as Muriel slowly smiled, charging her face with a great sweetness. The tight scowl disappeared. Her hand was dry and warm as I shook it, and I saw how very beautiful her eyes were when they came alive.

I bought a beer and we moved to the front and sat at a table.

"Those look like gambling pants," I said.

She smiled shyly, pleased. "Yeah, that's right. How'd you know? Not many people notice things like that."

I smiled back. "Well, I had a friend once and we used to get dressed up a lot, all the time." I surprised myself; usually I never talked about Gennie.

She told me a little bit about herself and her life; how she had come to New York City two years ago shortly after her friend, Naomi, had died; how she had fallen in love here, gotten "sick," and gone home again. She was twenty-three years old. She and Naomi had met in high school. I said I was thirty-five.

Then, I told her a little bit about Gennie. And on that first Sunday night in the Page Three on Seventh Avenue, Muriel and I put our heads forehead to forehead, over a small table in the front, and shed a few tears together over our dead girls.

We shyly exchanged the thin sheaf of poems we each had brought as an introductory offering. Once on the street, we promised to write to each other as we separated, Muriel going off to meet Ginger and catch the train back to Stamford.

"Here, take my gloves," she'd said, impulsively, just as she ran into the subway. "Your hands are gonna get cold walking home." I hesitated as she tucked the suede gloves into my hands with an almost pleading smile. "Keep them for me till next time." Then she was gone.

Something in her face reminded me of Gennie giving me her notebooks.

The strongest and most lasting sense I had of Muriel after she was gone was of great sweetness hidden, and a vulnerability which surpassed even my own. Her gentle voice belying her dour appearance. I was intrigued by her combination of opposites, by her making no attempt to hide her weaknesses, nor even seeming to consider them shameful or suspect. Muriel radiated a quiet self-knowledge which I mistook for self-acceptance.

Her sense of humor was sudden and appealing, with only a trace of the gallows behind it, and her frequent joking asides were insightful and without malice.

From our very first meeting and without explanation, Muriel made me feel that she was understanding whatever I was saying, and, given the massive weight of my inarticulate pain, a great deal of all that I could not yet put into words.

Rhea was still up as I came back into the house, whistling.

"What's making you so happy all of a sudden?" she asked jokingly, and I realized that for the first time since I'd come home from Mexico, I felt lighthearted and excited again.

Two weeks later on a Sunday night, Muriel and I met for dinner, and then went to the Bagatelle. Fast and crowded, it was a good place for cruising, but had always seemed a little too rich for my blood, or too threatening to face alone. Laurel's and the Sea Colony and the Page Three and the Swing were called bars, but the Bag was always The Club.

The first room we entered was already smoky, although it was still early in the evening. It smelled like plastic and blue glass and beer and lots of good-looking young women.

Muriel ordered her inevitable bottle of beer so I did, too, pretending to drink it for the rest of the evening. Neither Muriel nor I danced, and the tiny dance floor at the rear of the club was already crowded. We stood in the archway between the tables and the dancers, talking to each other, and drinking in the feeling of the other women around us, some of whom, like us, were no doubt coming to love.

I soon adapted to Muriel's fascination with gay bars. Whenever she came to the city, she explained to me, she came to go barring. She never felt truly alive except in gay bars, she said, and needed them like a shot in the arm.

What we both needed was the atmosphere of other lesbians, and in 1954, gay bars were the only meeting places we knew.

When Muriel and I weren't talking, we stood feeling a little out of place, trying to look cool and a bit debonair. Every other woman in the Bag, it seemed, had a right to be there except us; we were pretenders, only appearing to be cool and hip and tough like all gay-girls were supposed to be. Totally unapproachable in our shyness, we were never approached, and besides, in those days gay-girls were usually not very sociable outside of their own little group.

You never could tell who was who, and the protective paranoia of the McCarthy years was still everywhere outside of the mainstream of blissed-out suburban middle america. Besides, there were always rumors of plainclothes women circulating among us, looking for gay-girls with fewer than three pieces of female attire. That was enough to get you arrested for transvestism, which was illegal. Or so the rumors went. Most of the women we knew were always careful to have on a bra, underpants, and some other feminine article. No sense playing with fire.

The evening ended all too quickly, and Muriel returned to her part-time job in a denture lab in Stamford, promising more of her ribald and creative letters.

I was still looking for work, any work, and the bleakness of prospects was discouraging. I had survived McCarthy and the Korean War, and the Supreme Court had declared desegregated schools illegal. But racism and recession were still realities between me and a job, as I crisscrossed the city day after day, answering ads.

Wherever I went, I was told that I was either overqualified—who wants to hire a Black girl with one year of college?—or underexperienced—what do you mean, dear, you don't type?

Jobs were scarce for everyone in New York that autumn, and for Black women, they were scarcer still.

I knew I could not afford the luxury of hating to work in another factory or at a typewriter. I applied for a practical nursing program, but was told that I was too nearsighted. Whether this was concern for me or another excuse for racist choices, I never knew.

Through an employment agency, I finally got a job at a hospital in the accounting department, by lying about my bookkeeping skills. But that didn't matter too much because they had lied about what I was supposed to do. I was not to be a bookkeeper at all, but girl-friday-step-n-fetch-it for the head of the accounting department.

Mrs. Goodrich was an overbearing and awe-inspiring woman, who was the first woman ever to head the accounting department of a major hospital in the state. She had fought hard to achieve her position and the wars had left her with a harsh cold manner and little tact. In my spare time, when I wasn't delivering her messages or buying her coffee or sharpening her pencils, I sat at a separate desk near the door of the typists' pool, and typed insurance company letters while I waited to be buzzed for another errand. I answered Mrs. Goodrich's telephone when her secretary was at lunch, and she ranted and raved at me until I learned to remember those people to whom she would speak and those to whom she would not.

Mrs. Goodrich was a tartar, a woman who had fought long and hard to make herself a place in a world hostile to her as a woman accountant. She had won by the same terms as the men whom she had fought. Now she was wedded to those terms, particularly in dealing with other women. For some unstated reason, we took immediate and deep exception to each other. Whatever the recognition was that passed between us, it did not serve to make us allies. Yet our positions were clearly unequal. As my boss, she had the power, and I would not retreat. It was much more complex than simple aversion. I was outraged by her attitude towards me, and despite the fact that she found me clearly unsatisfactory, Mrs. Goodrich would not release me to the clerical pool, nor would she leave me alone.

Mrs. Goodrich told me I walked like a lumberjack, and made too much noise in the halls. I was too uppity for my own good and would never get ahead. I would have to learn to be prompt, even though my "people" were never on time. Anyway, I didn't belong in the hospital, and should quit work and go back to school. In one of our few civil conversations, I told her I couldn't afford to.

"Well, then, you'd better straighten out around here or you'll be out on the street in short order."

I cringed secretly as she bawled me out for typing errors, in front of the whole typing pool, then called me across the hall into her private office to pick up a pencil she'd dropped.

I dreamed of stepping on her face with an ice pick between my toes. I felt trapped and furious. I had gotten the job a week before Thanksgiving, and the last weeks of the year were agony for me. Mrs. Goodrich became the symbol of a job which I hated (I had never really learned to type) and I came to hate her with the same passion.

I was hungry for the sun in my days. I walked west through Union Square and up through Stuyvesant Park to work. Coming across 14th Street, some mornings I could catch a glimpse of it over near the river, but the sun was never really up past the buildings before I went into the grey stone building. It had gone down by the time I left work. We were given free lunch in the hospital cafeteria, so I couldn't go out at noon. It was a recurring sadness to me as I walked home in the winter evenings, cars' rear lights along Second Avenue flickering like those on a Christmas tree. I thought if I had to spend the rest of my life working in places like Keystone Electronics and Manhattan Hospital I would surely go mad. I couldn't figure it out, but I knew there had to be some other way.

At work, my only weapon was retreat, and I used it with the indiscriminateness of any adolescent rebel. I fell asleep at my desk at every opportunity, and upon the slightest provocation, usually in the middle of typing Mrs. Goodrich's letters. In these mini-sleeps, I would type snatches of poems or nonsense phrases into the middle of straight formal sentences. I never bothered to proofread my letters, but only checked them as a work of art, brushing my eye over the paper for correct margins and no strike-overs. Letters would arrive upon Mrs. Goodrich's desk for her signature neatly and correctly typed, but with appalling sentences tucked into them.

Dear Sir:
  Claim forms may be obtained strange gods worship the evening hours by writing the Main Office at. . .

I had nightmares of the sound of Mrs. Goodrich's buzzer, followed by her deep bellow from across the hall, summoning me into her office.

In the meantime, Muriel and I corresponded. To be more exact, Muriel wrote long and beautiful letters and I read and cherished them in silence.

Muriel's lyrical and revealing letters held a hunger and an isolation that matched my own, and a precious unfolding of her humorous and prismatic vision. I came to marvel and delight in the new view she afforded me of simple and unexpected things. Re-seeing the world through her unique scrutinies was like re-seeing the world through my first pair of glasses when I was a child. Endless and wonderful re-discoveries of the ordinary.

There was a pain in Muriel to become herself that engaged my heart. I knew what it was like to be haunted by the ghost of a self one wished to be, but only half-sensed. Sometimes her words both thrilled me and made me weep.

Snail-sped an up-hill day, but evening comes; I dream of you. This shepherd is a leper learning to make lovely things while waiting out my time of despair. I feel a new kind of sickness now, which I know is the fever of wanting to be whole.

My hands shook a little as I put the letter down and poured myself another cup of coffee. Each day I would rush to my mailbox after work, looking for one of her thick blue envelopes.

Slowly but surely, Muriel became more and more like a vulnerable piece of myself. I could cherish and protect this piece because it was outside of me. Hedging my emotional bets, inside safe and undisturbed. With each of Muriel's letters there blossomed within me the need to do for her what I never really believed I could do for myself, even while I was in the midst of doing it.

I could take care of Muriel. I could make the world work for her, if not for myself.

With no intent and less insight, I fashioned this girl of wind and ravens into a symbol of surrogate survival, and fell into love like a stone off a cliff.

I sent Muriel little scraps of paper with pieces of poems on them. Some were about her, some were not. Nobody could tell the difference. Muriel told me later she was convinced I was quite mad, also. I counted the days between her letters which brought me pieces of herself like special and anticipated gifts On December 21st, in answer to her entreaties and the solstice, I sent her a greeting card of a greek urn filled with stones which read, "I must have rocks in my head."

By that I meant I loved her.

More than twenty years later I meet Muriel at a poetry reading at a women's coffee-house in New York. Her voice is still soft, but her great brown eyes are not. I tell her, "I am writing an unfolding of my life and loves."

"Just make sure you tell the truth about me," she says.

It was New Year's Eve, the last day of 1954. Rhea was in love again, and had gone out for the evening and I imagined for the rest of the night. I had settled down to reading and writing and music when the phone rang.

"Happy New Year!" It was Muriel. "Are you going to be in this old evening?"

My voice was jittery with anticipation and unexpected surprise. "Yes, some friends are coming over later. Can you come too? Where are you?"

"At home, but I'm catching the next train." I heard her warm half-laugh and could almost see the trickle of smoke and the fold between her eyes. "I've got something to ask you."

"What is it?" I asked, wondering.

"Nope, have to do it in person. I gotta run now."

Two hours later in she walked, bereted and smoking. The apartment was bustling with laughter and the voice of Rosemary Clooney.

Hey there,
you with the stars
in your eyes
love never made
a fool of you

I ran to take her jacket. "It's so good to see you," I said.

"Yeah? That's what I came down to find out, because I couldn't understand that card. What did it mean?"

Bea and Lynn and Gloria had dropped by with wine and reefer, and I introduced them to Muriel as I poured her a glass of Chianti. Bea and Lynn were dancing belt-to-belt in the middle room; Muriel, Gloria, and I munched over the cartons of savory chinese food which they had brought with them.

At a few minutes to midnight, we switched off the tinny portable phono and turned on the radio to hear the cheer go up in Times Square to greet 1955, even while we were saying how square that all was. Muriel gave me a copy of Tolkien's *Lord of the Rings*, an underground bestseller which she'd lifted, she said, from a Stamford bookstore. Then we all kissed each other, and had some more wine.

We turned the music back on, and people told wild stories about other New Year's Eves. I had to admit that this was my first New Year's Eve party ever, but I managed to say it in a way that nobody believed me.

By 3:00 A.M., everybody had decided to spend the night. I
rolled out Rhea's double bed in the front room, and opened up
my couch in the middle room. There was a place for everyone.
I finally had to slip Lynn a sleeping pill from my hoard of doctor's samples, because she kept insisting she wasn't sleepy, and
I was determined to be the last one awake. It had been a heady
evening for me, and even with amphetamine, I was getting sleepy.

Muriel had gone to bed in the middle room with all her
clothes on, because this was a strange house filled with strange
people, she said, drolly, and she was very shy. The other three
sacked out in the front room. I had assumed Rhea would stay
over at her boyfriend's house. Unfortunately, Rhea and Art had
their big fight that night.

At 4:00 A.M., just about the time everyone had finally settled
down and I had crawled into my faded green studio couch beside Muriel, just about that time I heard Rhea's key in the door.

I jumped up, instantly awake. Oh shit. Pulling on my shirt, I
tiptoed into the kitchen to find my roommate standing forlorn-
ly, her bright party dress wrinkled and sad. Rhea was addicted
to having affairs with men who were only interested in shafting
her, literally and figuratively. She was in tears. Art had told her,
while they were in bed, that he was going to be married to the
nineteen-year old daughter of one of their progressive comrades.
At thirty-one, Rhea was sure it was her age. On the other
hand, I was sure it was because he was getting some from
Rhea and not getting some from his teenager. But I couldn't
say that to Rhea in her condition.

Half my mind, besides, was on the collection of people in the
house and how was I going to explain them to Rhea? Not that I
had to explain, really, but after all it was her bed that Bea and
Lynn and Gloria were sharing.

"That's awful, Rhea," I said as I took her coat. "Let me
heat up some coffee."

"It'll be all right," Rhea said abstractedly, wiping her eyes
and managing a brave little smile. Her long voluptuous black
hair was all awry. "I just want to go to bed for now."

"Well," I hesitated only a moment, "There're some people in
your bed, honey; some friends came over and you said you
didn't think you'd be home. . ."

Tears welled up in Rhea's eyes again as she reached distract-
edly for her pocketbook and the shoes which she'd so gallantly
dyed to match her dress, an electric-blue taffeta, just a few
hours before.

"But I'll wake them right up," I said hurriedly, as I saw her heading for the front door. Her cousin lived two floors down, but I could never bear to see Rhea cry. "I'm getting them right up."

And that's exactly what I did, posthaste.

Sleepily, the three girls moved, and we all crawled back into bed, spoon-wise, in the middle room with Muriel. Rhea went to her troubled sleep in her own bed. By this time, it was almost dawn and too late for me to sleep any more. Anyway, I had gotten my second wind. And I loved being the first one up in the mornings. I took some obetrol and sat reading in the john until dawn.

Tiptoeing past the sleeping women, I leaned out of the seventh-story front window, looking eastward through the still streets to the lightening sky. The air was mild for January, and I caught a faint whiff of malt from the Hartz Mountain birdseed factory across the East River. The January thaw. It reminded me with a start that spring was only three months away. Yet it seemed forever. I was tired of winter.

I switched on the radio softly; on this holiday morning it was mostly stale news, except for the automobile fatalities and the results of the recent congressional censure of McCarthy. As I listened to the weather report, unseasonably warm, I cleaned my sneakers with a dash of dry Dutch Cleanser, rubbed in with an old toothbrush. Cleaned shoes was a New Year's Day ritual that I carried over from my parents' house without question or consideration.

At 8:30 A.M. I woke everyone except Rhea. I was eager to start the day. "Who needs a toothbrush?" I called, breaking out the little store of them which I kept for such occasions. I was secretly pleased to have Muriel see how in charge I was of all situations. Always prepared, too. Just like the Marines' motto.

Everybody knew a thirty-five-year old woman could run any world, and I considered myself to be permanently in practice.

I made coffee the way I used to do it in Mexico, using very little coffee and straining it through the little fabric net which I'd brought home with me. I turned off the radio and started the phonograph, putting on Roberta Sherwood's "Cry Me a River" real low, so as not to disturb Rhea's fretful, sighing sleep. The rest of us sat around the table in the kitchen near the shaft window drinking coffee. Muriel's sturdy feet stuck out beneath the cuffs of her jeans, her broad toes moving up and down in time to the music as her soft musical laugh moved through the smoke of her ever-present cigarette. Bea and Lynn in their dungarees and flannel shirts; and Gloria, her flamboyant spanish huaraches over woolen stockings and her baggy peasant pants made from handwoven magenta cotton. The click of Gloria's fruitwood necklaces and bracelets was a contrapuntal echo behind the morning's conversations of politics, gay-girl gossip, and the advent and use of the new tranquilizers in mental hospitals.

The house grew even warmer as the steam came up, and I got up to fix us a beautiful New Year's breakfast. I mixed our last two eggs, well-beaten, into the leftover chinese food, added a drizzle of the foo yong gravy and some powdered milk, and scrambled it all together with a healthy amount of chopped onions quailed in margarine with lots of paprika and a dash of dill for color. It was a dish reminiscent of the Sunday-morning concoction of eggs, onions, and scraped chicken livers which my father called entre and which he used to cook for us each weekend while my mother and the three of us were at Sunday Mass.

After breakfast, we exchanged long goodbyes and Happy New Years, and the other three left. Muriel and I sat talking in the kitchen over cups of black coffee, because all the powdered milk was used up.

Rhea woke up about noon, and I introduced her to Muriel. We made Rhea some coffee, and she and Muriel argued the pros and cons of Marxism (although Muriel insisted she was apolitical, which I translated as naïve) for about an hour while I took a bath. Rhea dressed and went off to her parents' house for dinner, only a little sodden around the eyes.

I turned off the record player and double-locked the door. Then Muriel and I, with no more to-do about it, went to bed with each other in the New Year's watery sunlight in Rhea's front room double bed. The afternoon unfolded into a blossom of loving from which she rose to me like a flame.

I had not been close to a woman since those nights with Eudora in Cuernavaca more than six months before.

We lay entwined and exhausted afterward, laughing and talking excitedly. The camaraderie and warmth between us breached places within me that had been closed off and permanently sealed, I thought, when Genevieve died.

When Muriel and I talked, as we did, about Naomi and Genevieve, each dead at fifteen, the spirit of those two dead girls seemed to rise up from the earth, bless us, and then depart. A particular and terrible loneliness seemed at last about to give way.

We made love over and over and over again, pausing only to turn on the lights in the early dusk and to feed the cat. The sun went down and the steam came up, and the whole room seemed alight with the fragrance of our bodies.

For every secret hurt of Muriel's, there was one of mine to match, and the similarities of our lonelinesses, as well as of our dreams, convinced us that we were made for each other.

January 2, 1955.

I rolled over and raised myself up on one arm, regarded the sleep-sweet cheek and tousled hair of the woman curled away from me, one arm under her head. I bent to kiss the curl that swept over her ear, and ran my tongue slowly down the nape of her dark hair to where the covers draped her shoulders.

With a sigh and a slow smile, Muriel opened one eye as I advanced, whispering, toward her ear. "In the West Indies, they call this raising your zandalee."

Later, I called Mrs. Goodrich from bed, Muriel drowsing beside me. I explained that I was sick and could not come in to work. The whole department had been warned by Mrs. Goodrich the last day before the holidays to make sure that such "sicknesses" did not occur, under any circumstances.

Mrs. Goodrich fired me on the spot.

25 Rhea had all the cues she needed about my relationships with women. She had witnessed the melodrama with Bea. But on the surface, Rhea did not *know* I was gay, and I did not *tell* her. Homosexuality was outside the party line at that time; therefore, Rhea defined it as "bad," and her approval was important to me. Without words, we both more or less agreed never to allude to what was obviously the guiding passion of my life, my involvement with those female friends to whom Rhea always referred as "your cool-voiced young women."

Rhea and I loved each other, yet she would have professed horror had she been forced to imagine an extension of our love into the physical.

Fortunately, or maybe because of her attitudes, I was never physically attracted to Rhea. She was a beautiful, strong, and vivacious woman, but I have never found straight women physically appealing. Self-protective as this mechanism is, it also has served me as a sixth sense. In those days, whenever two or more lesbians got together, the most frequent topic of conversation was "Do you think she's gay?" It was a constant question about any woman we happened to be interested in. Nine times out of ten, if I felt a strong physical pull toward a woman, whatever her protective coloration might be, she would usually turn out to be either gay, or so strongly women-oriented that being gay became only a question of time or opportunity.

Always before, the few lesbians I had known were women whom I had met within other existing contexts of my life. We shared some part of a world common to us both—school or work or poetry or some other interest beyond our sexual identity. Our love for women was a fact that became known only *after* we were already acquainted and connected through some other reason.

In the bars, we met women with whom we would have had no other contact, had we not all been gay. There, Muriel and I were pretty well out of whatever was considered important. That was namely drinking, softball, dyke-chic fashion, dancing, and who was sleeping with whom at whose expense. All other questions of survival were considered a very private affair.

When Muriel came into the city on weekends that spring, she stayed at the YWCA over on Hudson Street in the West Village, which is now a nursing home. We spent the weekend in her tiny room making love, in between barring and trips back to Seventh Street for something to eat. Sometimes, we didn't have the money to rent a room at the Y, because I was not working again and she only had a part-time job in Stamford. Then, we braved Rhea's bewildered and questioning glances and stayed at the apartment. After Muriel left one Sunday, Rhea and I talked.

"Muriel's around a lot, isn't she?" I could see Rhea remembering the weeping Bea in the stairwell.

"I love Muriel very much, Rhea."

"I can see that." Rhea laughed. "But *how* do you love her?"

"In every way I know how!" And Rhea turned back to the dishes, shaking her head, trying to find some correlation between my loving Muriel and her own painful love affairs. She did not dare to see the similarities and so she could not see the differences. And the words were never spoken. I was too chicken to come right out and say, "Hey, look, Rhea, Muriel and I are lovers."

Rhea could not bear the heartbreak of her affair with Art, and began to make plans to move to Chicago later in the spring. The idea that I would soon have the apartment all to myself delighted me. I made up my mind that I would never live with anyone else again, unless we were lovers.

Muriel and I were beginning to envision the world together. I didn't know how I was going to bring my personal and political visions together, but I knew it had to be possible because I felt them both too strongly, and knew how much I needed them both to survive. I did not agree with Rhea and her progressive friends when they said that this was not what the revolution was about. Any world which did not have a place for me loving women was not a world in which I wanted to live, nor one which I could fight for.

One Friday night, Muriel and I spent the evening making love on my studio couch in the middle room of the apartment. Dusk crept away from the window on the air shaft and night came in. We were just resting briefly when we heard Rhea's key in the front door in the kitchen. Muriel and I lay curled into each other's arms on the now-familiar single couch. Without moving much, we simply pulled the covers up over us, closed our eyes, and pretended to be asleep.

We heard Rhea come into the kitchen and turn on the light. I could feel the glow of the sudden brightness from the room next door as it shined through the arched doorway and along the floor of my room, parallel to where the two of us lay. Rhea entered, proceeding across my room to hers at the front of the house. Her footsteps stopped beside the bed where Muriel and I were, our eyes squeezed shut like children. She stood there for a moment looking down at our supposedly sleeping figures under the covers entwined within the narrow space, lit by the dim reflected light from the kitchen.

And then, without warning, Rhea burst into tears. She stood over us sobbing wildly as if her heart was being broken by what she saw. She wept over us for at least two minutes while we both lay there, our arms around each other and our eyes closed tightly. There was nothing else we could do; I felt it would just be too embarrassing to Rhea for me to look up and say, "Hey, what's going on here?" Besides, I thought I knew. Our obvious

happiness in our "incorrect" love was so great besides her obvious unhappiness in her "correct" ones, that the only response
to such cosmic unfairness was tears.

Finally, Rhea turned and ran into her own room, closing the
door. We could hear her sobbing through the closed door until
we both fell asleep.

I never discussed that night with Rhea, nor whether those
furious tears had been for her own loneliness or for the joy that
Muriel and I were finding in each other. Perhaps, if I had, both
of our lives might have been different. Rhea left New York City
one week later, and I did not see her again for many years.

Much later, I discovered the real reason why Rhea left New
York that spring to take a job in Chicago, on what seemed at
the time to be such short notice. A visiting higher-up in progressive circles had come to the house one evening while I was there.
She later returned to headquarters in New Jersey with the
shocking report that Rhea shared a house with a homosexual,
and a Black one, at that. In other words, Rhea had been de-
nounced for her association with me. A progressive in good
standing could not afford such questionable company in 1955.
I had become an embarrassment.

I was totally oblivious to all this, immersed as I was in the
fact of Muriel and me. I only knew that Rhea was becoming
more and more troubled, culminating in the scene over my
couch. But the word had come down to her; get rid of me or
give up her work. Rhea loved me, and valued our friendship, but
her work was more important and she had to protect herself.
Her last affair was a perfect excuse. Rather than ask me to leave
or let me know what was going on, Rhea decided to give me the
apartment and move to Chicago.

The Last of My Childhood Nightmares

My Mother's House,
July 5, 1954

*Hickory-skinned demons with long white hair and handsome
demonical eyes stretch out arms wide as all tomorrow, across
the doorway exit from a room through which I run, screaming,
shrieking for exit. But I cannot stop running. If I collide with
those long arms barring my pathway out, I will die of electrocu-*

tion. As I run I start to shout in despair, "Our father who art
in heaven. . ." and the arms start to dissolve and drip down the
walls and the air between the door and me.

I then pass into another room of my parents' home—their
bedroom, the room in which I am now asleep. It is dark and
silent. There is a watermelon shaped like an egg on the bureau.
I lift the fruit up and it drops down upon the linoleum floor.
The melon splits open, and at the core is a brilliant hunk of
turquoise, glowing. I see it as a promise of help coming for me.

Rhea is asleep, still, in my parents' large bed. She is in great
danger. I must save her from the great and nameless evil in this
house, left here by the hickory-faced devils. I take her hand. It
is white and milky in the half-dark.

And then suddenly I realize that in this house of my childhood I am no longer welcome. Everything is hostile to me. The
doors refuse to open. The glass cracks when I touch it. Even the
bureau drawers creak and stick when I try to close them. The
light bulbs blow out when I switch on the light. The can-opener
won't turn; the eggbeater jams mysteriously.

This is no longer my home; it is only of a past time.

Once I realize this, I am suddenly free to go, and to take
Rhea with me.

26 In March, I got a job as a library clerk in the
New York Public Library Children's Services,
and I was truly delighted. Not only was I relieved
to be making money again, but I loved libraries and books, and
was so pleased to be able to do work which I enjoyed. Muriel
and I saw each other as often as we could now, and we began to
discuss her coming back to New York to live.

When she was animated, with her tousled dark hair and her
round monkish head, Muriel reminded me of a chrysanthemum,
always slightly bent over upon itself. She talked incessantly
about her "sickness" of the years before, and about what being
schizophrenic meant. I listened but did not know enough to
realize that, out of her love, she was also warning me.

On the few occasions that we smoked reefer together, she
waxed most eloquent and I was most open.

"Electric shock treatments are like little deaths," Muriel said,
reaching across me for the ashtray. "They broke into my head

like thieves with official sanction and robbed me of something precious that feels like it's gone forever."

Sometimes she sounded angry, and sometimes she sounded curiously flat, but however she sounded it made my arms ache to hold her. Pieces of her memory had gone too, she told me, and that made Suzy, her old New York lover, keeper of that piece of her past.

It was the equinox, and we lay smoking in bed in the evenness of springtime, with summer already coming.

"Did it make anything better?" I asked.

"Well, before shock, I used to feel this deep depression covering me like a huge bushel basket, but somewhere inside at the very core of it all, there was a little feeble light shining, and I knew it existed, and it helped illuminate chaos." She shuddered and lay silent for a moment, her lips tight and pale over her front teeth.

"But the thing I can never forgive the doctors for, is that after shock, the bushel only lifted a little; you know what I mean? But that little light had gone out, and it just wasn't worth it. I never wanted to trade my own little flame, I don't care however crazy it was, for any of their casual light from outside."

All this made me very sad. The only answer I had was to hold her tight. I swore to myself that I would never let that happen to her again. I would do anything in the world to protect Muriel.

That night, lying in the front room on Rhea's bed, Muriel warned, "If I give up my job in Stamford to come down here, I don't know how I'll ever be able to get another one. I just can't ask someone to hire me and run the risk of their saying no. I don't know why, but I know I can't take that. It will break me."

Having gone through the horrors of looking for work just recently myself, I thought I knew what she was talking about. But I did not, for the depths of her shaky reality were alien to me, although I never considered that possibility. I felt confident that eventually, out of our love, Muriel would find the strength to face that hurdle, too. So I did not heed her words as a warning, the only kind she could give me.

Rhea left, and in the beginning of April, Muriel returned to New York City to live. I painted the kitchen and bathroom and put up new bookshelves in anticipation.

Once Muriel quit work in Stamford, the physical transition to New York began in trickles. For months, every time she went back home for a visit, Muriel would reappear on Sunday afternoon with a stool or a box of tools or some wood or a shopping bag of books. Sometimes her friend Rupert would drive her down in his Volkswagen beetle with a load of books and papers.

Although the change from "staying over" to "living together" was a gradual one, I knew I had made a major decision. And I knew that decision would affect the rest of my life, although exactly how was not really clear to me then. When I had moved into the apartment with Rhea, I had merely scratched my name beside hers on the slip of paper stuck into the slot of our mailbox in the hall.

But one blustery day in the first week of April, on my lunch hour, I walked around to Hite's Hardware on East Broadway and ordered a proper metal mailbox tag, with Muriel's and my names upon it. I stood watching as the machine stamped the two names into the shiny brass rectangle, feeling proud, excited, and a little bit scared. It felt like a ritual joining, a symbolic marriage.

Afterward, I bought an egg cream on Chatham Square to celebrate, and stood looking at the little shiny plate with our two names side by side, separated only by a little dash. This would be my surprise for Muriel when she came down to New York on her birthday, the following week.

No more playing house.

For me, this was the real thing, a step from which there was no turning back. I wasn't just playing around any more, gay-girl. I was living with a woman and we were lovers. I had done, silently and easily, what I had longed and feared to do, I had made a commitment which was irrevocable. Without conscious articulation of why, I knew *together* meant *forever* for me, even though there was no troth plighted, no wedding ceremony, no paper signed. Muriel and I were united together by our loving and our wills, for good or ill.

Through the spring, I had thought long and hard about whether or not I could live that closely with anyone, and for the rest of my life, as I felt this was going to be—without question. Once I decided I could make that commitment, I never doubted for a minute that Muriel was the person I wanted to make it with.

We made our own vows of love and forever. As the spring evenings turned warmer, Muriel met me at the Chatham Square Library. Sometimes we went wandering through the back streets of Chinatown, buying strange succulent vegetables and peculiar fragrant pieces of dried meat to experiment with, along with hard wrinkled mushrooms by the piece. Each of us knew a different New York, and we explored together, showing each other secret treasured places in the middle of the alleyways south of Canal Street.

Sometimes she met me for lunch and we munched Musli apples leaning up against the Catherine Slip tenements in the strengthening sunlight, watching the sparks fly as workmen continued the complex task of dismantling the last great piece of the Third Avenue El, the Chatham Square Station. Sometimes we walked home together on the nights I worked late.

We talked about leaving New York, about homesteading somewhere in the west where a Black woman and a white woman could live together in peace. Muriel's dream was to live on a farm and it felt like a good life to me. I borrowed pamphlets from the library, and we wrote to all the appropriate government offices to find out if there were any homestead lands still available anywhere in the continental United States.

Sadly enough for us, the word came back that there was not, except in some of the more desolate northern reaches of Alaska, which was not yet a state. Neither Muriel nor I could stand the thought of living in a cold climate, and that far away from the sun. Besides, since we would not be able to support ourselves by farming, northern Alaska was definitely out.

When I came home from work with my arms full of the latest books and my mouth full of stories, sometimes there was food cooked, and sometimes there was not. Sometimes there was a poem, and sometimes there was not. And always, on weekends, there were the bars.

Early Saturday and Sunday mornings, Muriel and I wandered the streets of the Lower East Side and the more affluent West Village, scavenging the garbage heaps for treasures of old furniture, wonders that the unimaginative had discarded. We evaluated their future possibilities and dragged our finds back up six flights of stairs, to add them to the growing pile in the kitchen of things we were one day going to repair. There were wooden radio cabinets, gutted, that could be fitted with shelves for a fine record-holder. Old dresser drawers supplied stout wood for bookcase shelves, supported by scavenged bricks. There were brass lamps and rococo fixtures to be rewired, and a magnificent old dentist's chair with only one arm support missing. Occasionally we found something that needed no repair (my bed-lamp still sits on a Victorian lampstool that we dug out of a junkheap in Chelsea on our way home from the Grapevine one Sunday morning).

Ordering and re-ordering our world, Muriel and I sat up into the small hours reading the books I would sneak out of the cataloguing bins at the library, and eating pasta with margarine and oregano when we were poor. Other times we had wondrous meals concocted from our adventurous buys in Chinatown, together with a scrap of meat or a few chicken feet or a piece of fish or whatever we could afford and took a fancy to in the First Avenue Public Market. Around the corner from us, we did most of our food shopping there in the many stalls of busy hawkers.

I met the few of Muriel's friends that she could remember from the old days, and she met mine. There were Mick and Cordelia whom I had met in high school. Nicky and Joan, friends of Suzy, Muriel's old lover. We were poor and always hungry, and always being invited to dinner. Going to Suzy's house for dinner was always chancy. Suzy had once heard that pork fat was nutritious, so she kept a skillet of bacon drippings permanently on the back of her stove and cooked everything in it.

There were Dottie and Pauli, two skinny blonde artists from our neighborhood whom we met at Laurel's; Bea and Lynn, her new girl; Phyllis, who wanted to be an architect, but only talked about it when she was drunk; and, of course, there was Felicia, my adopted little sister, as I called her, and the only other Black woman in our group. Together, we formed a loosely knit, emotionally and socially interdependent set, sharing many different interests, some overlapping. On the periphery there existed another larger group of downtown gay-girls, made up of congenial acquaintances and drinking buddies and other people's past lovers, known by sight and friendly enough, but not to be called upon except in emergencies, when of course everybody knew everybody else's business anyway.

But the fact of our Blackness was an issue that Felicia and I talked about only between ourselves. Even Muriel seemed to believe that as lesbians, we were all outsiders and all equal in our outsiderhood. "We're all niggers," she used to say, and I hated to hear her say it. It was wishful thinking based on little fact; the ways in which it was true languished in the shadow of those many ways in which it would always be false.

When Muriel and I received stares and titters on the streets of the West Village, or in the Lower East Side market, it was a toss-up as to whether it was because we were a Black woman and a white woman together, or because we were gay. Whenever that happened, I half-agreed with Muriel. But I also knew that Felicia and I shared both a battle and a strength that was unavailable to our other friends. We acknowledged it in private, and it set us apart, in a world that was closed to our white friends. It was even closed to Muriel, as much as I would have liked to include her. And because that world was closed to them, it was easy for even lovers to ignore it, dismiss it, pretend it didn't exist, believe the fallacy that there was no difference between us at all.

But that difference was real and important, even if nobody else seemed to feel that way, sometimes not even Flee herself, tired as she was of explaining why she didn't go swimming without a bathing cap, or like to get caught in the rain.

Between Muriel and me, then, there was one way in which I would always be separate, and it was going to be my own secret knowledge, if it was going to be my own secret pain. I was Black and she was not, and that was a difference between us that had nothing to do with better or worse, or the outside world's craziness. Over time I came to realize that it colored our perceptions and made a difference in the ways I saw pieces of the worlds we shared, and I was going to have to deal with that difference outside of our relationship.

This was the first separation, the piece outside love. But I turned away short of the meanings of it, afraid ιο examine the truths difference might lead me to, afraid they might carry Muriel and me away from each other. So I tried not to think of our racial differences too often. I sometimes pretended to agree with Muriel, that the difference did not in fact exist, that she and all gay-girls were just as oppressed as any Black person, certainly as any Black woman.

But when I did think about it, it was as something that set me apart, but also protected me. I *knew* there was nothing I could do, including wearing skirts and being straight, that would make me acceptable to the little old Ukrainian ladies who sunned themselves on the stoops of Seventh Street and pointed fingers at Muriel and me as we walked past, arm in arm. One of these old ladies, who ran the cleaners across the street, tried to give Muriel a used woolen skirt one day. "For nothing," she insisted, pressing it into Muriel's hands. "No money, for nothing. Try it on, is nice. Make you look nice, show you legs little bit."

I had gone in and out of that store in dungarees for years, and this little old Ukrainian lady had never tried to reform me. She knew the difference, even if Muriel did not.

Somehow, I knew that difference would be a weapon in

my arsenal when the "time" came. And the "time" would certainly come in one way or another. The "time" when I would have to protect myself alone, although I did not know how or when. For Flee and me, the forces of social evil were not theoretical, not long distance nor solely bureaucratic. We met them every day, even in our straight clothes. Pain was always right around the corner. Difference had taught me that, out of the mouth of my mother. And knowing that, I fancied myself on guard, safe. I still had to learn that knowing was not enough.

Every one of the women in our group took for granted, and would have said if asked, that we were all on the side of right. But the nature of that right everyone was presumed to be on the side of was always unnamed. It was just another way of silently avoiding having to examine what our living positions were within our small group of lesbians, dependent as we were upon each other for support. We were too afraid those differences might in fact be irreconcilable, for we had never been taught any tools for dealing with them. Our individuality was very precious to each one of us, but so was the group, and the other outsiders whom we had found to share some more social aspects of our lonelinesses.

Being gay-girls without set roles was the one difference we allowed ourselves to see and to bind us to each other. We were not of that *other* world and we wanted to believe that, by definition, we were therefore free of that *other* world's problems of capitalism, greed, racism, classism, etc. This was not so. But we continued to visit each other and eat together and, in general, share our lives and resources, as if it were.

One evening coming home from work I ran into Nicky and Joan on Houston Street and invited them home to dinner on the spot. There was only $1.50 in my pocket and no food in the house. We stopped off in the market on First Avenue and bought a pound of extra-thin spaghetti, some fresh parsley, half a pound of chicken hearts, and a packet of powdered milk. With the other seventy-five cents I bought a huge bunch of daffodils and we all had a fine dinner, although I forget what we were celebrating. Because we were always celebrating something, a new job, a new poem, a new love, a new dream.

For dessert, we had a home-cooler: tall glasses of skim milk poured over cubes of frozen coffee heavily laced with cinnamon and almond extract.

The bars on weekends were a ritual of togetherness that I only came to fully understand years later when I was tired of being alone. Every Friday night, it was the same.

"Hurry up, Audi, let's try to get a table tonight." In Laurel's,
like in most of the other bars, the tiny tables lining the dance
area were first come, first served. Sometimes we'd run into Vida
and Pet, two of the few Black gay-girls we knew. They preferred
the word "dyke," and it seemed much more in charge of their
lives to be dykes rather than gay-girls, but we were still a little
scared of the way the word was used to badmouth someone.
Vida and Pet shared a house with another dyke named Gerri,
and we went to parties at their house out in Queens. Vida and
Pet were older than most of our friends, and more settled. They
were both very kind to Muriel and me, sometimes even buying
us food when we had no money, and mothering us in a way that
I both resented and appreciated, like making sure after their
parties that we had a ride back to the city or somewhere to stay
over for the night.

One warm Saturday evening, Muriel and I stood eyeing the
ripe melons piled high on the sidewalk stands in front of Bal-
ducci's. Cartons and crates of beautiful and expensive fruits and
vegetables extended out onto the sidewalks of Greenwich Avenue. Across the Village street in the early summer dusk, a handful of impatient husbands and lovers stood, calling up back and
forth to unseen but well-heard inmates within the grated windows of the Women's House of Detention on the west side of
Greenwich Avenue. Information and endearments flew up and
down, the conversants apparently oblivious to the ears of the
passersby as they discussed the availability of lawyers, the length
of stay, family, conditions, and the undying quality of true
love. The Women's House of Detention, right smack in the middle of the Village, always felt like one up for our side—a defiant
pocket of female resistance, ever-present as a reminder of possibility, as well as punishment.

"Think we can cop a honeydew?" My mouth was watering
for the fresh sweet fruit. I looked up Greenwich, which was
growing more crowded with evening strollers. I made up my
mind, more daring than scared.

"I don't know, but let's try. I'll get one from the side and go
down Sixth. If he comes after me, yell 'Cheeko!' then meet me
around the corner on Waverly."

We separated with elaborate casualness and Muriel walked
over to the oranges, feeling them in deep consideration. The

fruit vendor approached her expectantly. I sidled around the other side of the crates behind his back, snatched the ripest golden green melon that caught my eye, then took off. First rule of snatching anything outdoors: try to do it on one-way streets and always run against the flow of traffic. I sprinted down Sixth Avenue, avoiding startled pedestrians, turning into Waverly Place a block away only slightly winded. Pleased with my feat, I leaned against a railing to observe the luscious spoils and wait for Muriel.

Suddenly, a hand grabbed my arm from behind. My heart in my mouth, I tried to wrench free without even looking, still clutching our melon. Oh shit!

"Take it easy, girl, you're lucky it's just me!" I recognized Vida's rough kindly voice with a wave of relief. I sagged against the railing, unable to talk. "I *thought* that was you. I'm driving up Sixth and I see you tear-assing along, said to myself, lemme park this car and see what my buddy's doin'."

Muriel sauntered around the corner, stopping short with surprise at the sight of Vida. She and I exchanged quick glances. This was not exactly what we'd have preferred Vida find us doing. Uncool, definitely, stealing fruit on Saturday night. Vida laughed a broad laugh.

"Scared you good, didn't I?" Her voice changed, earnestly. "Well, I'm glad. You-all better stop this jiveass shit before next time it isn't me. Come on, Pet's in the car, let's go for a ride."

Muriel and I talked endlessly. I knew who I was going to spend the rest of my life with, yet it seemed as if there was never enough time to talk and share and catch up with all the pieces of each other that had existed before we met. As our newness became more known to each other, I marveled at how very dear Muriel's face was becoming to me. The fact of us was a most wonderful and novel idea, one that I pondered over, examining and savoring every aspect of what it meant to be permanently connected to another human being.

To go to bed and to wake up again day after day besides a woman, to lie in bed with our arms around each other and drift in and out of sleep, to be with each other—not as a quick stolen pleasure, nor as a wild treat—but like sunlight, day after day in the regular course of our lives.

I was discovering all the ways that love creeps into life when two selves exist closely, when two women meet. Like the smell of Muriel on my sweatshirt, and the straight black hairs caught in my glove. One night, I cried to think of how lucky we both were to have found each other, since it was clear that we were the only ones in the world who could understand what we understood in the instantaneous manner which we understood it. We both agreed ours was a union made in heaven, for which each of us had already paid several hells.

For our close friends, we were Audi and Muriel without definition. For our other friends, we were just another young gay couple in love, maybe a little more peculiar than most, traipsing around with notebooks under our arms, all the time. For the regulars at the Colony and the Swing we were Ky-Ky girls because we didn't play roles. And for the fast set at the Bag we were weirdos who deserved each other because Muriel was crazy and I was Black.

Meanwhile, Muriel and I built bookcases and had writing bees and adopted two little scrawny Black kittens which we named Crazy Lady and Scarey Lou.

Muriel was very much the dandy about her clothes. Like everything else about her, what she wore had to be precisely so, according to some secret guide in her own head, or Muriel would not go out. As long as something was not touched by her inner rules, it didn't matter, but Muriel's rules were inflexible and unmoving and once you came up against one of them, it was unmistakable. What those various rules were, I only found out slowly.

When I lived in Stamford, I had worn old dungarees and men's shirts to work. Just before Thanksgiving, I bought some corduroy and Ginger's mother helped me make a skirt for the holidays. When I lived in Mexico, I wore the full peasant skirts and blouses so readily available in the marketplaces of Cuernavaca. Now I had my straight clothes for working at the library— two interchangeable outfits of skirts, sweaters, and a warm-weather blouse or two. I had a pair of shoes for work, and a flamboyantly cut woolen suit which I had made out of the old coat my sister had given me to wear at my father's funeral. Since I never wore stockings, I stood waiting for the bus some days in the icy winds blowing down East Broadway and prayed for the warm protection of my dungarees or riding pants.

I had very few clothes for my real life, but with the addition of Muriel's quixotic wardrobe, we developed quite a tidy store of what the young gay-girl could be seen in. Mostly I wore blue or black dungarees which were increasingly being called *jeans*. I fell in love with a pair of riding pants which Muriel gave me, and they became my favorite attire. They became my uniform, along with cotton shirts, usually striped.

Muriel had her gambler's pants for winter, and in the warmer weather she preferred Bermuda shorts and knee-socks, usually black. Winter chic demanded our navy surplus turtleneck sweaters, and we pressed the point, often wearing them into the late spring on any air-conditioned occasion. I loved the deep dark secure feel of wool against my body, and the freedom of casual clothes. I always fancied that they made my large breasts look smaller.

Other than army-navy stores, for which both of us had an absolute passion, we did most of our other clothes shopping at John's Bargain Store. For each of us, there was a positive virtue in being able to live poor and well at the same time, and this took effort and ingenuity and a sharp eye for real bargains. When John's failed us, there were always the little open shops along Rivington and Orchard Streets on Sunday mornings. In these side streets near the Public Market on Essex, men in yarmulkes hawked their wares. A sale on sneakers for $1.98, or solid-color sweatshirts selling for ninety-nine cents were finds to boast about.

We were reinventing the world together. Muriel opened me to a world of possibilities that felt like a legacy left me by Eudora's sad funny eyes and patient laugh. I had learned from Eudora how to take care of business, be dyke-proud, how to love and live to tell the story, and with flair. Muriel and I were making the lessons become real together.

When I recall the time Muriel and I spent together, I remember the assurances we gave each other, the sense of a shared niche out of the storm, and the wonder grounded in magic and hard work. I remember always the feeling that it could continue forever, this morning, this life. I remember the curl of Muriel's finger and her deep eyes and the smell of her buttery skin. The smell of basil. I remember the openness of our loving that was a measurement against which I held up whatever was called love; and which I came to recognize as a legitimate demand between all lovers.

Muriel and I loved tenderly and long and well, but there was no one around to suggest that perhaps our intensity was not always too wisely focused.

Each one of us had been starved for love for so long that we wanted to believe that love, once found, was all-powerful. We wanted to believe that it could give word to my inchoate pain

and rages; that it could enable Muriel to face the world and get
a job; that it could free our writings, cure racism, end homophobia and adolescent acne. We were like starving women who
come to believe that food will cure all present pains, as well as
heal all the deficiency sores of long standing.

27 In that golden summer of 1955 we were very
busy and full of light. During the week I worked
at the library and Muriel built beds across town
for Mick and Cordelia. On the weekends, we wrote and read and
studied Chinese calligraphy and went to the beach and the bars.

Jonas Salk announced his new vaccine for polio at my sister
Helen's graduation from City College, and since so many of the
girls I knew from Hunter High School had varying degrees of
disabilities from polio, this news had a personal meaning.

Life had so many different pieces. *Jet* was a girlie magazine
trying to be a Black newsmagazine which I borrowed from my
brother-in-law Henry on my infrequent visits to the Bronx, read
avidly on the long subway ride downtown, and then surreptitiously dropped onto the next seat as I got off. When I mentioned at the library that I wrote poetry, somebody was bound
to mention Anne Morrow Lindbergh's *Gift from the Sea*, the
runaway bestseller that year. It had no more to do with my
work than a scallop to a whale. Spurred on by Muriel, I sent
some of my poems to *The Ladder*, a magazine for lesbians pub-
lished by the Daughters of Bilitis. Their prompt and unaccom-
panied return crushed me.

I supplemented our reading from the library with a steady
trade in the used bookstores over on Fourth Avenue. Muriel
spent a lot of her time over there too, where used copies of
Byron and Gertrude Stein could be bought at the Strand one
week and traded in for a little less at the Pine down the street
a week later. Books were not so much in excess then; I remember trading a birthday copy of Lindbergh for a handful of used
paperbacks, two hardcover volumes of minor poets, and a first
issue of *MAD* magazine, which cost ten cents.

In June, Lynn came to live with us. We hadn't planned it that
way, that's just the way it worked out. Muriel and I had re-
established a guarded communication with Bea, and Lynn was

her ex-lover whom we had first met on that infamous New Year's Eve.

She came to call unexpectedly from Philadelphia one Sunday evening in early summer, her long blonde hair streaming around her short sturdy neck, and an overstuffed duffle bag slung across one shoulder. Rumpled army fatigues covered her ample hips. Lynn had a sly smile and screwed up her face whenever she laughed. She was broad, and squat, and very sexy, and in terrible emotional shape. She was the same age I was, twenty-one, but had lived a very hectic life.

Lynn's young husband, on army leave, had died three months before, burned in a truck accident from which he had thrown her clear. They had been moving Lynn's belongings to her new lover's house in Philly.

Lynn arrived on our doorstep with no place to go. She and Bea had broken up for reasons I knew only too well, and Lynn had followed the gay lorelei to New York. Jittery with dexedrine and crazed with exhaustion, she was afraid to go to sleep because of her nightmares of death and dying and the burning wreck from which arose billows of guilt over Ralph's death.

Nobody I knew could have remained immune to this game little girl-woman's piteous story. This was a chance to put into practice the kind of sisterhood that we talked and dreamed about for the future.

Muriel and I took Lynn into our home to live with us. For a while that summer, we had a vision and possibility of women living together collectively and sharing each other's lives and work and love. It almost worked. But none of us knew quite enough about ourselves; we had no patterns to follow, except our own needs and our own unthought-out dreams. Those dreams did not steer us wrong, but sometimes they were not enough.

I found myself day-dreaming over the library catalogue, imaging Lynn's malocclusion, and I had to finally admit to myself how physically attracted to her I was. I was frightened and embarrassed as well as perplexed by this strange and unexpected turn of events. I loved Muriel like my own life; we were pledged to each other. How could I desire another woman physically? But I did. Naturally, the thing to do was to examine this new state of affairs in all of its endless ramifications, and to discuss each one of them in detail.

That is what the three of us did, endlessly, over and over until all hours of the morning. Muriel thought it was an exciting

idea, possible in a new world of women. Lynn wanted to sleep
with us both and no more to-do about it. I knew what I wanted,
which was everybody one at a time, and since my wants felt
contradictory, I had to figure out some way I could have everything that I wanted and still be safe. That was very difficult, because we were in uncharted territory.

What we were trying to build was dangerous, and could have
enormous consequences for Muriel and me. But our love was
strong enough to be tested, strong enough to provide a base for
loving and extended relationships. I always used to say that I
believed in sleeping with my friends. Well, here was a chance to
put theory into practice. Besides, every time Lynn laughed her
slightly hysterical laugh or wrinkled her nose, my knees turned
to pudding. I could smell her like wilted fall flowers throughout
the house as soon as I opened the door of the apartment from
work.

Our conversations went on all night. Sometimes I arrived at
the library without having slept at all, looking like something the cat dragged in and the kittens wouldn't eat. I said that
my boyfriend Oliver had a fatal disease and had been sick all
night and his sister Muriel and I had stayed up to nurse him.
Mrs. Johnson, head of the children's room, looked at me with a
very funny eye, but never said a word. I think she was gay too.

So all in all, I was rather relieved one day when I opened the
door after work to find Muriel and Lynn just getting out of bed
together. A piece of me was furious (What, another woman's
hands on Muriel's body?), and another piece of me was afraid
(Well! Now I'd really have to fish or cut bait). But a large piece
of me was just relieved that we had moved beyond talking, and
that the direction of that movement was out of my hands.

The three of us kissed and held hands and had dinner, which
Lynn cooked for the first time. Then Muriel went to Laurel's
for a beer, and I found out that Lynn was every bit as delicious
as I had fantasized her to be.

Our new living arrangement called for a celebration, so I
took the next two days off from work. I called the library and
told Mrs. Johnson that Muriel and I were taking Oliver to a
nursing home in Connecticut because we couldn't care for him
any longer.

Muriel and I decided that nothing could break the bonds between us, certainly not the sharing of our bodies and our joys
with another woman whom we had come to love, also. Our

taking Lynn to our bed became, not merely a fact to be integrated into our living, but a test for each one of us of our love and our openness.

It was a beautiful vision but a difficult experiment. At first Lynn seemed to be having the best of it. She had both of us totally focused upon her and her problems, as well as upon her little horsewoman's body and her ribald lovemaking.

I helped Lynn get a job at the library, in another branch. She rented a basement space over on West Bleecker Street to store her furniture, but mostly she lived at Seventh Street.

We were certainly the first to have tried to work out this unique way of living for women, communal sex without rancor. After all, nobody else ever talked about it. None of the gay-girl books we read so avidly ever suggested our vision was not new, nor our joy in each other. Certainly Beebo Brinker didn't; nor Olga, of *The Scorpion*. Our much-fingered copies of Ann Bannon's *Women in the Shadows* and *Odd Girl Out* never so much as suggested that the perils and tragedies connected with loving women could possibly involve more than two at a time. And of course none of those books even mentioned the joys. So we knew there was a world of our experience as gay-girls that they left out, but that meant we had to write it ourselves, learn by living it out.

We tried to make it all work out gracefully and with a certain finesse.

Muriel, Lynn, and I made spoken and unspoken rules of courtesy for ourselves that we hoped would both allow for and help allay hurt feelings: "I thought you were staying with me tonight." The pressures of close quarters: "Hush, she's not asleep yet." And of course, guilt-provoking gallantry: "I'll go on ahead and the two of you meet me later; but don't be too long, now."

Sometimes it worked; sometimes it didn't. Muriel and I attempted to examine why, endlessly. For all her manipulative coolness, Lynn was seldom alone with either of us for any length of time. Increasingly, she got the message that, try as we might to make it otherwise, this space on Seventh Street was Muriel's and my space, and she, Lynn, was a desired and sought-after visitor, but a visitor forever.

I had wanted it to be different. Muriel had wanted it to be different. Lynn had wanted it to be different. At least in all the places we consciously touched. Somehow, it never was, but

neither Muriel nor I wanted to notice that, nor how unfair such
a stacked deck was. She and I had each other; Lynn had only a
piece of each of us, and was here on sufferance.

We never saw nor articulated this until much later, despite
our endless examinations and theme-writing about communal
living. And by then it was too late, at least for this experiment
in living out our visions.

Muriel and I talked about love as a voluntary commitment,
while we each struggled through the steps of an old dance, not
consciously learned, but desperately followed. We had learned
well in the kitchens of our mothers, both powerful women who
did not let go easily. In those warm places of survival, love was
another name for control, however openly given.

One Sunday night in the beginning of August, Muriel and I
came home from Laurel's to find that Lynn had left. Her knapsack and the boxes in which she kept her assortment of memen-
tos from different lives were gone. In the middle of the kitchen
table was Muriel's Cassell's german dictionary, the book in
which we kept our savings, ninety dollars to date. It was open,
and the pages were empty.

That ninety dollars was all the money we had, and it represented a huge loss to us. Our roommate was gone, our house-
keys were gone, our savings were gone. The loss of the dream
was even greater.

Even many years afterward, Lynn was never able to say to
us why she had done it.

28 That fall, Muriel and I took a course at the
New School in contemporary american poetry,
and I went into therapy. There were things I did
not understand, and things I felt that I did not want to feel,
particularly the blinding headaches that came in waves sometimes.

And I seldom spoke. I wrote and I dreamed, but almost never
talked, except in answer to a direct question, or to give a direction of some sort. I became more and more aware of this the
longer Muriel and I lived together.

With Rhea, as with most of the other people I knew, my pri-
mary function in conversations was to listen. Most people never

get a chance to talk as much as they want to, and I was an attentive listener, being really interested in what made other people tick. (Maybe I could squirrel it off and examine their lives in private and find out something about myself.)

Muriel and I communicated pretty much by intuition and unfinished sentences. Libraries are supposed to be quiet, so at work I didn't have to talk, except to point out where books were, and tell stories to the children. I was very good at that, and I loved to do it. It felt like reciting the endless poems I used to memorize as a child, and which I would retell to myself and anybody else who would listen. They were my way of talking. To express a feeling, I would recite a poem. When the poems I memorized fell short of the occasion, I started to write my own.

I also wanted to go back to college. The course we were taking at the New School didn't make too much sense to me, and the idea of studying was not a familiar one to me. I had managed high school without it, and nobody had bothered to notice. I entered college believing one learned by osmosis, and by concentrating intently on what everybody said. That had meant survival in my family's house.

When I left college, I said to myself at the time that one year of college was more than most Black women had and so I was already ahead of the game. But when Muriel came to New York, I knew I was not going back to Mexico any time soon, and I wanted a degree. I had had tastes of what job-hunting was like for unskilled Black women. Even though I had a job which I enjoyed, I wanted someday not to have to take orders from everybody else. Most of all, I wanted to be free enough to know and do what I wanted to do. I wanted not to shake when I got angry or cry when I got mad. And the city colleges were still free.

I started therapy on the anniversary of the first day Muriel and I met the year before.

On Thanksgiving Day, we fixed a great feast in celebration and invited Suzy and Sis for dinner. Since even at student rates therapy was a luxury, and we had only one income between us, money became even tighter. The day before Thanksgiving, I took my mail-pouch pocketbook and Muriel put on her loosest fitting jacket, and we went across town to the A&P next to Jim Atkins's, the all-night diner in the Village. We came back with a little capon, two pounds of mushrooms, a box of rice, and asparagus. The asparagus was the hardest of all to get, and some of the tips were broken from being tucked so quickly into Muriel's waistband. But we managed without mishap or detection, and walked home whistling and pleased.

About stealing food from supermarkets—I felt that if we needed it badly enough, we would not get caught. And truth to tell, I stopped doing it when I no longer had to, and I never did get caught.

On our way home we splurged on a pint of cherry-vanilla ice cream for dessert, and Suzy and Sis brought the wine. Muriel made an italian pepper and egg pie, and we had a wonderful feast. I brought out all my Mexican rugs and *rebozos*, and decorated the walls and the chairs and the couch with bright colors. The house looked and smelled holiday happy.

That night, I announced that I had made up my mind to register for college at night in the spring term.

Muriel and I kept Christmas on Christmas Eve, such keeping as we did. We exchanged our presents, grumbled a lot, and prepared to go our separate families' ways the next day. We wrapped their presents, and worried about what we could wear home that would not be too uncomfortable, yet appropriate enough to forestall questions and comments.

On Christmas Day, with many kisses and long goodbyes, Muriel went to Stamford and I went up to the Bronx to my sister Phyllis's home to have dinner with her and Henry and the children, along with my mother and Helen. Phyllis had a family and a real house, not an apartment, so it was tacitly agreed that she keep Christmas. It relieved me of another direct confrontation with my mother's house, and gave me a chance to enjoy my two nieces, whom I loved but did not often see. I made a big project of inviting them down to Seventh Street afterward, but they never came.

Christmas we gave to our families; New Year's we kept for ourselves. They were two separate worlds. My family knew that I had a roommate named Muriel. That was about all. My mother had met Muriel, and as usual, since I had left her house, knew it was wise to make no comment about my personal life. But my mother could make "no comment" more loudly and with more hostility than anyone else I knew. Muriel and I had been to Phyllis's house for dinner once, and whatever Phyllis and Henry thought about our relationship, they kept it to themselves. In general, my family only allowed themselves to know whatever it was they cared to know, and I did not push them as long as they left me alone.

On New Year's Eve, Muriel and I went to a party at Nicky and Joan's house. They lived in a brownstone in the eighties near Broadway. Nicky was a writer who worked on a fashion newspaper and Joan was a secretary at Metropolitan Life. Nicky was tiny and tight; Joan was lean and beautiful, with dark spaniel eyes. Unlike Muriel and I, they looked very proper and elegant in their straight clothes, and for that reason, and because they lived so far uptown, it felt like they lived a far more conventional life than we did. In some ways, this was true, for Nicky in particular. Joan was talking about quitting her job and becoming a bum for a while. I envied her the freedom of choice that allowed her to consider this, knowing she could get another job whenever she wanted one. That was what being white and knowing how to type meant.

This was to be a holiday fete, not simply a wash-your-foot-and-come. I never enjoyed parties much if Muriel and I weren't giving them, although I had started to really enjoy the parties out in Queens that we went to with Vida and Pet and Gerri. Those parties given by Black women were always full of food and dancing and reefer and laughter and high-jinks. Vida with her dramatic voice and sense of the absurd, and Pet with her dancing feet that were never still, made it easy not to be shy, to move with the music and laughter. It was at those parties that I finally learned how to dance.

Joan and Nicky's parties were different. Usually there wasn't much music, and when there was, it was not for dancing. There was always lots of wine around, both red and white, because Nicky and Joan were more Bermuda shorts than dungarees. One of the noticeable differences between the two sets was wine versus hard liquor. But more than one glass of any kind of wine gave me heartburn, and besides it was all too dry for my taste. It was not sophisticated to like sweet wine, and that became another one of my secret vices, like soft ice cream, to be indulged only around tried and true friends.

And there was never enough food. Tonight, for the holidays, a beautifully laid table graced the corner of Nicky and Joan's great, high-ceilinged parlor. Upon an old linen tablecloth that had belonged to Nicky's mother, and bright red poinsettia mats cut from felt, sat little plates of potato chips and pretzels and crackers and cheeses, a bowl of sour cream and onion dip made from Lipton's onion soup mix, and tiny little jars of red caviar with bright green bibs around them. There were saucers of olives and celery and pickles on the edges of the table, and in

various corners of the room, baskets of mixed nuts. I kept
thinking of the pigs-in-a-blanket and fried chicken wings and
potato salad and hot corn bread at Gerri and them's last "do,"
knowing it wasn't a question of money, because red caviar cost
a lot more than chicken wings.

The feeling in the room was subdued. Mostly, women sat
around in little groups and talked quietly, the sound of modera-
tion—thick and heavy as smoke in the air. I noticed the absence
of laughter only because I always thought parties were supposed
to be fun, even though I didn't find them particularly so, never
knowing what to say. I busied myself looking through the bookshelves lining the room.

Muriel circulated with ease. She seemed in her element, her
soft voice and fall-away chuckle moving from group to group,
cigarette and bottle of beer in hand. I studied the books, uncomfortable and acutely aware of being alone. Pat, a friend of
Nicky's from the paper, came over and started to talk. I listened
appreciatively, greatly relieved.

Muriel and I left shortly after midnight, walking over to the
subway on Central Park West arm in arm. It was good to be out
in the sharp cold air, even good to be a little tired. We frolicked
through the almost empty streets, talking and laughing about
nonsensical things, joking about our uptown friends who
drank dry wine. Occasional blasts from party horns were still
erupting from gaily lit windows, holiday open.

In the freshness and nip of the winter's late night, alone now
with Muriel, something powerful and promising inside of me
stretched, excited and joyful. I thought of other New Year's
Eves that I had spent, alone, or wandering through Times Square.
I was very lucky, very blessed.

I squeezed Muriel's hand, and felt her tight squeeze back. I
was in love, a new year was beginning, and the shape of the
future was a widening star. It was one year to the day that
Muriel and I had locked the door of Seventh Street behind Rhea
and turned off the fire under the coffee on the stove and laid
down together with our hearts against each other. This was our
first anniversary.

We went home and ushered it in quite properly, until dawn
sang with the rhythms of our bodies, our heat.

Later, we got up, and Muriel cooked a huge pot of hoppin'
john, black-eyed peas and rice, which Suzy's friend Lion from
Philly had taught her how to do, and of which she was very

proud. I laughed to see her strutting around the kitchen rosy-cheeked, waving her wooden spoon aloft in triumph as the food reached exactly the right consistency without becoming mushy.

Evening moved upon us, and as our friends dropped by, we wished each other good times and ate and ate. Some of the women were hung-over, and some were depressed, and some were just plain sleepy from being out all night and thinking of work tomorrow. But we all agreed that Muriel's pot was the best hoppin' john we'd ever tasted, and that it was going to be a super year for us all.

Nicky and Joan were the last to leave. After they had gone, Muriel and I put the dishes and pots to soak in the covered part of the sink, and we climbed back into bed with our notebooks and wrote New Year themes. Muriel chose a subject—A Man from the Land Where Nobody Lives. When we finished, we exchanged our notebooks and read each other's work before moving on to the next theme.

Muriel had written:

The Year 1955

Audi	*Me*
got a new job	
started therapy	
sent out some poems	NOTHING!
is going back to school	

I stared at the notebook page in silence, feeling like cold water had been thrown at me. I reached over and took her hand. It lay cool and still beneath my fingers, without movement. I did not know what to say to Muriel. The idea that anyone could measure herself against me and find that self wanting was truly shocking. The fact that it was my beloved Muriel who was doing it was nothing less than terrifying.

I thought of our life as a mutual exploration, a progress through the strength of our loving. But as I read and re-read the stark outline in her notebook, I realized that Muriel saw that joint becoming in terms of achievements of mine which somehow defined her inabilities. They were not mutual triumphs, the notebook said in inescapable terms, and there was nothing either I or our loving could do to shield her from the implications of that truth, as she saw it.

29 I walked down those three little steps into the Bagatelle on a weekend night in 1956. There was an inner door, guarded by a male bouncer, ostensibly to keep out the straight male intruders come to gawk at the "lezzies," but in reality to keep out those women deemed "undesirable." All too frequently, undesirable meant Black.

Women stood three-deep around the bar and between the tables, and in the doorway to the postage-stamp-sized dance floor. By 9:00 P.M., the floor was packed solid with women's bodies moving slowly to the jukebox beat of Ruth Brown's

When your friends have left you all alone
and you have no one to call your own

or Frank Sinatra's

Set 'em up, Joe
I got a little story. . .

When I moved through the bunches of women cruising each other in the front room, or doing a slow fish on the dance floor in the back, with the smells of cigarette smoke and the music and the hair pomade whirling together like incense through charged air, it was hard for me to believe that my being an outsider had anything to do with being a lesbian.

But when I, a Black woman, saw no reflection in any of the faces there week after week, I knew perfectly well that being an outsider in the Bagatelle had everything to do with being Black.

The society within the confines of the Bagatelle reflected the ripples and eddies of the larger society that had spawned it, and which allowed the Bagatelle to survive as long as it did, selling watered-down drinks at inflated prices to lonely dykes who had no other social outlet or community gathering place.

Rather than the idyllic picture created by false nostalgia, the fifties were really straight white america's cooling-off period of "let's pretend we're happy and that this is the best of all possible worlds and we'll blow those nasty commies to hell if they dare to say otherwise."

The Rosenbergs had been executed, the transistor radio had been invented, and frontal lobotomy was the standard solution for persistent deviation. For some, Elvis Presley and his stolen Black rhythms became arch-symbols of the antichrist.

Young america's growing pains, within the Bagatelle, were represented by the fashion conflicts between the blue-jeans set and the bermuda-shorts set. Then, of course, there were those who fell in between, either by virtue of our art or our craziness or our color.

The breakdown into the mommies and the daddies was an important part of lesbian relationships in the Bagatelle. If you asked the wrong woman to dance, you could get your nose broken in the alley down the street by her butch, who had followed you out of the Bag for exactly that purpose. It was safer to keep to yourself. And you were never supposed to ask who was who, which is why there was such heavy emphasis upon correct garb. The well-dressed gay-girl was supposed to give you enough cues for you to know.

For some of us, however, role-playing reflected all the depreciating attitudes toward women which we loathed in straight society. It was a rejection of these roles that had drawn us to "the life" in the first place. Instinctively, without particular theory or political position or dialectic, we recognized oppression as oppression, no matter where it came from.

But those lesbians who had carved some niche in the pretend world of dominance/subordination, rejected what they called our "confused" life style, and they were in the majority.

Felicia was so late one Sunday afternoon for our photography lesson, that Muriel and I went off to Laurel's without her, because you had to be early on Sundays to get something to eat. The Swing Rendezvous had closed its table, but at Laurel's on Sunday afternoons there was free brunch with any drink, and that meant all you could eat. Many of the gay bars used this to get Sunday afternoon business at a traditionally slow time, but Laurel's had the best food. There was a Chinese cook there of no mean talent, who cooked back and kept it coming. After the word got around, every Sunday afternoon at four o'clock, there would be a line of gay-girls in front of Laurel's, smoking and talking and trying to pretend we had all arrived there at that time by accident.

When the doors opened, there was a discreet but determined stampede, first to the bar and then to the food table, set up in the rear of the lounge. We tried to keep our cool, pretending that we couldn't care less for barbecued spareribs with peach and apricot sweet sauce, or succulent pink shrimp swimming in thick golden lobster sauce, dotted with bits of green scallion and bright yellow eggdrops, tiny pieces of pork and onion afloat on top. There were stacked piles of crispy brown eggrolls filled with shredded ham and chicken and celery, rolled together and fried with a touch of sesame paste. There were fried chicken bits, and every once in a great while, a special delicacy such as lobster or fresh crab. Only the first lucky few got to taste those special dishes, so it was worthwhile being first in line and pushing your cool image a little bit askew.

We were healthy young female animals mercifully more alive than most of our peers, robust and active women, and our blood was always high and our pockets empty and a free meal in convivial surroundings—meaning around other lesbians—was a big treat for most of us, even if purchased at the price of a bottle of beer, which was fifty cents, with many complaints.

Dancing wasn't allowed at Laurel's so it never got to be as popular as the Bag, except on Sunday afternoons. Muriel preferred it because it was always quieter. Trix ran the place, and always had a hand for "her girls." Tiny and tough, with a permanent Florida tan and a Bronx accent, she took a shine to Muriel and me, and sometimes she would buy us a beer, and sit down and talk with us if the place wasn't too crowded.

We all knew the situation with gay bars, how they came in and out of existence with such regularity and who really profited from them. But Trix was pretty and bright and hard and kind all at the same time, and her permanent tan particularly endeared her to me. She looked like one of the nicer hickory-skinned devils who used to people my dreams of that period.

Actually, the life span of most gay bars was under a year, with the notable exception of a few like the Bag. Laurel's went the way of all the other gay bars—like the Swing and Snooky's and the Grapevine, the Sea Colony and the Pony Stable Inn. Each closed after a year or so, while another opened and caught on somewhere else. But for that year, Laurel's served as an important place for those of us who met and made some brief space for ourselves there. It had a feeling of family.

On summer Sunday afternoons, Muriel and I would split from the gay beach at Coney Island or Riis Park early, take the subway back home in time to wash up and dress and saunter over to Laurel's in time for the food at 4:00. I had my first open color confrontation with a gay-girl one Sunday afternoon in Laurel's.

Muriel and I had come back that day from Riis Park, full of sun and sand. We loved with the salt still on our skins, then bathed, washed our hair, and got ready to go out. I put on my faded cord riding britches with the suede crotch, and a pale blue short-sleeved sweatshirt bought earlier that week at John's on Avenue C for sixty-nine cents. My skin was tanned from the sun and burnished ruddy with the heat and much loving. My hair was newly trimmed and freshly washed, with the particular crispness that it always develops in sustained summer heat. I felt raunchy and restless.

We walked out of the hot August afternoon sun into the suddenly dark coolness of Laurel's downstairs. There was Muriel in her black Bermuda shorts and shirt, ghost pale, her eternal cigarette in hand. And I was beside her, full of myself, knowing I was fat and Black and very fine. We were without peer or category, and on that day I was conscious of being very proud of it, no matter who looked down her nose at us.

After Muriel and I had gotten our food and beer and copped one of the tables, Dottie and Pauli came over. We saw them a lot at the Bag and in the supermarket over on Avenue D, but we'd never been to their house nor they to ours, except for New Year's food, when everyone came.

"Where you guys been?" Pauli had an ingenuous smile, her blonde hair and blue eyes incandescent against the turquoise mandarin shirt she wore.

"Riis. Gay Beach." Muriel's finger crooked over the bottle as she took a slug. All of us eschewed glasses as faggy, although I sometimes longed for one because the cold beer hurt my teeth.

Pauli turned to me. "Hey, that's a great tan you have there. I didn't know Negroes got tans." Her broad smile was intended to announce the remark as a joke.

My usual defense in such situations was to ignore the overtones, to let it go. But Dottie Daws, probably out of her own nervousness at Pauli's reference to the unmentionable, would not let the matter drop. Raved on and on about my great tan. Matched her arm to mine. Shook her pale blonde head, telling whomever would listen that she wished she could tan like that instead of burning, and did I know how lucky I was to be able to get such a tan like that? I grew tired and then shakingly furious, having enough of whatever it was.

"How come you never make so much over my natural tan most days, Dottie Daws; how come?"

There was a moment of silence at the table, punctuated only by Muriel's darkly appreciative chuckle, and then we moved on to something else, mercifully. I was still shaking inside. I never forgot it.

In the gay bars, I longed for other Black women without the need ever taking shape upon my lips. For four hundred years in this country, Black women have been taught to view each other with deep suspicion. It was no different in the gay world.

Most Black lesbians were closeted, correctly recognizing the Black community's lack of interest in our position, as well as the many more immediate threats to our survival as Black people in a racist society. It was hard enough to be Black, to be Black and female, to be Black, female, and gay. To be Black, female, gay, and out of the closet in a white environment, even to the extent of dancing in the Bagatelle, was considered by many Black lesbians to be simply suicidal. And if you were fool enough to do it, you'd better come on so tough that nobody messed with you. I often felt put down by their sophistication, their clothes, their manners, their cars, and their femmes.

The Black women I usually saw around the Bag were into heavy roles, and it frightened me. This was partly the fear of my own Blackness mirrored, and partly the realities of the masquerade. Their need for power and control seemed a much-too-open piece of myself, dressed in enemy clothing. They were tough in a way I felt I could never be. Even if they were not, their self-protective instincts warned them to appear that way. By white america's racist distortions of beauty, Black women playing "femme" had very little chance in the Bag. There was constant competition among butches to have the most "gorgeous femme" on their arm. And "gorgeous" was defined by a white male world's standards.

For me, going into the Bag alone was like entering an anomalous no-woman's land. I wasn't cute or passive enough to be "femme," and I wasn't mean or tough enough to be "butch." I was given a wide berth. Non-conventional people can be dangerous, even in the gay community.

With the exception of Felicia and myself, the other Black women in the Bag came protected by a show of all the power symbols they could muster. Whatever else they did during the week, on Friday nights when Lion or Trip appeared, sometimes with expensively dressed women on their arms, sometimes alone, they commanded attention and admiration. They were well-heeled, superbly dressed, self-controlled high-steppers who drove convertibles, bought rounds of drinks for their friends, and generally took care of business.

But sometimes, even *they* couldn't get in unless they were recognized by the bouncer.

My friends and I were the hippies of the gay-girl circuit, before the word was coined. Many of us wound up dead or demented, and many of us were distorted by the many fronts we had to fight upon. But when we survived, we grew up strong.

Every Black woman I ever met in the Village in those years had some part in my survival, large or small, if only as a figure in the head-count at the Bag on a Friday night.

Black lesbians in the Bagatelle faced a world only slightly less hostile than the outer world which we had to deal with every day on the outside—that world which defined us as doubly nothing because we were Black and because we were Woman—that world which raised our blood pressures and shaped our furies and our nightmares.

The temporary integration of war plants, and the egalitarian myth of Rosie the Riveter had ended abruptly with the end of World War II and the wholesale return of the american woman to the role of little wifey. So far as I could see, gay-girls were the only Black and white women who were even talking to each other in this country in the 1950s, outside of the empty rhetoric of patriotism and political movements.

Black or white, Ky-Ky, butch, or femme, the only thing we shared, often, and in varying proportions, was that we dared for connection in the name of woman, and saw that as our power, rather than our problem.

All of us who survived those common years had to be a little strange. We spent so much of our young-womanhood trying to define ourselves as woman-identified women before we even knew the words existed, let alone that there were ears interested in trying to hear them beyond our immediate borders. All of us who survived those common years have to be a little proud. A lot proud. Keeping ourselves together and on our own tracks, however wobbly, was like trying to play the Dinizulu War Chant or a Beethoven sonata on a tin dog-whistle.

The important message seemed to be that you had to have a place. Whether or not it did justice to whatever you felt you were about, there had to be some place to refuel and check your flaps.

In times of need and great instability, the place sometimes became more a definition than the substance of why you needed it to begin with. Sometimes the retreat became the reality. The writers who posed in cafés talking their work to death without writing two words; the lesbians, virile as men, hating women *and* their own womanhood with a vengeance. The bars and the

coffee-shops and the streets of the Village in the 1950s were full
of non-conformists who were deathly afraid of going against
their hard-won group, and so eventually they were broken between the group and their individual needs.

For some of us there was no one particular place, and we
grabbed whatever we could from wherever we found space,
comfort, quiet, a smile, non-judgment.

*Being women together was not enough. We were different.
Being gay-girls together was not enough. We were different.
Being Black together was not enough. We were different. Being
Black women together was not enough. We were different. Be-
ing Black dykes together was not enough. We were different.*

Each of us had our own needs and pursuits, and many different alliances. Self-preservation warned some of us that we could
not afford to settle for one easy definition, one narrow individ-
uation of self. At the Bag, at Hunter College, uptown in Harlem,
at the library, there was a piece of the real me bound in each
place, and growing.

It was a while before we came to realize that our place was
the very house of difference rather the security of any one
particular difference. (And often, we were cowards in our learning.) It was years before we learned to use the strength that
daily surviving can bring, years before we learned fear does not
have to incapacitate, and that we could appreciate each other
on terms not necessarily our own.

The Black gay-girls in the Village gay bars of the fifties knew
each other's names, but we seldom looked into each other's
Black eyes, lest we see our own aloneness and our own blunted
power mirrored in the pursuit of darkness. Some of us died inside the gaps between the mirrors and those turned-away eyes.

*Sistah outsiders. Didi and Tommy and Muff and Iris and Lion
and Trip and Audre and Diane and Felicia and Bernie and Addie.*

Addie was Mari Evans beautiful, a wasted sister-soul. Driven
as we all were driven, she found ways out that were still alien to
some of the rest of us—harsher, less hidden.

That Sunday afternoon while Muriel and I waited for Flee
and our photography lesson, Addie was turning Flee onto
smack for the first time in a borrowed apartment across Second
Avenue.

30

The spring of 1956 came with a plethora of ambiguous omens. I had stopped therapy because of our shortage of money. What had seemed just enough to get by on a year ago had shrunk through inflation or recession or whatever they chose to call it in the *New York Times*. Fingering over my private structures became a luxury I could not afford. Therapy was the last possible cut to be made. Neither of us said a word about Muriel's inability to look for work. She did not deal with her self-loathing, and I did not deal with my resentment. My physiology professor at Hunter College tried to help my financial problems by offering me a job as a live-in maid in her Park Avenue house.

The night before my last session in therapy, I dreamt that Muriel and I stood waiting for a train in a midnight-blue subway station. There are clusters of people about, but their backs are turned and I cannot see their faces. As the train pulls into the station, Muriel falls off the platform beneath its wheels. I stand on the platform as the train rolls over her, powerless to do anything, my heart breaking beneath the wheels. I awake to tears and a sense of mourning too deep for words, that would not go away.

Muriel was having trouble sleeping. Night after night she sat up on the couch in the middle room, reading and smoking and writing in her journal, and sometimes I woke to hear her talking to herself. I found out only later the desperate quality of those hallucinations which she hid from me under irascibility or humor.

Other nights she stayed out drinking until I had gone to sleep. I could wake and look through the doorway of our bedroom to find her, night after night, leaning against the pillows on the couch propped up against the wall. Her dear dark head outlined in a circle of lamplight, Crazy Lady and Scarey Lou curled up together against the warmth of her thighs. Sometimes I felt we were as lost to each other as if one of us were dead.

In the morning when I got up to dress for work, I would find her asleep on the couch looking worn and vulnerable, her pale hand still holding the book fallen upon her breast, the two little kittens entwined, asleep, upon her tummy. She was getting thinner and thinner, eating less and less, insisting she was not hungry, even though it seemed very dangerous to me to be living on beer and cigarettes. I turned off the lamp over her head, pulled the covers over her, and went on to work.

Que Será, Que Será,
Whatever will be, will be. . .

Spring came in with extraordinary fervor, and the sounds of
Doris Day's wide-mouthed rendition of "Whatever Will Be, Will
Be" resounded from every jukebox and soda fountain radio.

One brisk Sunday evening in early April, Muriel and I ran
into my old school friend Jill crossing East Houston Street, huddled into a worn pea coat two sizes too big for her. I had not
seen her for almost two years, since she and The Branded had
used my Spring Street apartment after I left for Stamford to
work. Both poets, renegades, and very determined young
women, there was much that connected Jill and me across our
differences. There was also a lot of unfinished business that
separated us. It made us wary of each other, at the same time
as we valued each other's insights.

Jill was on her way to her father's law office downtown to
use his electric typewriters after business hours. Muriel and I
joined her, and for several Sundays thereafter, we typed our
poems and themes on elegant IBM machines. There was a
guarded truce between Jill and me, as if we had decided to forget whatever had occurred before without speaking of it, as if
the connections and the history we shared were enough to bridge
the differences between us. At least Jill was a fighter too, another confirmed outsider. As infants, we had grown up in the
subliminal echo of Franklin Delano Roosevelt's determinedly
optimistic fireside chats. We each had absorbed some of his
prescription for progress: When times are hard, do something.
If it works, do it some more. If it does not work, do something
else. But keep doing.

The next week, coming out of my german class one evening,
I heard someone calling me by name. Turning, surprised, I saw
Toni, ex-varsity star of Hunter High School. We had only been
bare acquaintances before, but here in the inhospitable waste-
lands of Hunter College, we greeted each other's familiar face
warmly and with welcome relief.

"Let's go for coffee next week," I suggested, as the bell rang
for the next class and we dashed for the elevator. Toni laughed
and shook her close-cropped blonde head.

"Why coffee? How about a drink! There's a great bar downtown on the West Side called the Sea Colony. We can drive
down after class, and it's not too far from where you live, is
it?"

So Toni was gay. Another welcome not-quite-surprise. And she had her own car, no mean accomplishment three years out of high school.

Toni was by now a registered nurse, teaching a course in Hunter's nursing program once a week. I was amazed. It seemed as if she had gotten on about the business of making her life work while we were still trying to reconstruct the world. Toni seemed so grown-up and capable and settled and prosperous in comparison to Muriel and me. She was a year younger than I was, and she owned her own car and rented a summer house at Huntington Station and never had to worry about what she spent for food. Very much in the closet at work and school, Toni still had a reputation for having "unconventional" friends.

We saw a lot of Toni; Muriel saw more of her than I did, since I was in school until 10:00 four nights a week.

I had just finished my advanced algebra homework, still confused about the function of sines, and climbed into bed when I heard Muriel's key in the door. I felt the rush of damp air around her from the spring storm outside before I saw her now-gaunt face, glistening with wet from the long walk across town.

"You still up?" She shed her navy sweater onto the couch and came in to sit down on the edge of our bed. Happy to see her home before I slept and in a good mood, I sat up and reached for my glasses. Her note had said that she and Toni were going for a beer.

"Where's Toni; why didn't she drive you home?" I kissed her. She smelled of beer and smoke and April rain.

"She got a flat near the hospital today so she didn't have the car." Neither of us was used to including wheels in our lives.

"I got an eight on my quadratics exam tonight." Trig had been a major stumbling block in math that term. "Where did you-all go?"

"We went to the Swing but it was closed up, and I don't know if it's for tonight or for good. So then we went to a new place over on Bleecker called the Mermaid, but they had a dollar minimum which is shit-for-the-birds during the week, so we wound up at the Riv." The Riviera was not primarily a gay bar, but its sawdust floors and cheap beer made it everybody's standby on Sheridan Square.

"How's Toni?"

Muriel chuckled. "Getting looser all the time. She didn't even have her head-nurse's cap with her tonight." Muriel reached over and took a puff from my cigarette. "How would you feel if Toni and I slept together?"

I looked at her deep brown eyes, shining and open for the first time in so long. So that was it. Her expectant half-smile helped cushion my surprise at how easily this whole question had arisen, again.

"Well, have you?"

"Not yet, of course not. You know I'd tell you."

She spoke with such animation and lightness of spirit that I had to smile in spite of myself. Old Muriel had come back to town. I butted my cigarette and settled back into bed. "Well, I'm glad you asked. Come on to bed." Muriel was taking off her sneakers.

My stabs of jealousy were tempered by my lessening sense of guilt; for what, I could not say. I lay beside Muriel, listening to her gentle snoring, still not really sure of what I felt. I liked Toni, and what was even more important, I trusted her. Trusted her to take care of Muriel.

I loved to see Muriel's eyes alight. I recalled the disruption Lynn had caused in our lives last year. But this felt very different. I had learned a lot. Muriel certainly needed something.

But another piece of myself turned over in the darkness, filled with a great sadness. I suddenly thought about my last year at home. One morning going into my parents' bedroom to get the iron in the pre-dawn hours before I left for school. Turning in the dimness of the early-morning light, I was startled suddenly to find my mother's open eyes silently regarding me as I crept around quietly. I sensed that she had been awake for a long while, listening to me going about my adolescent business in the quiet apartment. Our eyes met for a moment, and it was the only time that I felt the full weight of my mother's pain at the hostilities forever between us.

That moment was short and sharp and incredibly poignant.

I stood there with my hand on the bedroom doorknob. No word passed between us, but I suddenly remembered the day I first menstruated, and I felt like I was about to cry. I tucked the iron under my arm and closed the door softly behind me.

In the dim glow from the Seventh Street streetlamps, I turned my head to regard Muriel's sleeping face. What did my mother think about at night now that I had gone away?

More and more of my own energies were being focused elsewhere. I thought of life between Muriel and me, certainly not as idyllic, but as something precious to both of us that we were still committed to build. And besides, we had said *forever*.

Muriel seemed to gain a new lease on life. She began to sleep better, and she spent less and less time on the couch in the middle room.

Soon, big brusque Toni became a part of our lives, with her gymnastic jackets and her lacy RN cap perched incongruously on her aggressive head. She would come over on Sunday afternoon bringing homemade blintzes and charts from school, upon which we would try to diagram the interpersonal relationships possible in our future world of women.

School was going better for me than I had ever hoped. For the first time in my life, I began to know, really know, I was smart—smart as defined by being able to do the white man's work, being able to study. I was finally learning german, and doing a fine job of it. Mostly, with the help of Muriel and my old therapist, I had learned to study. Muriel, who had studied german in school, also helped me with german conversation, and for a while I was more articulate in german than I was in english.

Sometimes Toni stayed over on Seventh Street. In the chilly exultations of middle spring, the three of us would wake at dawn, pick up Nicky and Joan, and go fishing in Sheepshead Bay on Saturday mornings. We returned in the afternoon, the boats heavy with flounder and blackfish.

And on Sundays, often, there was Jill and her daddy's typewriters.

Muriel, Jill, and I walked back to Seventh Street through the darkening Sunday city—the unmistakable smell of early May was on the warming air. It was late when we got home, and Jill stayed over. The next day was Monday, which meant work as usual. I went to bed and left them both still talking in the middle room.

Sometime between midnight and morning I woke with a start in horror and disbelief. The muffled sounds coming from the next room were unmistakable. Muriel. Muriel and Jill were making love on the middle-room couch. I lay rigid, trying not to hear, trying not to be awake or there at all, trapped like some wild animal between a seven-story drop out the front windows and the activity going on in the next room. NO EXIT.

Had it been anyone else on our couch with Muriel my pain and fury might have been less. There was so much unsettled history between Jill and me. The cruelest weapon at hand, or so it felt. In our own house. With me in the next room. A veil of red fury settled over my consciousness which I had not felt since those days in my mother's house when I used to burst into nosebleeds instead of tears. I bit down on a mouthful of woolen blanket, feeling like I had to commit murder, only there was no one to kill. I fell asleep again immediately in desperate self-protection.

When I got up the house was quiet and empty. I could not even say, "How could you, you little bitch, with her of all people?" We couldn't even talk about it. Muriel wasn't there.

I walked back and forth through the apartment wringing my hands until the fingers tingled and grew red. How was I going to manage this day? Where was she? I wanted to wring her neck. Slowly I got dressed, and engineered myself out onto the street.

The street and the sky and the people I passed were all covered with a veil of rage fastened to an iron ring that was anchored with a steel bolt through the middle of my chest.

I had to get to work, which was now at a library in the Bronx. I huddled against the back wall in the Astor Place Station, afraid I was going to push someone or myself under an approaching train.

I rode up to Morris Avenue, my eyes filmed in red, my hands shaking. I could not separate the pain of betrayal from the pain of raw fury. Fury at Muriel, fury at Jill, fury at myself for not killing them both. The train rocketed on, with a delay at 34th Street. If I could not let this poison out of me I would die. A blinding headache came and went, without increasing or lessening my agony. My nose started to bleed around Grand Central Station. Somebody gave me a tissue and a seat and I leaned my head back, closing my eyes. The pictures of mayhem that flashed across the screen of my eyelids were too terrifying. I kept my eyes open for the rest of the way.

That morning, there was a staff meeting at the library. On these days, the staff took turns preparing tea, an old library custom. This week it was my turn. In the sparsely furnished, immaculate staff kitchen, I lifted a large pot of boiling water from the stove to pour it into the teapot standing in the sink.

Out of the kitchen window I could see fuzzy buds on the acacia tree in the tiny backyard that separated the library from the row of tenements fronting on the next street. In the dampness of this overcast Monday morning, the brightness of the new green was startling. Spring was coming on inexorably and Muriel had slept with Jill on our middle-room couch a few hours ago.

My left hand closed around the open mouth of the teapot as the steaming pot of boiling water rested in my other hand against the edge of the sink. The snake ring that Muriel had given me for my birthday curled around my left index finger, silver against my brown skin. I considered the back of my hand and my wrist as it disappeared into the cuff of my shirt and sweater. Almost casually, I realized what was about to happen, as if all of this was a story in some book that I had read thoroughly some time before.

I felt the tension rising in my right arm, and my right hand began to shake. I watched as the pot slowly rose from the edge of the sink, and the boiling water poured over the lip of the pot in slow motion onto my left hand as it rested upon the teapot. The water cascaded down, bounced off the back of my hand and flowed down the drain. I watched the brown skin cloud with steam, then turn red and shiny, and the poison began to run out of me like water as I fumbled at the buttons of my shirt cuff and peeled back the wet cloth from my scalded wrist. The steamed flesh had already started to blister.

Walking into the staff room next door where the rest of my colleagues sat discussing book orders. "I've burned myself by mistake." Then pain erupting into the space left empty by the draining away of the poison.

Someone took me home in a taxi from the doctor's office. It was Muriel who opened the door for me, and helped me off with my clothes. She did not ask what had happened. Next to the pain in my hand and wrist, everything else felt like it had never been. I fell immediately asleep. The next day I went to St. Vincent's burn clinic, where the snake ring had to be cut away from the scalded swollen flesh.

During the next few days, when I felt anything at all other than pain, it was guilt and embarrassment, as if I'd done an unforgivable and unmentionable act. Self-mutilation. Displaying a rage that was neither cool nor hip. Otherwise, I was quite empty of passion.

Muriel and I never spoke of Jill nor of the accident. We were very guarded and tender with each other, and a little bit mournful, as if we were both acknowledging with our silence what was irretrievable.

Jill had gone, to appear again some other time when one least expected her. She was not really important here, only what she represented. Now, most of all, when we needed the words between us, Muriel and I were both silent. What was lying between us had moved beyond our old speech, and we were both too lost and too frightened to attempt a new language.

We went out with Joan and Nicky to celebrate Nicky's birthday. My burns were healing. Luckily, there was no infection, and I had returned to work, wearing a white glove to hide the ugly scarring around my wrist and the back of my hand, oddly intertwined with new high-pink flesh. My mother had told me that cotton gloves and daily rubs with cocoa butter would keep the heavy keloid scars from forming, and she was right.

Muriel and I made love for the last time on May 20th. It was the night before my final exams at college.

The house was empty when I got home the next day. I'd come home early to study. It was empty when I left in the late twilight to catch the subway up to Hunter, and it was empty when I came home that night and finally went to bed. No one to exult with, no one to worry with, my first term back at school. It felt very lonely.

When we realized Muriel and Joan were having an affair, Nicky and I both predicted it would come to no good in the end. Neither Joan nor Muriel was working.

Summer became a nightmare of separation and endings. Muriel was going and I could not let her go, even though so much of me wanted to. An old dream of us together forever in a landscape blinded me.

Nightly, the floor around my lonely bed was carpeted and pitted with volcanoes through which Muriel wandered with great bravado and little caution. I tried to warn her, but my tongue was mute. My bed was safety, but my life, too, was bound up in where she put her feet. Molten fire flowed across the linoleum. If only she would do it my way, if only she could hear me, walk where I could see paths shining dully through the flames, then we would both be safe, forever. Dear god, make her listen to me before it's too late!

But we were unknowing partners in an intimate and complicated minuet. Neither one of us could break out. Neither one of us had the tools to recognize nor to alter the steps and the tone of our tight little dance. We could destroy each other, but we could not move beyond our pain. Our living together now was no longer even a matter of convenience, but neither of us would let go, nor admit to needing the devastating contact. If we did, we would have to ask the question, why; obviously, love was no longer enough of an answer.

Muriel spent most of her time now over at Nicky and Joan's in their new street-level apartment on Sixth Street and Avenue

B. Whenever we were alone together, venom and recriminations leaped out of my mouth like wild frogs, raining down upon her sullen, unresponsive head.

Before the summer solstice, Muriel was wildly in love again. I used to lie awake nights wondering how I could have lost my girl to thin willowy Joan, with the indecisive smile and the air of permanent potential.

The day I got my final marks from Hunter, there were riots in Poland. We lived in a Polish neighborhood, and the neighboring stoops were buzzing with excitement and apprehension as I took my grade cards from the mailbox. I had received a C in math and an A in german. This was the first A I had ever gotten in any subject other than english.

Of course, I was convinced that I had nothing to do with that grade. As soon as a challenge was overcome, it ceased to be a challenge, becoming the expected and ordinary rather than something I had achieved with difficulty, and could, therefore, be justly proud of. I could not own my own triumphs, nor give myself credit for them. Getting the A became not an achievement won by my hard work and study, but only something that had happened—probably, german must be getting easier to understand than it used to be. And besides, if Muriel was leaving me, obviously I couldn't be a person who did anything right, certainly not get an A in german under her own steam.

Some nights I couldn't sleep. Dawn found me walking up and down in front of the building where Joan and Nicky lived, the sharp edge of a fingered butcher knife up my sleeve. Muriel was in there, and most likely not asleep. I had no idea what I was planning to do. I felt like an actor in some badly written melodrama.

My heart knew what my head refused to understand. Our life together was over. If not Joan, then someone else. Another piece of me insisted this could not possibly be happening, while images of murder, death, earthquake harrowed my dreams. The psychic discord was ripping my brain apart. There must be something I could do differently that would take care of everything, end my agonies of bereavement, return Muriel to reason. If only I could figure out how to convince her this was all ridiculous behavior, unnecessary. We could start from there.

Other times, fury, cold as dry ice, strummed behind my eyes. When she did not come home for days, I stalked the streets of the Village, hunted and hunting her and Joan, at the mercy of emotional typhoons over which there was no control. Hate. I blew through summer pre-dawn streets like a winter wind, surrounded by a cloud of pain and rage so intense that no sane person would dare to intrude upon it. Nobody approached me on those journeys. I was sometimes sorry about that; I longed for an excuse to kill. My piercing headaches went away.

I called my mother to see how she was doing. Out of a clear blue sky, she inquired as to how Muriel was doing. "How's your friend? She's all right?" My mother was nothing if not psychic.

"Oh, she's fine," I said hurriedly. "Everything's fine." Desperate that my mother not know of my failure. Determined to hide this shame.

Summer school started and I registered for english and german. I was dropped in the first two weeks because I never attended classes. I was now working half-day at the library, which meant less money but more time.

I mourned Muriel in a wildness of grief with which I had never mourned Gennie. This was the second time in my life that something intolerable was happening; I could do nothing to affect it, nothing to help myself in it. I could do nothing to encompass it, nor to alter it. I was too beside myself to consider altering me.

For if knowing what we knew, and sharing all that we shared, Muriel and I could not make it together, then what two women on earth could? For that matter, what two people on earth could possibly make it together? The heartbreak of holding on seemed preferable to the heartbreak of ever having to try again, of ever again attempting to connect with another human being.

All the pains in my life that I had lived and never felt flew around my head like grey bats; they pecked at my eyes and built nests in my throat and under the center of my breastbone.

Eudora, Eudora, what was it you used to say to me?

Waste nothing, Chica, not even pain. Particularly not pain.

I rubbed cocoa butter onto the keloid scars on the back of my wrist and hand, and they gradually grew smaller. I started to wear the West Indian bangles my mother had brought back from Grenada for me. They covered up the scars and the discolored skin, and I no longer had to give explanations of what had happened.

Most of our friends had been through the trauma of the breakup of an affair. But this one was different, I thought. Muriel and I had actually lived together, for almost two years, and we had said forever.

"You'll get over it," Toni said, the day she taught me to swim underwater at Huntington Station. "Open your eyes, goddammit, open your eyes!" Toni was yelling at me through the chill water. "It's always easier with your eyes open." I dipped under again. Coming up. "Anyway, you know Muriel's crazy. She's not worth all this."

But to me, she was.

One steamy August midnight a voice from the past came over the telephone. Marie called quite suddenly after a year's absence. She was in Detroit. She had been in hiding, eluding police across country with her husband Jim, the white-slaver from Texas. Marie had finally run away from him and was now living under an assumed name in Detroit. Our giggled confidences on the daybed in her mother's living room seemed centuries ago.

I borrowed money from Toni and went to Detroit for a week, by bus.

The trip was a welcome change. Marie's problems were external, and solvable on some manageable plane: evading Jim's search for her, finding a new job, fending off inquisitive family and friends. We had a good time in Detroit.

Back in New York, Muriel stayed at the apartment to feed the cats and to straighten out her messes in the kitchen, which over the summer, through both of our lacks of concern, had become an archeological dig of remains from other people's lives. She tidied up our collections of tools and nails and old wood, and the potentially lovely results of our once idyllic Sunday scavenging through the city. She also refinished the wooden cabinet which we had been building to store the stuff.

To top it all off, as a surprise, she decided to paint the whole kitchen. But Muriel had difficulty in finishing any project.

I got back from Detroit two days later. It was late afternoon as I dragged my valise back up the familiar flights of stairs and unlocked my front door. Open cans of dried-out paint stinking in the summer heat. The half-painted kitchen, brilliant yellow on one wall, pale cream on the others. And the kittens, who had gotten into the turpentine looking for something to eat. Little Crazy Lady and Scarey Lou were quite dead and rigid on the floor under the kitchen table.

I packed their small bodies into a toolbox lined with an old pillowcase, and took them down Seventh Street to the East River Park in the beginning twilight. I left them there, in a scrambled grave, under a bush as close to the muddy river waters as I could get, piling stones and dirt around the heap to keep the dogs away. The ballplayers in the park opposite watched curiously.

On my walk home through the late summer evening, I thought of the rapid transition from Detroit back to the same old New York. But something had given inside of me. I did not stop by Sixth Street to ask Muriel what had happened. No need; she'd loved the kittens, and she'd let them die. Suddenly, and curiously without drama, the two stiff little black bodies in the tool-box under the bush became tangible evidence I needed, the last sacrifice.

When two women construct a relationship they enter to-gether, the anticipated satisfactions are mutual if not similar. Sometimes that relationship becomes unsatisfactory, or ceases to fulfill those separate needs. When that happens, unless there is a mutual agreement to simultaneously dissolve the relation-ship, there must always be one person who decides to make the first move.

The woman who moves first is not necessarily the most in-jured nor the most at fault.

The first week in September. The *Journal-American* was predicting that Elvis Presley, whose voice decorated every juke-box and radio, would be only a flash-in-the-pan. Muriel's clothes were still at the house, although I saw little of her.

I stood on the corner of Second Avenue waiting for the bus. Already, even though the weather was still quite warm, the days were getting visibly shorter. The pain of the early summer had dulled. I had never before wanted a summer to end, but now, the bleakness of this year's approaching winter seemed like a relief.

The bus door opened and I placed my foot upon the step. Quite suddenly, there was music swelling up into my head, as if a choir of angels had boarded the Second Avenue bus directly in front of me. They were singing the last chorus of an old spiritual of hope:

> Gonna die this death
> on Cal—va—ryyyyy
> BUT AIN'T GONNA
> DIE
> NO MORE. . . !

Their voices sweet and powerful over the din of Second Avenue traffic. I stood transfixed on the lower step of the bus.

"Hey girlie, your fare!" I shook myself and dropped my two coins into the fare-box. The music was still so real I looked around me in amazement as I stumbled to a seat. Almost no one else was in the late-morning bus, and the few people who were there were quite ordinarily occupied and largely silent. Again the angelic orchestration swelled, filling my head with the sharpness and precision of the words; the music was like a surge of strength. It felt rich with hope and a promise of life—more importantly, a new way through or beyond pain.

> I'll die this death
> on Calvary
> ain't
>> gonna
>>> die
>>>> no
>>>>> more!

The physical realities of the dingy bus slid away from me. I suddenly stood upon a hill in the center of an unknown country, hearing the sky fill with a new spelling of my own name.

Muriel moved out of Seventh Street the same way she had moved in, in trickles. She packed the last of her books just before Christmas. I came home from school one night and she was there, come to finish packing. Muriel had fallen asleep in her clothes on the couch. This was where she used to sit and write until dawn whenever she couldn't sleep, that last winter we were together. Her arm was raised against the light. On the back of one of her hands she had doodled a little pattern of stick-figure daisies, the way children write upon themselves when they are bored or lonely.

The lamplight shone down upon her form in a tight circle, illuminating her as vulnerable and untouched. Looking down at Muriel asleep in the light, even after all of the pain and anger, a remembered love at the core of me made my heart move. She opened her eyes, asked me what I was looking at. "Nothing," I answered, turning away, not wanting another angry exchange. She was not my creation. She had never been my creation. Muriel was herself, and I had only aided that process, as she had mine. I had released her anger in much the same way as she had released my love, and we were precious to each other because of that. It was only the Muriel in my head I had to give up, or keep forever; the Muriel peering up from the couch belonged to herself, whoever she wished to be.

Alone, I began to drop by the bars during the week—the Bag, the Page Three, the Pony Stable, the Seven Steps. . . A few times that winter, after Joan had run away from her, I found Muriel sitting in a corner of some bar, crying. I had never seen her crying in public before. Her voice had lost its sweetness. Sometimes, she yelled or made a scene and got thrown out of a club. I had never seen her drunk before, either. I remembered the night in Cuernavaca when I listened to Eudora roaring in the compound gardens, sodden with tequila.

Drunk, with her dark hair disheveled and falling about her face, her crooked pinkie at half-mast, Muriel looked like a buttery angel, fallen from grace, become all too human. Nicky said she was finally recovering from the effects of electroshock. Sometimes I took Muriel back to her apartment and put her to bed; sometimes I took her to my house. One night, as she slept at Seventh Street, I lay awake in the next room, listening to her crying out in her sleep for Joan to come play in the snow. Finally, one night I started downstairs into the Seven Steps and spotted Muriel, slumped over the far corner of the bar, her back towards me. I swung around, walking quickly out before she could turn around and see me. I was tired of playing keeper.

The stolen, bastardized yet familiar rhythms of Presley drape like garlands over that winter.

> Now that my baby's left me I've found a new place to dwell
> It's down at the end of Lonely Street in Heartbreak Hotel

Muriel went home to Stamford for Christmas. She did not come back, in any real sense. The following spring she signed herself into a state hospital insulin unit, where Toni was working in an experimental program for schizophrenics.

The last thing Muriel did before she left Seventh Street for the last time was to burn all of her poetry and her journals in a galvanized tin bucket which she set on the floor in front of the green couch in the middle room. The bottom of the pail left a permanent burn in the shape of a ring upon the old flowered linoleum. Felicia and I cut out the old square and pieced in a remnant of the same pattern which we found on Delancey Street the following spring.

31 Gerri was young and Black and lived in Queens and had a powder-blue Ford that she nicknamed Bluefish. With her carefully waved hair and button-down shirts and grey-flannel slacks, she looked just this side of square, without being square at all, once you got to know her.

By Gerri's invitation and frequently by her wheels, Muriel and I had gone to parties on weekends in Brooklyn and Queens at different women's houses.

One of the women I had met at one of these parties was Kitty.

When I saw Kitty again one night years later in the Swing Rendezvous or the Pony Stable or the Page Three—that tour of second-string gay-girl bars that I had taken to making alone that sad lonely spring of 1957—it was easy to recall the St. Alban's smell of green Queens summer-night and plastic couch-covers and liquor and hair oil and women's bodies at the party where we had first met.

In that brick-faced frame house in Queens, the downstairs pine-paneled recreation room was alive and pulsing with loud music, good food, and beautiful Black women in all different combinations of dress.

There were whip-cord summer suits with starch-shiny shirt collars open at the neck as a concession to the high summer heat, and white gabardine slacks with pleated fronts or slim ivy-league styling for the very slender. There were wheat-colored Cowden jeans, the fashion favorite that summer, with knife-edge creases, and even then, one or two back-buckled grey pants over well-chalked buckskin shoes. There were garrison belts galore, broad black leather belts with shiny thin buckles that originated in army-navy surplus stores, and oxford-styled shirts of the new, iron-free dacron, with its stiff, see-through crispness. These shirts, short-sleeved and man-tailored, were tucked neatly into belted pants or tight, skinny straight skirts. Only the one or two jersey knit shirts were allowed to fall freely outside.

Bermuda shorts, and their shorter cousins, Jamaicas, were already making their appearance on the dyke-chic scene, the rules of which were every bit as cutthroat as the tyrannies of Seventh Avenue or Paris. These shorts were worn by butch and femme alike, and for this reason were slow to be incorporated into many fashionable gay-girl wardrobes, to keep the signals clear. Clothes were often the most important way of broadcasting one's chosen sexual role.

Here and there throughout the room the flash of brightly colored below-the-knee full skirts over low-necked tight bodices could be seen, along with tight sheath dresses and the shine of high thin heels next to bucks and sneakers and loafers.

Femmes wore their hair in tightly curled pageboy bobs, or piled high on their heads in sculptured bunches of curls, or in feather cuts framing their faces. That sweetly clean fragrance of beauty-parlor that hung over all Black women's gatherings in the fifties was present here also, adding its identifiable smell of hot comb and hair pomade to the other aromas in the room.

Butches wore their hair cut shorter, in a D.A. shaped to a point in the back, or a short pageboy, or sometimes in a tightly curled poodle that predated the natural afro. But this was a rarity, and I can only remember one other Black woman at that party besides me whose hair was not straightened, and she was an acquaintance of ours from the Lower East Side named Ida.

On a table behind the built-in bar stood opened bottles of gin, bourbon, scotch, soda and other various mixers. The bar itself was covered with little delicacies of all descriptions; chips and dips and little crackers and squares of bread laced with the usual dabs of egg-salad and sardine paste. There was also a platter of delicious fried chicken wings, and a pan of potato-and-egg salad dressed with vinegar. Bowls of olives and pickles surrounded the main dishes, with trays of red crab apples and little sweet onions on toothpicks.

But the centerpiece of the whole table was a huge platter of succulent and thinly sliced roast beef, set into an underpan of cracked ice. Upon the beige platter, each slice of rare meat had been lovingly laid out and individually folded up into a vulval pattern, with a tiny dab of mayonnaise at the crucial apex. The pink-brown folded meat around the pale cream-yellow dot formed suggestive sculptures that made a great hit with all the women present, and Pet, at whose house the party was being given and whose idea the meat sculptures were, smilingly acknowledged the many compliments on her platter with a long-necked graceful nod of her elegant dancer's head.

The room's particular mix of heat-smells and music gives way in my mind to the high-cheeked, dark young woman with the silky voice and appraising eyes (something about her mouth reminded me of Ann, the nurse I'd worked with when I'd first left home).

Perching on the edge of the low bench where I was sitting, Kitty absently wiped specks of lipstick from each corner of her mouth with the downward flick of a delicate forefinger.

"Audre. . . that's a nice name. What's it short for?"

My damp arm hairs bristled in the Ruth Brown music, and the heat. I could not stand anybody messing around with my name, not even with nicknames.

"Nothing. It's just Audre. What's Kitty short for?"

"Afrekete," she said, snapping her fingers in time to the rhythm of it and giving a long laugh. "That's me. The Black pussycat." She laughed again. "I like your hairdo. Are you a singer?"

"No." She continued to stare at me with her large direct eyes.

I was suddenly too embarrassed at not knowing what else to say to meet her calmly erotic gaze, so I stood up abruptly and said, in my best Laurel's-terse tone, "Let's dance."

Her face was broad and smooth under too-light make-up, but as we danced a foxtrot she started to sweat, and her skin took on a deep shiny richness. Kitty closed her eyes part way when she danced, and her one gold-rimmed front tooth flashed as she smiled and occasionally caught her lower lip in time to the music.

Her yellow poplin shirt, cut in the style of an Eisenhower jacket, had a zipper that was half open in the summer heat, showing collarbones that stood out like brown wings from her long neck. Garments with zippers were highly prized among the more liberal set of gay-girls, because these could be worn by butch or femme alike on certain occasions, without causing any adverse or troublesome comments. Kitty's narrow, well-pressed khaki skirt was topped by a black belt that matched my own except in its newness, and her natty trimness made me feel almost shabby in my well-worn riding pants.

I thought she was very pretty, and I wished I could dance with as much ease as she did, and as effortlessly. Her hair had been straightened into short feathery curls, and in that room of well-set marcels and D.A.'s and pageboys, it was the closest cut to my own.

Kitty smelled of soap and Jean Naté, and I kept thinking she was bigger than she actually was, because there was a comfortable smell about her that I always associated with large women. I caught another spicy herb-like odor, that I later identified as a combination of coconut oil and Yardley's lavender hair pomade. Her mouth was full, and her lipstick was dark and shiny, a new Max Factor shade called "WARPAINT."

The next dance was a slow fish that suited me fine. I never knew whether to lead or to follow in most other dances, and

even the effort to decide which was which was as difficult for
me as having to decide all the time the difference between left
and right. Somehow that simple distinction had never become
automatic for me, and all that deciding usually left me very little energy with which to enjoy the movement and the music.

But "fishing" was different. A forerunner of the later one-
step, it was, in reality, your basic slow bump and grind. The low
red lamp and the crowded St. Alban's parlor floor left us just
enough room to hold each other frankly, arms around neck and
waist, and the slow intimate music moved our bodies much
more than our feet.

That had been in St. Alban's, Queens, nearly two years before, when Muriel had seemed to be the certainty in my life.
Now in the spring of this new year I had my own apartment all
to myself again, but I was mourning. I avoided visiting pairs of
friends, or inviting even numbers of people over to my house,
because the happiness of couples, or their mere togetherness,
hurt me too much in its absence from my own life, whose
blankest hole was named Muriel. I had not been back to Queens,
nor to any party, since Muriel and I had broken up, and the only people I saw outside of work and school were those friends
who lived in the Village and who sought me out or whom I ran
into at the bars. Most of them were white.

"Hey, girl, long time no see." Kitty spotted me first. We
shook hands. The bar was not crowded, which means it probably was the Page Three, which didn't fill up until after midnight. "Where's your girlfriend?"

I told her that Muriel and I weren't together any more.
"Yeah? That's too bad. You-all were kinda cute together. But
that's the way it goes. How long you been in the 'life'?"

I stared at Kitty without answering, trying to think of how to
explain to her, that for me there was only one life—my own—
however I chose to live it. But she seemed to take the words
right out of my mouth.

"Not that it matters," she said speculatively, finishing
the beer she had carried over to the end of the bar where I was
sitting. "We don't have but one, anyway. At least this time
around." She took my arm. "Come on, let's dance."

Kitty was still trim and fast-lined, but with an easier loose-
ness about her smile and a lot less make-up. Without its camou-
flage, her chocolate skin and deep, sculptured mouth reminded
me of a Benin bronze. Her hair was still straightened, but shorter, and her black Bermuda shorts and knee socks matched her

astonishingly shiny black loafers. A black turtleneck pullover completed her sleek costume. Somehow, this time, my jeans did not feel shabby beside hers, only a variation upon some similar dress. Maybe it was because our belts still matched—broad, black, and brass-buckled.

We moved to the back room and danced to Frankie Lymon's "Goody, Goody," and then to a Belafonte calypso. Dancing with her this time, I felt who I was and where my body was going, and that feeling was more important to me than any lead or follow.

The room felt very warm even though it was only just spring, and Kitty and I smiled at each other as the number ended. We stood waiting for the next record to drop and the next dance to begin. It was a slow Sinatra. Our belt buckles kept getting in the way as we moved in close to the oiled music, and we slid them around to the side of our waists when no one was looking.

For the last few months since Muriel had moved out, my skin had felt cold and hard and essential, like thin frozen leather that was keeping the shape expected. That night on the dance floor of the Page Three as Kitty and I touched our bodies together in dancing, I could feel my carapace soften slowly and then finally melt, until I felt myself covered in a warm, almost forgotten, slip of anticipation, that ebbed and flowed at each contact of our moving bodies.

I could feel something slowly shift in her also, as if a taut string was becoming undone, and finally we didn't start back to the bar at all between dances, but just stood on the floor waiting for the next record, dancing only with each other. A little after midnight, in a silent and mutual decision, we split the Page together, walking blocks through the West Village to Hudson Street where her car was parked. She had invited me up to her house for a drink.

The sweat beneath my breasts from our dancing was turning cold in the sharpness of the night air as we crossed Sheridan Square. I paused to wave to the steadies through the plate glass windows of Jim Atkins's on the corner of Christopher Street.

In her car, I tried not to think about what I was doing as we rode uptown almost in silence. There was an ache in the well beneath my stomach, spreading out and down between my legs like mercury. The smell of her warm body, mixed with the smell of feathery cologne and lavender pomade, anointed the car. My eyes rested on the sight of her coconut-spicy hands on the steering wheel, and the curve of her lashes as she attended the roadway. They made it easy for me to coast beneath her sporadic bursts of conversation with only an occasional friendly grunt.

"I haven't been downtown to the bars in a while, you know? It's funny. I don't know why I don't go downtown more often. But every once in a while, something tells me go and I go. I guess it must be different when you live around there all the time." She turned her gold-flecked smile upon me.

Crossing 59th Street, I had an acute moment of panic. Who was this woman? Suppose she really intended only to give me the drink which she had offered me as we left the Page? Suppose I had totally misunderstood the impact of her invitation, and would soon find myself stranded uptown at 3:00 A.M. on a Sunday morning, and did I even have enough change left in my jeans for carfare home? Had I put out enough food for the kittens? Was Flee coming over with her camera tomorrow morning, and would she feed the cats if I wasn't there? If I wasn't there.

If I wasn't there. The implication of that thought was so shaking it almost threw me out of the car.

I had had only enough money for one beer that night, so I knew I wasn't high, and reefer was only for special occasions. Part of me felt like a raging lioness, inflamed in desire. Even the words in my head seemed borrowed from a dime-store novel. But that part of me was drunk on the thighed nearness of this exciting unknown dark woman, who calmly moved us through upper Manhattan, with her patent-leather loafers and her camel's-hair swing coat and her easy talk, from time to time her gloved hand touching my denimed leg for emphasis.

Another piece of me felt bumbling, inept, and about four years old. I was the idiot playing at being a lover, who was going to be found out shortly and laughed at for my pretensions, as well as rejected out of hand.

Would it be possible—was it ever possible—for two women to share the fire we felt that night without entrapping or smothering each other? I longed for that as I longed for her body, doubting both, eager for both.

And how was it possible, that I should be dreaming the roll of this woman's sea into and around mine, when only a few short hours ago, and for so many months before, I had been mourning the loss of Muriel, so sure that I would continue being broken-hearted forever? And what then if I had been mistaken?

If the knot in my groin would have gone away, I'd have jumped out of the car door at the very next traffic light. Or so I thought to myself.

We came out of the Park Drive at Seventh Avenue and 110th Street, and as quickly as the light changed on the now deserted avenue, Afrekete turned her broad-lipped beautiful face to me, with no smile at all. Her great lidded luminescent eyes looked directly and startlingly into mine. It was as if she had suddenly become another person, as if the wall of glass formed by my spectacles, and behind which I had become so used to hiding, had suddenly dissolved.

In an uninflected, almost formal voice that perfectly matched and thereby obliterated all my question marks, she asked,

"Can you spend the night?"

And then it occurred to me that perhaps she might have been having the same questions about me that I had been having about her. I was left almost without breath by the combination of her delicacy and her directness—a combination which is still rare and precious.

For beyond the assurance that her question offered me— a declaration that this singing of my flesh, this attraction, was not all within my own head—beyond that assurance was a batch of delicate assumptions built into that simple phrase that reverberated in my poet's brain. It offered us both an out if necessary. If the answer to the question might, by any chance, have been no, then its very syntax allowed for a reason of impossibility, rather than of choice—"I can't," rather than "I won't." The demands of another commitment, an early job, a sick cat, etc., could be lived with more easily than an out-and-out rejection.

Even the phrase "spending the night" was less a euphemism for making love than it was an allowable space provided, in which one could move back or forth. If, perhaps, I were to change my mind before the traffic light and decide that no, I wasn't gay, after all, then a simpler companionship was still available.

I steadied myself enough to say, in my very best Lower East Side Casual voice, "I'd really like to," cursing myself for the banal words, and wondering if she could smell my nervousness and my desperate desire to be suave and debonair, drowning in sheer desire.

We parked half-in and half-out of a bus stop on Manhattan Avenue and 113th Street, in Gennie's old neighborhood.

Something about Kitty made me feel like a rollercoaster, rocketing from idiot to goddess. By the time we had collected her mail from the broken mailbox and then climbed six flights of stairs up to her front door, I felt that there had never been anything else my body had intended to do more, than to reach inside of her coat and take Afrekete into my arms, fitting her body into the curves of mine tightly, her beige camel's-hair billowing around us both, and her gloved hand still holding the door key.

In the faint light of the hallway, her lips moved like surf upon the water's edge.

It was a 1½ room kitchenette apartment with tall narrow windows in the narrow, high-ceilinged front room. Across each window, there were built-in shelves at different levels. From these shelves tossed and frothed, hung and leaned and stood, pot after clay pot of green and tousled large and small-leaved plants of all shapes and conditions.

Later, I came to love the way in which the plants filtered the southern exposure sun through the room. Light hit the opposite wall at a point about six inches above the thirty-gallon fish tank that murmured softly, like a quiet jewel, standing on its wrought-iron legs, glowing and mysterious.

Leisurely and swiftly, translucent rainbowed fish darted back and forth through the lit water, perusing the glass sides of the tank for morsels of food, and swimming in and out of the marvelous world created by colored gravels and stone tunnels and bridges that lined the floor of the tank. Astride one of the bridges, her bent head observing the little fish that swam in and out between her legs, stood a little jointed brown doll, her smooth naked body washed by the bubbles rising up from the air unit located behind her.

Between the green plants and the glowing magical tank of exotic fish, lay a room the contents of which I can no longer separate in my mind. Except for a plaid-covered couch that opened up into the double bed which we set rocking as we loved that night into a bright Sunday morning, dappled with green sunlight from the plants in Afrekete's high windows.

I woke to her house suffused in that light, the sky half-seen through the windows of the top-floor kitchenette apartment, and Afrekete, known, asleep against my side.

Little hairs under her navel lay down before my advancing tongue like the beckoned pages of a well-touched book.

How many times into summer had I turned into that block from Eighth Avenue, the saloon on the corner spilling a smell of sawdust and liquor onto the street, a shifting indeterminate number of young and old Black men taking turns sitting on two upturned milk-crates, playing checkers? I would turn the corner into 113th Street towards the park, my steps quickening and my fingertips tingling to play in her earth.

And I remember Afrekete, who came out of a dream to me always being hard and real as the fire hairs along the under-edge of my navel. She brought me live things from the bush, and from her farm set out in cocoyams and cassava—those magical fruit which Kitty bought in the West Indian markets along Lenox Avenue in the 140s or in the Puerto Rican *bodegas* within the bustling market over on Park Avenue and 116th Street under the Central Railroad structures.

"I got this under the bridge" was a saying from time immemorial, giving an adequate explanation that whatever it was had come from as far back and as close to home—that is to say, was as authentic—as was possible.

We bought red delicious pippins, the size of french cashew apples. There were green plantains, which we half-peeled and then planted, fruit-deep, in each other's bodies until the petals of skin lay like tendrils of broad green fire upon the curly darkness between our upspread thighs. *There were ripe red finger bananas, stubby and sweet, with which I parted your lips gently, to insert the peeled fruit into your grape-purple flower.*

I held you, lay between your brown legs, slowly playing my tongue through your familiar forests, slowly licking and swallowing as the deep undulations and tidal motions of your strong body slowly mashed ripe banana into a beige cream that mixed with the juices of your electric flesh. Our bodies met again, each surface touched with each other's flame, from the tips of our curled toes to our tongues, and locked into our own wild rhythms, we rode each other across the thundering space, dripped like light from the peak of each other's tongue.

We were each of us both together. Then we were apart, and sweat sheened our bodies like sweet oil.

Sometimes Afrekete sang in a small club further uptown on Sugar Hill. Sometimes she clerked in the Gristede's Market on 97th Street and Amsterdam, and sometimes with no warning at all she appeared at the Pony Stable or Page Three on Saturday night. Once, I came home to Seventh Street late one night to find her sitting on my stoop at 3:00 A.M., with a bottle of beer in her hand and a piece of bright African cloth wrapped around her head, and we sped uptown through the dawn-empty city with a summer thunder squall crackling above us, and the wet city streets singing beneath the wheels of her little Nash Rambler.

There are certain verities which are always with us, which we come to depend upon. That the sun moves north in summer, that melted ice contracts, that the curved banana is sweeter. Afrekete taught me roots, new definitions of our women's bodies—definitions for which I had only been in training to learn before.

By the beginning of summer the walls of Afrekete's apartment were always warm to the touch from the heat beating down on the roof, and chance breezes through her windows rustled her plants in the window and brushed over our sweat-smooth bodies, at rest after loving.

We talked sometimes about what it meant to love women, and what a relief it was in the eye of the storm, no matter how often we had to bite our tongues and stay silent. Afrekete had a seven-year-old daughter whom she had left with her mama down in Georgia, and we shared a lot of our dreams.

"She's going to be able to love anybody she wants to love," Afrekete said, fiercely, lighting a Lucky Strike. "Same way she's going to be able to work any place she damn well pleases. Her mama's going to see to that."

Once we talked about how Black women had been committed without choice to waging our campaigns in the enemies' strongholds, too much and too often, and how our psychic landscapes had been plundered and wearied by those repeated battles and campaigns.

"And don't I have the scars to prove it," she sighed. "Makes you tough though, babe, if you don't go under. And that's what I like about you; you're like me. We're both going to make it because we're both too tough and crazy not to!" And we held each other and laughed and cried about what we had paid for that toughness, and how hard it was to explain to anyone who didn't already know it that soft and tough had to be one and the same for either to work at all, like our joy and the tears mingling on the one pillow beneath our heads.

And the sun filtered down upon us through the dusty windows, through the mass of green plants that Afrekete tended religiously.

I took a ripe avocado and rolled it between my hands until the skin became a green case for the soft mashed fruit inside, hard pit at the core. *I rose from a kiss in your mouth to nibble a hole in the fruit skin near the navel stalk, squeezed the pale yellow-green fruit juice in thin ritual lines back and forth over and around your coconut-brown belly.*

The oil and sweat from our bodies kept the fruit liquid, and I massaged it over your thighs and between your breasts until your brownness shone like a light through a veil of the palest green avocado, a mantle of goddess pear that I slowly licked from your skin.

Then we would have to get up to gather the pits and fruit skins and bag them to put out later for the garbagemen, because if we left them near the bed for any length of time, they would call out the hordes of cockroaches that always waited on the sidelines within the walls of Harlem tenements, particularly in the smaller older ones under the hill of Morningside Heights.

Afrekete lived not far from Genevieve's grandmother's house.

Sometimes she reminded me of Ella, Gennie's stepmother, who shuffled about with an apron on and a broom outside the room where Gennie and I lay on the studio couch. She would be singing her non-stop tuneless little song over and over and over:

> Momma kilt me
> Poppa et me
> Po' lil' brudder
> suck ma bones. . .

And one day Gennie turned her head on my lap to say uneasily, "You know, sometimes I don't know whether Ella's crazy, or stupid, or divine."

And now I think the goddess was speaking through Ella also, but Ella was too beaten down and anesthetized by Phillip's brutality for her to believe in her own mouth, and we, Gennie and I, were too arrogant and childish—not without right or reason, for we were scarcely more than children—to see that our survival might very well lay in listening to the sweeping woman's tuneless song.

I lost my sister, Gennie, to my silence and her pain and despair, to both our angers and to a world's cruelty that destroys its own young in passing—not even as a rebel gesture or sacrifice or hope for another living of the spirit, but out of not noticing

or caring about the destruction. I have never been able to blind
myself to that cruelty, which according to one popular definition of mental health, makes me mentally unhealthy.

Afrekete's house was the tallest one near the corner, before
the high rocks of Morningside Park began on the other side of
the avenue, and one night on the Midsummer Eve's Moon we
took a blanket up to the roof. She lived on the top floor, and in
an unspoken agreement, the roof belonged mostly to those who
had to live under its heat. The roof was the chief resort territory
of tenement-dwellers, and was known as Tar Beach.

We jammed the roof door shut with our sneakers, and spread
our blanket in the lee of the chimney, between its warm brick
wall and the high parapet of the building's face. This was before
the blaze of sulphur lamps had stripped the streets of New
York of trees and shadow, and the incandescence from the
lights below faded this far up. From behind the parapet wall
we could see the dark shapes of the basalt and granite outcrop-
pings looming over us from the park across the street, outlined,
curiously close and suggestive.

We slipped off the cotton shifts we had worn and moved
against each other's damp breasts in the shadow of the roof's
chimney, making moon, honor, love, while the ghostly vague
light drifting upward from the street competed with the silver
hard sweetness of the full moon, reflected in the shiny mirrors
of our sweat-slippery dark bodies, sacred as the ocean at high
tide.

I remember the moon rising against the tilted planes of her
upthrust thighs, and my tongue caught the streak of silver reflected in the curly bush of her dappled-dark maiden hair. *I
remember the full moon like white pupils in the center of your
wide irises.*

*The moons went out, and your eyes grew dark as you rolled
over me, and I felt the moon's silver light mix with the wet of
your tongue on my eyelids.*

*Afrekete Afrekete ride me to the crossroads where we shall
sleep, coated in the woman's power. The sound of our bodies
meeting is the prayer of all strangers and sisters, that the discarded evils, abandoned at all crossroads, will not follow us
upon our journeys.*

When we came down from the roof later, it was into the
sweltering midnight of a west Harlem summer, with canned
music in the streets and the disagreeable whines of overtired and

overheated children. Nearby, mothers and fathers sat on stoops or milk crates and striped camp chairs, fanning themselves absently and talking or thinking about work as usual tomorrow and not enough sleep.

It was not onto the pale sands of Whydah, nor the beaches of Winneba or Annamabu, with cocopalms softly applauding and crickets keeping time with the pounding of a tar-laden, treacherous, beautiful sea. It was onto 113th Street that we descended after our meeting under the Midsummer Eve's Moon, but the mothers and fathers smiled at us in greeting as we strolled down to Eighth Avenue, hand in hand.

I had not seen Afrekete for a few weeks in July, so I went uptown to her house one evening since she didn't have a phone. The door was locked, and there was no one on the roof when I called up the stairwell.

Another week later, Midge, the bartender at the Pony Stable, gave me a note from Afrekete, saying that she had gotten a gig in Atlanta for September, and was splitting to visit her mama and daughter for a while.

We had come together like elements erupting into an electric storm, exchanging energy, sharing charge, brief and drenching. Then we parted, passed, reformed, reshaping ourselves the better for the exchange.

I never saw Afrekete again, but her print remains upon my life with the resonance and power of an emotional tattoo.

Epilogue

Every woman I have ever loved has left her print upon me, where I loved some invaluable piece of myself apart from me— so different that I had to stretch and grow in order to recognize her. And in that growing, we came to separation, that place where work begins. Another meeting.

A year later, I finished library school. The first summer of a new decade was waning as I walked away from Seventh Street for the last time, leaving that door unlocked for whatever person came after me who needed shelter. There were four half-finished poems scribbled on the bathroom wall between the toilet and the bathtub, others in the window jambs and the floorboards under the flowered linoleum, mixed up with the ghosts of rich food smells.

The casing of this place had been my home for seven years, the amount of time it takes for the human body to completely renew itself, cell by living cell. And in those years my life had become increasingly a bridge and field of women. *Zami.*

Zami. A Carriacou name for women who work together as friends and lovers.

We carry our traditions with us. Buying boxes of Red Cross Salt and a fresh corn straw broom for my new apartment in Westchester: new job, new house, new living the old in a new way. Recreating in words the women who helped give me substance.

Ma-Liz, DeLois, Louise Briscoe, Aunt Anni, Linda, and Genevieve; MawuLisa, thunder, sky, sun, the great mother of us all; and Afrekete, her youngest daughter, the mischievous linguist, trickster, best-beloved, whom we must all become.

Their names, selves, faces feed me like corn before labor. I live each of them as a piece of me, and I choose these words with the same grave concern with which I choose to push speech into poetry, the mattering core, the forward visions of all our lives.

Once *home* was a long way off, a place I had never been to but knew out of my mother's mouth. I only discovered its latitudes when Carriacou was no longer my home.

There it is said that the desire to lie with other women is a drive from the mother's blood.

ALSO BY AUDRE LORDE

Sister Outsider: Essays and Speeches

The essential writings of Black lesbian poet and feminist writer Audre Lorde. In this charged collection of fifteen essays and speeches, Lorde takes on sexism, racism, ageism, homophobia, and class, and propounds social difference as a vehicle for action and change. Her prose in incisive, unflinching, and lyrical, reflecting struggle but ultimately offering messages of hope.

"Audre Lorde is a passionate sage. I say 'is' and not 'was' because her keen insights continue to provoke and sustain us and give us courage."
> —VALERIE MINER, author of *After Eden* and professor of feminist studies at Stanford University

"[Lorde's] works will be important to those truly interested in growing up sensitive, intelligent, and aware."
> —THE *NEW YORK TIMES*

ISBN: 978-1-58091-186-3
eISBN: 978-0-307-80904-9

CROSSING PRESS
www.tenspeed.com